MONTE IRVIN
Nice Guys Finish First

MONTE IRVIN
Nice Guys Finish First

Monte Irvin with
James A. Riley

Carroll & Graf Publishers, Inc.
New York

First edition 1996.

Carroll & Graf Publishers, Inc.
260 Fifth Avenue
New York, NY 10001

ISBN 0-7867-0254-0

Library of Congress Cataloging-in-Publication Data is available.

Manufactured in the United States of America.

This book is dedicated to my family.
First, to my wife Dee.
Also to Pam, Patti and Craig
Stacie and Erika
Milt and Dorothy, Cal and Kay, Irene and John, Panola
and to all my aunts, uncles, cousins, nephews, nieces
and other members of my extended family.

And, posthumously to
Carl, Mack, Bob, Curtis, Pearl, Eulalia, and Arline.

Most especially,
to my parents, Cupid Alexander and Mary Eliza Irvin.

—M. I.

This book is dedicated to my family.
Especially to my wife Dottie.
Also to Josh, Jube and Kathy,
Wayne and Kathy, Penny, Pat and Joe,
Mike, Mardi and Mike, Patti, Merri and Tracy, Laura, Joey,
and to all my aunts, uncles, cousins
and other members of my extended family.

And in remembrance of my parents, Jim and Martha Riley,
and in appreciation of my wife's mother and late father,
Lena and Allen Taylor.

—J. R.

Contents

Preface

One generation passeth away, and another generation cometh . . .

—Ecclesiastes 1:4

This shall be written for the generation to come . . .

—Psalm 102:18

THIS BOOK IS more than a chronicle of my life. It is a tribute to my family and is dedicated to them and their accomplishments. Most especially, it is dedicated to our parents, Mary Eliza and Cupid Alexander Irvin, who had the nerve, determination, strength and foresight to leave their agrarian homestead and opt for a better life in the North for themselves and their ten children. They never imagined that, with help, the wheels of justice would grind slowly but exceedingly successfully. Thanks to God for His help in guiding them all the way.

Our mother was the spiritual leader, determined, fearless, strong-willed and always in control. There was no democracy or debate when it came to her rules. You either did it the right way or not at all. Our father was a tireless worker in support of his family, compassionate, hardworking, mild mannered, congenial and cooperative.

With all the bonding, self reliance, faith, hard work, determination, luck and the support of relatives and friends, we were able to overcome the traumatic vicissitudes of life in an urban setting and ultimately prosper. In order to progress and keep busy and keep out of trouble, all of the younger ones turned to the church and athletics.

My brother Bob, who was eight years older than I am, was a

wonderful all-around baseball player and excelled as a pitcher, hitter and fielder. His dream to become a Negro League star was never fulfilled because he worked hard to help my mother and father to support the rest of the family.

Milton, the second youngest, finished Orange High School and was awarded a football scholarship to Virginia State University of Petersburg, Virginia until he was inducted into the Armed Services.

Cal, the youngest of the family, played three varsity sports in high school and became a star basketball player and was the valedictorian of his class. He later matriculated to Morgan State University, where he earned all CIAA honors in baseball, basketball and football, and co-captained the 1944 championship basketball team. He finished his college education at the University of Illinois, and then started his teaching and coaching career.

Preston Grimsley, my nephew, also attended Morgan State University at the same time and was the star tackle on the football squad until he left school after gaining Hall of Fame recognition.

My other nephew, Harvey Grimsley, starred for the Rutgers football team in 1946 and, in 1993, he was inducted into the Rutgers football Hall of Fame at Rutgers University, New Brunswick, New Jersey.

Another nephew, Milton Irvin, Jr., was an Essex Catholic High School cross country champion and, in 1967, was inducted into their Hall of Fame. He went to Wharton School of Business in Philadelphia where he earned his M.B.A. and recently became a general partner in the Saloman Brothers investment firm.

Educationally, Robert Irvin, Jr., attended East Orange High School and matriculated at Drexel College in Philadelphia, where he became an audio expert and is now running his own business.

My niece, Sally Grimsley, was an excellent athlete at Orange High School and Morgan State University and became an area supervisor for the state of New Jersey.

Debbie Irvin became a high school teacher and will soon begin working on her Ph.D. at Montclair State College.

Beverly Giscombe became an attorney and judge, and now runs her own law firm in East Orange, New Jersey.

Daryl Frazier became a chemist with a pharmaceutical company in New Jersey, and his sister Karen runs her own business as a franchise operator in East Orange, New Jersey.

My sister Panola Grimsley is 95 as of this writing and living in East Orange, New Jersey.

My sister Irene Steward was accomplished in her own right by attending a beauty culture school and, after finishing, she became a teacher for the school until she retired some fifteen years ago and is living in Daytona Beach, Florida.

My two daughters, Pamela Fields Irvin and Patricia Irvin Gordon, have made me very proud. Both Pam and Patti attended Fiske University in Nashville, Tennessee.

Pamela became an elementary grade teacher and, for nearly twenty years, she has been working for AT&T as an area supervisor for special markets.

Patti completed her master's degree in Elementary Education and is now married to Dr. Craig S. Gordon, a prominent gastroenterologist, and is the mother of two teenage daughters, Stacie and Erika. Presently, she is a housewife and living in Houston, Texas.

Collectively, seventeen Halls of Fame are represented in some combination by the children and grandchildren of our parents. And who is to know what honors and achievements await the great-grandchildren and future generations?

These are just some of our family's accomplishments. So we say, "God bless our parents. God bless Eliza and Cupid Alexander for being so brave, working so hard to help all of us to succeed. We can see you up there smiling and very satisfied for making all of these achievements possible. Rest easy because we think about you and pray for you all the time."

Monte Irvin

Introduction

Monte Irvin [is] a man unexcelled for decency.

—Bowie Kuhn in *Hardball*

Monte Irvin [is] a man for whom I've always had an enormous respect. . . . [He is the] nicest man in the whole world.

—Leo Durocher in *Nice Guys Finish Last*

To some people Monte Irvin may seem too good to be true. He survived a near fatal illness, lived through the Great Depression and World War II, and lost his prime years to racial injustice that kept him out of major-league baseball. Still, he forged a Hall of Fame career and played in two World Series with the New York Giants before embarking on a successful second career as a special assistant to the commissioner of baseball. Throughout his tribulations, he remained remarkably unembittered and in his triumphs, he remained humble. He is truly a man for all seasons.

I first became aware of Monte Irvin as a youngster clipping pictures from newspapers and collecting baseball cards, but more than thirty years passed before I had the pleasure of meeting him. In the summer of 1981, while trekking northward along the eastern seaboard from Miami to New York in search of former players from the Negro leagues, I met with Monte in the baseball commissioner's office in Rockefeller Plaza. From that day to the present, I have been impressed with the sensitivity and concern that Monte has shown for others, especially those baseball players whose careers were spent in the sundown shadows of black baseball.

Monte was one of those fortunate enough to make the transition to the major leagues after the color line was eradicated, but his empathy can be traced to his own experience in the Negro leagues. A man of lesser character might have forgotten those ball players who were less fortunate, but Monte chose instead to pursue a pioneering course by helping gain recognition for the contributions made by that generation of players.

In his youth, Monte had seen many of the great stars who were excluded from the major leagues by the "gentleman's agreement" that established the color line in organized baseball. A few years later, a rising star himself with the Newark Eagles, Monte was being promoted by the Negro League owners as the man best suited to break the color line and become the first black ball player in the majors. However, a man named Hitler and a place called Pearl Harbor interrupted those plans and sent him to war.

Following his service in World War II, Monte was signed by Branch Rickey, but when Newark Eagles owner Effa Manley demanded compensation, Rickey released his claim and Brooklyn's loss was the New York Giants' gain.

Without Monte's clutch basehits during the 1951 season, baseball would have been robbed of its most dramatic comeback, capped by the most exciting single play in the sport's history: "The shot heard around the world." The man who hit that famous home run, Bobby Thomson, credits Monte as being the player most responsible for the Giants getting to the playoffs, where Thomson attained baseball immortality.

Bobby Thomson is not alone in his recognition of Monte's contributions in the stretch drive as Monte was awarded the Giants' MVP trophy for the 1951 season. In addition to the acclaim granted him for his baseball achievements, Monte's New York Giants teammates are unanimous in voicing their respect for his integrity and admiration for the dignity and class with which he carried himself. Jackie Robinson may have been the first black American to play major-league baseball, but it was the pioneering presence of Monte Irvin and others like him that preserved a permanent place for black ball players in the American and National leagues.

Having starred in both the Negro leagues and the majors, Monte's career bridged the color barrier and provided him with a unique perspective. More than any other player, he is in a position to look at baseball from two distinctly different vantage points. His vision comes from having seen the promised land, both from afar in the wilderness of the Negro leagues and from the mountaintop of major-league stardom. Monte's life story encompasses baseball as it was *then*, when the racial barriers were firmly entrenched in America's game, and *now*, after those barriers have been removed to truly make baseball our National Pastime.

Family has always been an important part of Monte Irvin's life and in his acceptance speech at Cooperstown, when he was inducted into the National Baseball Hall of Fame, he paid homage to his parents, family, and friends. Although currently making his home in Homosassa, Florida, Monte still maintains ties with Newark and New York, where he spent most of his baseball career.

Memories from those past seasons in the sun are sweet, and the friendships endure. Monte retains a special feeling for his former New York Giants skipper, Leo Durocher, but his life has proven Leo's dictum to be wrong. *Nice Guys Finish First!*

James A. Riley

I

Beginnings

1 A Mission in Life

When Monte was seventeen, he was sick and near death, but our mother said that she had talked to a "Higher Doctor" and that Monte wasn't going to die. Maybe the Lord knew he had a mission to perform on earth.

—Cal Irvin, younger brother

I ALWAYS FELT that I had a mission in life. I thought I was born to play sports. Even now, I still feel that must have been my mission because I came through so many close calls where my life could very easily have been ended.

The first crisis occurred when I was only two years old and could have been trampled when I walked under a spirited horse's belly. Then, about a year later, a doctor had to be rushed to our farm to save my life because I had engorged such a great quantity of plums, pits and all.

Again, as a teenager, I survived two close calls that could have proved fatal. First, I was riding in a car that was missed by a speeding train by only a matter of seconds. Then, as a high school senior, I almost died from a streptococci infection when nearly everyone had given up on me.

The next incident came after I started playing professional baseball and had signed to play in Mexico. On the flight down there, the plane hit an air pocket going over the mountains to Mexico City and dropped about two or three hundred feet before righting itself.

A year later I was drafted, and during World War II, I had two more close calls where I could have been killed. I was in a troop convoy on the way to Europe that passed through waters in the north Atlantic where German submarines were operating, and we were without air cover for a time. And, after we had reached England, the German air force bombed a supply depot a few hours after my outfit had moved out of the area. If we hadn't moved, all of us might have been killed.

Looking back, it seems that what I have learned from my experiences down through life might benefit somebody, someplace, in some way. I'm sure there are people who will face some of the same problems that I had in my life. Maybe, by learning how I handled each situation, it will enable them to deal with their problems successfully.

Early in life I learned, just through observation, that right always wins out over wrong. If a person has good intentions in his heart and wants to do the right thing, then there are certain ways that any obstacle can be overcome. I was very fortunate to have the kind of parents that I had, who believed in doing the right thing, and always tried to be honest, trustworthy, and forthright. My mother was a Bible student and when I was a youngster, both my mother and father would say, "If people would only live by the Golden Rule, there wouldn't be the problems that there are." In other words, "treat people the way you want to be treated." If somebody mistreats you, two wrongs won't make a right.

That doesn't mean that you have to kowtow to a bully, or if someone physically abuses you, that you can't strike back. I'm not talking about that at all. You should be tough as nails when you have to be. For instance, when I was a youngster about nine years old, I was on my way to school on the very first day and a kid bigger and older than me beat me up. That night, after I got back home, I sat and thought about what I was going to do to make that kid sorry for what he did. So I decided that the first thing I had to do was to get bigger and stronger. That way, the next time we met, the situation would be a little more even.

So, I worked hard to get stronger and, sure enough, in about a year, I had grown and I had gotten stronger. Now I was ready to get even with this kid who had embarrassed me. One day I saw him and I told him, "You know the last time we met, you beat me pretty badly and I want a rematch. I think that I can make you sorry you ever did that." He said, "Anytime you're ready." I replied, "How about right now?" So we began fighting, just the two of us, but I had learned a little something since the first time. I didn't go for his face, I went for the body. Every time he would swing at me, I would hit him in the ribs or in the stomach. After about three or four minutes, I had hurt him so badly, he went down to one knee and said, "I give up. You're the best." "Okay," I replied, "but don't ever try to bully me again."

This was way back in 1928 and many years later we happened to meet at a gas station. He was glad to see me and I was glad to see him. We shook hands and kind of hugged and talked about what we had been doing for the past twenty years. Then he said, "By the way, you taught me a lesson." "How so?" I asked. "Well," he said, "I used to try to be bad, but after you evened the score, I found out I wasn't as bad as I thought I was. And, instead of becoming a bully, I tried to become a decent human being. But if you hadn't beaten the hell out of me the way you did, I probably would have taken the wrong path." "Well, I'm sorry it had to happen that way," I replied. "But I'm glad that we're friends now, and I just wish you the best." I'm certainly glad that the whole thing turned out the way it did.

You've got to be smart enough to do the things that are needed in a given situation. Do the very best you can and always try to improve yourself. Observe others who are successful in handling their affairs and take the good from a lot of people. If you admire someone, try to emulate them. My all-time heroes are Thurgood Marshall and Dr. Martin Luther King, Jr., two men who had to really work to achieve what they did. And I had the privilege of meeting them both.

I first met Thurgood Marshall at an affair in Harlem when I was with the New York Giants and he was a lawyer for the NAACP. I met Dr. King in 1961 when he spoke in Westchester County, New York, and I was working for Rheingold Brewery. Tickets for the occasion were quite expensive, but Rheingold sent me and my wife to represent them. Dr. King was a great baseball fan, and I was impressed that he was so knowledgable about the sport.

But there was a greater significance for me in our meeting because he presented his philosophy that you could win a person over through nonviolence. Sometimes if you don't strike back, that person feels bad about what he's done to you. I think the only way Dr. King could have succeeded in his movement was by it being nonviolent. He tried to affect the consciences of the people who were mistreating him and the cause.

Right until today, if I meet a person who is not particularly friendly, or if he seemingly doesn't like me or my kind, I try to do something to change his mind. I'll go a long way in trying to win this person over. If after a lengthy period I find out that it's an impossibility, I'll just leave him alone, hoping that one day he will soften and things will be okay.

There have been some people who didn't like me at first, but we later became good friends. Because they found out that I didn't hold grudges and that I tried to do the right thing. They also learned that I could go either way. I could be as tough as I had to be, or I could be mild. And we're good friends today because I won them over. I'm glad I handled it that way. It made them feel better and it made me feel better. They have mellowed and I'm really happy that I've lived long enough to see this kind of change.

But I'm just happy that things have worked out. You can get by without a lot of violence, just by being smart and trying to improve yourself, while also trying to impress those who oppose you. Consequently, from 1928 until today, I've never had another fight with an individual. So I must have done something right.

2 Family and Early Years

My parents were sharecroppers who lived on a white man's land. They gave the major part of their crops to him in lieu of cash for rent. . . . To move away from the South required money, and to accumulate money was not easy. . . . The habit of silence was still strong.

—Jackie Robinson in *Baseball Has Done It*

ALTHOUGH I SPENT most of my years in New Jersey, life for me began in the rural South. I was born February 25, 1919, in Haleburg, Alabama, the eighth child of Cupid Alexander Irvin and Mary Eliza Henderson Irvin. Both of my parents were born and reared in Alabama, and my father was a sharecropper like just about everybody else living around there. Haleburg was a small country community in the southeastern part of the state near the Georgia state line. Columbia is nearby and I always told everyone that I was from there.

We had a big farm about seven miles outside of town, and growing up on a farm in Alabama was really quite interesting. At the time, I was quite young and didn't know anything about hard times because the only times we ever had were hard. We didn't have very much, but we appreciated what we did have.

For instance, I remember a typical outing would be to get in our wagon and drive about eight miles into Columbia to get supplies for the month. The only thing we had to buy at that time was granulated sugar, salt, coffee, and maybe two or three other items that we didn't make or couldn't grow. Being way out in the country like we were, a trip into town was a special event. If we had been real good and done our chores, my father would say, "Well, come on, let's go." And he'd tell each of us, "*You* can go, and *you* can go, and *you* can go. You've done everything I've asked you to do and you're a good worker, so I'm going to reward you by taking you into town."

What we really liked, although it wasn't very much, was a candy cane. Our father would buy us each one, and we thought it was just wonderful. But when we'd get to town, first of all we wanted one of those big pretty red apples. We almost always had a knife with us and we would cut out the core. Then we would put that candy cane in the apple and twirl it around, and then suck out the juice. That was a real treat for us. And our father would only do it if we had been good.

It was the same way at Christmas. If we had been good, we would get candy canes. We didn't have a Christmas tree, but Santa Claus left us gifts by the fireplace because that was where he was supposed to come down the chimney. I remember one year we got up early Christmas morning and went in there, looking to see what Santa Claus had left. There were apples and oranges along with those candy canes. And we would cut out the center of the oranges and put the candy canes in, just the same as we did with the apples. That was all we wanted, and we didn't expect anything else. We didn't have to have toys. We were perfectly happy.

But we did wonder about how Santa Claus got to our house. One year I asked my mother, "Mom, how did Santa Claus get here?" She said, "Well, he comes on a sled." We only had one road leading north and one road leading west, so we went to the fork of the road to try to see the sled tracks that Santa Claus had left. We looked one way and we didn't see any tracks, and we looked the other way and didn't see any tracks there either. So we went back and told her, "We just couldn't find any tracks of the sled." She said, "Well, maybe the wind has covered them up, or maybe somebody in a wagon came by and erased them. But you can bet that he was in his sled, and this is what he left you."

We all believed that until we were older and knew better. After all, we were way out in the country and who was going to tell us any different? So Santa Claus came the whole time we lived in Alabama.

Also during that time I remember my father, brothers, and sisters all worked in the field. Sometimes my mother would too, but most of the time she would stay home and do the cooking. But everybody else worked out in the field picking cotton. They would put pads on their knees and they'd get down and straddle a row and pick from both sides as they went along. Now, that was hard work, and I'm glad that I left the South before I got old enough to pick cotton.

Since I was so young I was designated as the water boy. All I had to do was to supply the water. Of course, we were always glad when noontime came so we could get something to eat. We didn't have any kind of bell, or watch, or anything else, but we got so we knew when it was noon. All we had to do was look up, and when the sun was right directly overhead, that was time to eat. And we'd go back to the house and have some lunch. Many times my mother would bring the food out in the wagon, so we wouldn't even have to go back to the house. This was all in a day's work.

As the water boy, when we were in the field, it was my job to get the water. About every hour I'd have to bring fresh water to keep them cool and refreshed. Over near Tucker Branch, where I got the water, there was a wonderful plum tree with big delicious plums. One day, when the plums were ripe, my family made the mistake of leaving me over there by myself.

I tried to help myself to as many plums as I could eat, including the seeds. So, after eating all those plums, I went to my mother and said, "Mom, I don't feel good." "Well, what have you been eating?" she replied. I said, "I ate some plums." "Well, did you spit the seeds out?" she asked. "No, Ma'am, I didn't," I said. "Oh, boy!" my mother exclaimed. And immediately she told my brother, "Bob, get on Old Alice and go get the doctor."

Old Alice was one of our horses and that may have been her name, but she was the most spirted and fastest horse we had. Bob had to go about seven miles to Haleburg to get the doctor, and it took him about a half hour. While my family was waiting for the doctor to come, my mother rubbed my tummy and tried to console me. I was writhing in pain because I couldn't eliminate those plums.

In the country things don't get done right away and it seemed like a long time before Bob came back with the doctor. When the doctor got there he gave me something that relieved me and plums shot up in the air in all directions. But I tell you, I never felt better in my life. It came very close to being a serious incident, and I'm sure happy I survived that ordeal. From then on, when I would eat the plums, I made sure I spit out the pits.

Old Alice was the same horse that could have kicked me and killed me when I had walked underneath her a year earlier. I must have been about two years old when that occurred. It was in the evening and everybody was working at the mill. The men were grinding sugar cane and the women were serving refreshments. My parents had put me to bed because I was so small. They thought I was asleep, but I crawled out the window and joined the rest of the family at the cane mill. It must have been about seventy-five yards from the house to the mill. I just saw the light down there and started walking toward it.

The horses were tied near the mill, and when my family looked up I was standing under the belly of Old Alice. They said, "Isn't that Pete standing out there?" They still called me Pete then. My mother looked up frantically and said, "He's standing under Alice's belly." Fortunately, they were able to coax me out without touching the belly of the horse. Once they got me out, my mother grabbed me and held me in her arms. I can remember crawling out of the window, but I cannot remember being underneath the horse. I could have been kicked or trampled to death if I had touched Old Alice's belly.

Needless to say, I'll never forget Old Alice. But she was not the only animal that I remember from those days. One of the things that was intriguing to me was that we had a dog named Bob, who would help bring in the cows. When it was time to feed them, we would call all the cows in together. But we had one animal that was very obstinate. This cow was different and wouldn't come with the others. All we had to do was call Bob. We had him trained so that he would go and bring the cow back. If it wouldn't come, Bob would grab the cow by the ear with his teeth. And when they finally got to the house, they would both be bloody. The cow's ear was half chewed off and Bob had blood all over this mouth because he wouldn't let the cow loose until they got there.

From doing that constantly, I'm sure the cow had some kind of hearing problem because it got to the point where most of both ears were almost chewed off and Bob didn't have much to grab on to. But later on the dumb cow got smart, and when we would call her, she would come because she didn't want Bob to get after her. I still get a kick out of thinking about it.

On the farm we raised about everything we needed for subsistence. We would kill some hogs, slaughter some cows, and put the meat in the smokehouse during the winter months. We would also bury sweet potatoes and white potatoes and dig them up as they were needed. In addition to the meat that we had from the domestic animals, my father would go hunting and bring back something for my mother to cook.

On those occasions when the larder got kind of slim, my mother would take a look and if there wasn't very much to cook or if she wanted something a little bit different, she would say, "C. A., time to get your gun out. Time to go." My father was an excellent hunter and he would almost always respond by bringing back just about anything she wanted. He was that kind of a man.

Sometimes my father used to take me hunting with him. He would say, "Monte, come on, let's go. I'm going hunting. How'd you like to go with me?" I would say, "Sure," because I was always delighted to go with him. But shells cost money and we didn't have any to spare. So, my father would only take two shells. I would say, "Pop, why are you only taking two shells?" "That's all I need," he said, "I can do a lot of damage with two shells."

Sure enough we would go down in the woods, and with those two shells my father would come back with two squirrels or two rabbits or some birds. He was noted not to miss. Whenever he went out hunting, he would always come back with something, even if it was possums, raccoons, or something else.

I remember one time when one of the animals he shot was a flying squirrel. The squirrel was jumping from one tree to another and my father hit that squirrel in midair and down it came. It was the same thing with a bird. The birds would fly and he just wouldn't miss. He was just a great shot. I would go and pick them up and put them in a bag. We'd take them home to Momma, and she would make a big rabbit stew or cook those birds or whatever we had. My mother could make anything taste good.

When I was growing up, big families were popular because the children could share some of the chores on a farm, and parents didn't have to hire any help. Back then you stayed at home until you were grown or moved away and married. So, we really were one big, happy family.

My mother had thirteen children, but I only remember ten, six boys and four girls. The girls in order were Pearl, Panola, Arline, and

Irene. The boys were Carl, Mack, Bob, yours truly, Milt, and Cal. My mother also had a baby boy by the name of Curtis, who lived only a matter of months, and another baby who was stillborn. Both of these infant deaths happened before I was born.

My sister Eulalia also died at a young age. She was only seventeen and was getting ready to get married. But one night she had a pain in her side and my parents called the doctor to come over and look at her. He put on a hot compress and it caused her appendix to burst before she could get to the hospital. He was just a country doctor and didn't know any better. He didn't have the knowledge about proper treatment that they do now.

My sister passed away before we moved north in 1927. They say that I was crazy about her, but I was too young to remember. Eulalia was the one who gave me my name. When I was born my parents named me Hubert, and when I was real young, as I said, my nickname was Pete. But Eulalia didn't like the name, and she's the one who gave me the name Monford. When I was about eight years old, we officially had the name changed to Monford Merrill Irvin, but everyone called me Monty.

I changed the spelling myself many years later after I had started playing major-league baseball. Because, when I was autographing baseballs, every time I signed a ball the *y* ran down into another player's signature. I substituted an *e* so all the letters would be on one line. But it was Eulalia who was responsible for me ending up with the name Monte.

Our parents certainly set a good example for all of us children. My father had an excellent work ethic and he was a wonderful person. During his lifetime, he and I never had a cross word. My younger brother, Cal, looks just like him. My father was quite a man and everybody loved him. All the children still talk about him, and how much he meant to them. He was easygoing but never let anybody run over him.

My mother was a little more stern and when she spoke we jumped in a hurry. There was only one rule in our house and that was our mother's. I was fortunate in that I came from a caring family where I learned strong family values, which have stayed with me to this day.

I was also fortunate in that I came from a baseball family. Back then, the men and older boys used to work a half day on Saturdays.

Then they got a team together and went out in the fields and played baseball. They made their own balls and bats.

Some of the guys, just by pitching hay or throwing stones, could throw the ball real hard. Some of them were also fortunate enough to see some of the touring teams play, so they had a pretty good idea of how to play. One section of the region would play another, or this family would play some other families from nearby. Or maybe some guys from nearby towns would come over for a game and we'd get together and have a picnic afterward. That was the most fun they had.

I used to watch my father and my older brother, Bob, in those games, and that's how I first became interested in baseball. So my baseball interest came to some degree from my father, but mainly from my brother Bob.

Those were the good times that I remember from when I was very small and still living in the South. But there were some bad memories from that time, too. That's the reason why we left and came north. It had to do with a certain man named Buck Carter, who owned a lot of land around there. He had a lot of influence but he was a disreputable person and misused his power.

Buck Carter shared the farm with my father and cheated him whenever he could, like every day. At that time a black man had no recourse whatsoever in such a matter. If a white man said something was true, then that's the way it was. My father was a righteous man and he wanted to do the right thing. He knew he was being cheated and also knew that if he protested too much he would have trouble. After he spoke out about it he knew he had to leave, so he told us, "We've got to go someplace else to live." He had a relative in Waycross, Georgia, and he went there to stay for a while. The rest of us were going to join him later.

Before we left, a group of men who worked for Buck Carter came to our house. They drove up in a buggy looking for my father, but we told them he had left. They stopped the buggy under a big chinaberry tree. My oldest brother, Carl, was up in the fork of the tree and the plowshare was also up there to keep it from rusting. He was kind of hot-headed and, if the men started to rough up our mother, he was going to drop that plowshare on them.

The men grabbed our mother and made some threats. They said, "We know you know where he is. You'd better tell us." They tried to throw a scare into her but she just told them that my father was gone and didn't say where. They didn't hit her or anything, but my brother Carl was ready with the plowshare if they had done anything wrong.

We left soon after that incident. A black minister named William Stratton, a highly respected man in our community, heard about what was going on and he immediately came out to our place. He said, "It's not safe to be here anymore." So we packed a few clothes and left to join my father in Waycross.

My father had gotten a menial job in a five-and-dime store, and we stayed there about a month. Then he made his way on up to New Jersey to join my oldest sister, Pearl, who had been there awhile. He made some money and sent it back so we could have enough money to join him at the proper time. The trainfare cost $37.10, and I never will forget that amount because all the people in the area were trying to get together that amount of money. It was terrible around there the way things were, and everybody was trying to leave.

I didn't know how this man who cheated my father could have been so evil. A few years after we left, he passed away and most of the families moved away from the area. But because of him we had good reason to dislike Haleburg and we wanted to forget what had happened there. So after we got to New Jersey we sat down at the table one night and one of us said, "You know, when they ask me where I'm from, I'm not going to tell them I'm from Haleburg, I'm going to tell them I'm from Columbia." We were divided about half and half on that. Three of us, my sister and brother and I, told people we were from Columbia, and the others still said they were from Haleburg.

I've only been back twice since we left in 1927. About fifteen years ago the mayor of Haleburg wrote me a letter saying, "We don't know why you don't claim Haleburg as your hometown. We want to honor you." Grover C. Hall, a Pulitzer prize winner in journalism, was also from Haleburg and they put a sign at the entrance of the town with our names on it. They had a ceremony for the occasion and asked us to be their honored guests.

I went to Alabama with my sister, and we found that things were much different from the time when we had lived there. Our old homestead was covered by grass, and our house had fallen down. But there was a big clump there, and when we looked, we found that it was the chimney of our old home. That's how we knew where the house was.

When we lived there, the town was comprised mostly of blacks who worked for other people. The population was about two hundred and it has remained just about the same since that time. We had a few relatives stilll living in the area and we really enjoyed seeing them. During our visit, the mayor came around and talked to us and said, "Let bygones be bygones." I said, "That's fine with me."

I went back again on February 4, 1995, when I was inducted into the Wiregrass Sports Hall of Fame, which includes people from three towns, Dothan, Columbia, and Haleburg. It was only the third ceremony that the association had held. The first year they had inducted Johnny Mack Brown and some other noted people, and this year they added ten more to bring the membership to thirty-eight. It was an outstanding event and we had a great time. We spent three wonderful days there and the people were very hospitable.

I was impressed by how much things have changed in the area, especially the attitude of the people. I told them that I had left in 1927 as a very angry youngster but time had healed my anger and I felt no malice toward anyone. I'm glad that I have lived long enough to see things change as they have.

While we were there, we visited the Baptist church that I attended as a child, and made another trip to the old homestead. We had about three hundred acres and the Chattahoochee River runs right through it. It is prime land now. The fields were plowed, and every parcel was neat with hedgerows between them. Some of the fields were white with late cotton. We still have a relative named Stovall, who lives on some of the land that we owned.

We relinquished the property by not paying the taxes on the land around the year 1931. I remember, after we had been in New Jersey for a while, we received a tax bill, saying that if we didn't pay the taxes on our land in Haleburg the land would be auctioned off. We told them, "You can do whatever you want with it. We have no intention of ever coming back." That might have been a rash decision because later on they built a highway near there and we probably could have made a lot of money by selling the land at that time. We probably gave away a fortune, but we never thought the land would ever be worth anything and we were just glad to be away from there.

As I've gotten older, I've mellowed somewhat and things *have* changed since the spring of 1927 when we had to leave. Back then, I was too young to really understand how bad the conditions were. But I'm glad that my father did leave, and that I was able to grow up in the North, where there was more opportunity.

3 Formative Years

Monte served as a role model for me. He set the kind of examples that I wanted to follow, and he was the perfect kind of person to emulate. He set high standards in athletics, academics and conduct. He constantly gave me something to shoot at. He was a source of pride for the whole family and a beacon of happiness for us all.

—Cal Irvin, younger brother

I WAS EIGHT years old when we left the South and moved to Bloomfield, New Jersey. Growing up there was just great for all of us children. We had a pond nearby and we used to go down there every day and play. When I was about nine years old, we would get some flat rocks and have a contest to see who could skip the most rocks all the way across the pond. I became the champion because I could do it almost every time.

One day we were all down there and the guys said, "Come on, let's go swimming." I had never taken any swimming lessons, but everybody jumped in so I did too. I saw them doggie paddling to stay afloat and I started doing what they were doing. It was the first time I had ever tried it. I just did it. I just jumped in and started swimming simply because my buddies were doing it.

Things always came pretty naturally to me, so when I started school in Jersey, right away I wanted to play baseball. We used to watch the local black semipro team in Bloomfield, which would play the local white team. And we saw the black Jacksonville Red Caps when they came through on a tour. At that time there was no radio or TV, so when a prominent black team like this appeared there was a lot of interest and everybody would turn out to cheer because black people finally had something to cheer for. Sometimes the black guys would win and sometimes the white guys would win. But it was all in fun and everybody had a good time.

Our family had relatives in Orange, New Jersey, and the next year, my father got a job there. He wanted to be close to work and not have to travel great distances so we moved to Orange. That is where I spent most of my childhood and formative years. We lived in an integrated neighborhood and there were generally good feelings between whites and blacks. We played together, fought together, and had good times together. It was a rough-and-tough environment and I could easily have gone the wrong way. Fortunately, we had a lot of athletic activities and this was right up my alley. So I turned to sports to point me in a positive direction.

In Orange, they had a church baseball league, a semipro league, and something called the suburban league. The last was racially mixed and included teams from Orange, East Orange, West Orange, Nutley, Montclair, and Bloomfield. The team in Orange was named the Triangles and was a black ballclub. They had some pretty good players, and when they would play one of the other clubs, there was always a lot of interest because it was black against white.

At that time if you had any intention of playing sports, you automatically thought about baseball. Each community had its own team, and there was a lot of pride involved in the competition. The teams had meetings and players paid dues. At the games there was no admission charge, but we would pass the hat to pay for the balls, umpires, and transportation. Two, three, or sometimes four thousand people would attend. Games usually started at six o'clock in the evening and continued until about eight-thirty when it got too dark. Sometimes they would play a full game but other times they would only be able to get in about seven innings.

On a Sunday our team would travel to a neighboring city and people would come out in droves. I was only about ten years old and this was all very appealing to me. My brother Bob played on the team and he would take me along, so I really became interested in the game.

At that time I also had another interest other than baseball. I really wanted to become a saxophone player. When I told my mother I wanted to play a saxophone, she said, "Well, all right. You work hard and save your money and you can go down and pay on one, five dollars down and a dollar a week." Well, I worked real hard and saved up five dollars. On the way to the music shop, I had to pass by Davega Sporting Goods Store, which was a big chain in the Northeast at that time. As I went by Davega's I saw a catcher's mitt in the window that I liked. So instead of putting down a deposit on the saxophone, I went in and bought the glove for five dollars. When I came home with the mitt rather than the saxophone, my mother wanted to know what was going on. I said, "Well, I think I like baseball better anyhow."

My brother Bob was six years older than me and Bob had more experience playing baseball. He had bought me my first ball glove when I was about six, and now I had the new catcher's mitt. In order for me to improve, Bob and I would get out in the driveway, and he would pitch and I would catch. Bob provided the baseball, which I think at that time cost fifty cents. We would always just play catch with this one particular ball, and it would last a long time because we wouldn't hit it. Bob just wanted to practice his control. He was so fast that sometimes I could just barely get the glove up in time. He could throw the ball so hard that one time he knocked me over with the ball. Playing catch with my brother definitely helped me develop my skills.

Bob was a natural athlete. In addition to his pitching, he was a good hitter and was good at everything. In 1928 the Jacksonville Red Caps came through town, and he asked them for a tryout. Bob could throw so hard that they wanted to hire him right away. Since he was still living at home, he needed my mother's permission to play with them. "Well, do they play on Sunday?" she asked. Bob said, "Yeah." And she replied, "Well, if they play on Sunday, then you can't play, because Sunday is the Lord's day." My mother wouldn't let Bob play. He forgave her later on, but he never did forget it. Bob always used to say, "I wonder what my career would have been like if I had gone with the Jacksonville team." He could throw as hard as anybody, and it's a shame that his kind of talent was lost to baseball.

It was along about this time that I made my first trip to the Grove Street Oval in East Orange. In 1986 the park was recognized as an historic site and renamed Monte Irvin Field in my honor. Many times as a youngster I walked the five miles from my house to the field to watch the old-time great black baseball teams play. That's where I first saw John Henry Lloyd, Slim Jones, and Chino Smith play. Some of the happiest moments of my youth were spent right there. We went there and watched baseball played the way it *should* be played, and that certainly inspired me later on to become a ball player. That was where I also first saw the Pittsburgh Crawfords, sometime around 1932. The Crawfords that year had Satchel Paige, Josh Gibson, Judy Johnson, Oscar Charleston, and Bill Perkins.

This of course was during the Depression, and since the park was close by and nobody had much money, people would go there and enjoy themselves. Some fans would bring their own chairs and sit in an area parallel to the third-base line. Other fans would ring the outfield and sometimes sit on the roofs of surrounding buildings.

During this time my father, like many others of the Depression era, worked long hours to bring home wages of eighteen dollars a week to provide for his family. Some people look at famous athletes as heroes, but men like my father are the real heroes to me. We never went on relief because we were too proud, and we never went hungry a day in our lives. A dollar would go a long way back then.

Another thing we did to make ends meet, particularly during the Depression, was to have a family garden. My father had a green thumb. He could grow almost anything. He knew how to plant, what to plant, and how to take care of his garden. We would always have enough for our family, and then have some left over for our neighbors.

While my father always had a garden, my mother was great with the fruits. That was another thing that helped us have plenty of food to eat. She could can fruits and put fruits in the jar. And it was an all-day process. She would can enough fruit to last us three or four months. When we wanted some pears, apples, berries, or canned anything, it was always there. My mother would cook a few vegetables, too, and make a great meal out of it because she was such a good cook.

Her reputation for cooking was widely known. We lived right across the street from our church. We'd always go to Sunday school and most of the time to the regular service. After church our minister, Reverend Lawrence, would always stop by to eat. I can hear him now saying, "Mrs. Irvin, can I go home with you and sample some of that wonderful cooking of yours?" And she would say, "Reverend Lawrence, by all means, the invitation is always open."

You could look at him and tell that he was a chow hound. He had a big roll of fat on the back of his neck. I think it was because he ate so much of my mother's cooking. When he would come, she would make us wait until the minister and our father were finished eating, and then it was our turn.

One particular Sunday, the men took seemingly longer than ever to finish. And my brother Cal, who was about eight years old, was very hungry. And he thought that he was going to starve to death before they finished. So, when my father and the minister turned their heads, he sneaked under the table. We had a long tablecloth to cover the table and Cal was hidden by that tablecloth. Then, while they weren't looking, he reached up and grabbed three pieces of chicken, one for himself, one for my other brother, and one for me. But just as he was heading back to the other room, my mother saw him and made him bring all three pieces back.

"Momma, you don't know what you have done," he said. "Why can't we eat with you?" "Now just wait a minute," she said. "We'll be finished in a minute and then you can come on in." Cal said, "Yeah, but by then all the good stuff will be gone." "Well, you'll just have to wait until we finish," she said. Sure enough, they did finish very shortly, and this particular Sunday the food seemed to taste better than ever. I guess it was because we were so hungry from waiting for so long.

These are some of the little things that happened when our minister came to dinner. But soon he was transferred to another church. When we heard that, we couldn't have been happier because we didn't have to contend with Reverend Lawrence any longer.

Even after I started playing baseball with the Newark Eagles, my mother's cooking was still renowned. Roy Campanella, always one of my good friends, was playing with the Baltimore Elites. When we played the Elites at home, the team would usually stay around after the game because they would be going over to New York to play the next series. Some of the guys heard about what a great cook my mother was, and I told her about it. She said, "Well, you tell the boys to come on over because I'm ready for them." So I invited Leon Day, Lennie Pearson, and Campy up to the house to get some of my mother's home cooking.

She had smothered steak, fried chicken, corn on the cob, and some fresh-cut corn. And she had iced tea and candied sweets for dessert. After the guys finished, they said, "Mrs. Irvin, we've had a lot of meals and we've never had any kind of food like this." "Well, it's just my pleasure to feed a bunch of hungry baseball players," she replied. "The only thing I want you to do is to be sure you eat everything. And, if you do, I'll have Monte to invite you back."

So every time we played after that, they always asked me about her. In fact, they took up a little collection, and each of them gave her some money, which she didn't want to take. But they made her take it for serving such a great meal.

My mother was a super cook and she had this knack of improving the taste of anything. There are natural athletes, but she was a natural cook. She knew the little things that would improve the taste. Maybe she would add a little spice here, or a little sugar here, or a little salt there. Anyhow, she was known as the best cook in the area, and she kept that reputation for a long time.

Desserts were her specialty. She would always say, "Well, C. A., I think we should have something a little sweet." So, she became an expert on making peach cobbler, blueberry cobbler, and chocolate cake. And she made some roll cakes that people used to call tea cakes. They were kind of flat and puffy but were very filling and very tasty. My mother always kept us supplied with them and kept them in her tea-cake can. When we got hungry, or if there was nothing else for dessert, we could always have some tea cakes.

When we left Alabama to come north, my mother made sure that she had enough tea cakes to last all the way to New Jersey. Up until the day she died, she still used to make those tea cakes and we still enjoyed them. Family life sure was more close-knit back then. It was a totally different era.

While we lived in Orange, my father worked in a dairy. He was in charge of all the horses used to deliver the milk. He got jobs for my three older brothers, and all of them worked there, making about eighteen dollars a week each. That was fine for our family and we made out all right. Milk was free for us until some of the drivers got caught selling it for five cents a bottle. Then the dairy started charging five cents to the workers for each bottle.

But originally they gave the milk away and we got six quarts every morning. In the winter the milk would be setting at the front door, and the cream would come right to the top because of the coldness. I would get up early and go out there and top all six bottles before the rest of the family got up. They would get on me about doing that, but it didn't make any difference. I wanted to get big and strong and that's how I did it. I drank a lot of milk, I exercised, and I worked hard.

Then when we had a baseball team in school, I went out for the team right away. I was a pitcher and I could throw the ball hard. Anybody who could throw the ball hard and get it over the plate could win, so I won a lot of games. By then Bob was out of school and working, so the focus was now on me and my two younger brothers, Milt and Cal. Milt is three years younger than I am, and Cal is two years younger than Milt.

Later Bob married and moved away from home, and I taught Cal the things that Bob had taught me. By now there were only three of us, me, Milt, and Cal, left at home. All of my other brothers and sisters had moved away. We three boys had one heck of a time, all going to school and all playing athletics. We grew up in the Y and in the church. We would go to Sunday school and then to the regular church services afterward. And when we moved right across from the YMCA in Orange, we were always over there doing something. We were playing basketball, Ping-Pong, swimming or doing something.

So we grew up in an athletic atmosphere. And it became noted that Cal, Milt, and I were the best at almost anything we were playing. I became the marble champion and the tops champion. We'd put the marbles in a circle and I got so good that I didn't miss. I was like Pee Wee Reese, who got his nickname because he was so good at shooting marbles. In fact I would like to have played Pee Wee because nobody was better than me at that time.

We used to put tops in a ring. Then each of us would wind our top up and spin it, and try to knock another top out of the ring. If you did, then you would take that top. I had all the tops on the street and in the area. We had this big wardrobe trunk down in the basement where Cal, Milt, and I kept all our stuff, including the tops that we had won.

Football was Milt's best sport, and he later received a scholarship to Virginia State University. Cal was an excellent student and he became one of the greatest basketball players who ever came out of Orange High. But in baseball he didn't have the power that I did. He was a great fielder, could run like crazy, and was very graceful. I did get him a tryout with the Eagles. But eventually he said, "Monte, you may make a lot of money and become a star in baseball, but I don't think I will. You know good fielders are a dime a dozen." He was about a .280 hitter, which today would earn him a million dollars a year. He told me, "I think I'll concentrate on education. I think I'd like to teach and coach." So I said, "Okay, go for it."

Cal received a scholarship to Morgan State College, where he played baseball, basketball and football. He had never played football before in high school, but he went out for the team and he made All-CIAA (Central Intercollegiate Athletic Association) end. In his third year, he hurt his knee, but the coach wanted him to play football anyway. But Cal told him, "No, I can't play football any longer because I hurt my knee." So the football coach wanted to take his scholarship away if he didn't play football.

After that Cal decided to just quit and matriculate at the University of Illinois. He finished his course work out there, but he had to work like crazy. And he didn't have much money. He couldn't expect much help from my mother and father since they didn't have it to spare. They sent him a little money when they could, but it wasn't enough by itself.

In that regard my sister Arline was a godsend to both Cal and me because she was always there when we needed a few dollars. We could always go to her and she would sympathetically listen to our story and help us financially. She did that for years and years and that's why we were always so grateful to her. She passed away in 1994, not long after celebrating her eighty-second birthday. While she was still alive, not a year went by that we didn't go to see her because we knew how valuable she was to us and how much we loved her.

4 Four-Sport Star

Monte was an all-around athlete in high school and earned a football scholarship to Lincoln University. That's where I first met him, when we played on the basketball and baseball teams together. Later we were also teammates with the Newark Eagles.

—Max Manning, Newark Eagles

I JOINED THE Orange Triangles, the local black team, around 1932 as an oversized thirteen-year-old schoolboy. When I started to play with the Triangles, they already had a great reputation and a lot of good players. My brother Bob was pitching and playing outfield for the team. As I got older, he and I became quite a one, two punch. He would pitch and I would catch. If he wasn't pitching, he would play outfield, and I would pitch. When I wasn't pitching, I would catch or play shortstop. I always wanted to be in the center of everything where I could handle the ball each time. I got to where I could play all the positions and play them equally well.

After Bob left the team, along came Lennie Pearson from Akron, Ohio. Lennie's arm was as strong, or stronger, than mine, so we took turns pitching. He would pitch one day, and I would catch him. Then I would pitch the next day, and he would catch. We had a kind of double-duty situation and thought we were invincible. In fact, we *were* the best. No one could beat us because as hard as we threw, all we had to do was get it over the plate and nobody was going to hit us. It continued like that until I entered high school.

When I got to Orange High, I began to compete in other sports and gained a reputation as an all-around athlete. I could throw a javelin farther than anyone, I could hit a baseball farther than anyone, I was a good basketball player, and I had no peer as a football player. I was never second best in anything. Altogether, I earned sixteen varsity letters in baseball, basketball, football, and track.

In football I played both ways, like most players did back then. We ran a single-wing offense and I was the triple-threat tailback, a runner, a passer, and a punter. On defense, I sometimes played safety, but what I really enjoyed most was playing as a linebacker. I had a knack for tackling and enjoyed pursuing a runner or meeting one of those big fullbacks head on. I'd get down low and put my shoulder right into his mid-section and knock him back. If I had decided on going to the pros, I would rather have played defense than offense. At that time professional football wasn't the big attraction that it is now, and I had developed a little problem with water on my knee. It wasn't anything serious. All they did was stick a needle in there and drain it off. In a week I was all right again.

By the standards of that era, I had pretty good size for basketball and since I was the tallest player on the team I played center. I was strong and could jump, so I was a pretty good rebounder and could score my share of points. But Cal was the best all-around basketball player in our family. I had decided that, if I wanted to play professionally, baseball was the way to go. I had a knack for the game and had a feel for it. I could run, hit, and field the ball. After I learned how to play, I didn't even have to practice because everything came naturally.

When spring came around, I was playing baseball *and* was on the track team. In track I threw the javelin, the shotput, and the discus. I remember one time when we had a baseball game and a track meet on the same day. I hit a home run that went about four hundred fifty feet, and then went over to the track, where I threw the shotput one time to win that event, and still made it back to the ball game before the inning was over.

I got a particular thrill when I set a state record throwing the javelin. In fact, the coach asked me about trying out for the Olympics. I told him I was already doing too much and I didn't want to take on any added responsibilities. But I agreed to help him out by throwing the javelin for the school.

So we had the state meet up in Montclair, New Jersey, and I grabbed the javelin and went through the form of throwing it. The first time, I threw it a long way, but the trajectory was too low. My coach said, "Try to get it up. Throw it higher and get more arc." The next time, at the last minute, I was able to get that arc on it and I threw the damn thing practically out of the stadium. It was measured at one hundred, ninety-two feet, eight inches. According to the record book, the previous top mark was about one hundred, seventy feet. My new mark was the state record for a long time until some fresh kid from Trenton High School broke it a few years ago.

I was very proud of that record because I didn't have to throw the javelin that many times until I mastered the technique. I think the record today is around two hundred, eighty feet. New coaching techniques and the fact that the javelin is made of some kind of light metal rather than wood is probably the reason for the added distance. But in my time I was strong and could throw the javelin just about as good as any high school kid in the country.

At the same time that I was throwing the javelin, I was pitching *and* playing first base and shortstop on the baseball team. I did this for a couple of years and, by doing too much, I hurt my arm.

One day in 1936 I threw the javelin and felt this pain in back of my shoulder. The next day I couldn't move my arm above my head. It was so bad that I couldn't scratch my head or comb my hair. That's how sore my arm was. So I went to my mother and told her how much my arm was hurting. I said, "Mom, Dr. Usher is a chiropractor and I heard he was a good doctor. Maybe he can help me." She asked, "How much does it cost?" So again, I had to ask her for five dollars. And again, she went somewhere and somehow came up with a five-dollar bill. She gave me the money and said, "Here, you go to see Dr. Usher and tell him to please try to help you." So I went to see Dr. Usher, who was a friend of the family.

When he put me on an examining table, I told him how I hurt my arm and where it hurt. Then he started to examine me. Dr. Usher pressed on a nerve in my upper back, and I almost jumped off the table. He said, "You've got a strained muscle, but I think I can help you." I would go to him about once a week and every time he would manipulate my arm. He said, "I'll tell you what you do. You can play baseball this summer, but I want you to throw underhand. Don't throw overhand at all."

Dr. Usher also told me, "I want you to let a lot of hot water run over your arm, and I want you to tell your brother and your father to rub it." So my father said, "Well, I've got the perfect thing. I've got this horse liniment." So he massaged my arm with the liniment that he used to rub the horses at the dairy. I played the whole summer but I never did throw overhand. I would catch the ball and throw it back in underhand. In just a year, my arm came back stronger than before. I guess it was because I was young and in such good shape that it healed so quickly.

In the meantime, Lennie Pearson hurt his arm, too. I don't know what kind of treatment he received, but it never came back the way mine did. If Lennie's arm had responded like mine, he could have been a great catcher or a good pitcher. But when he hurt his arm, he became a first baseman and stayed there permanently. I kept playing shortstop, and later on center field, and I was just delighted to have such good fortune.

From then on I took special care of my arm. I would always warm up real well, and I wouldn't sleep on my right side, only on the left side. I wouldn't sit in a draft, and I just nursed it like a baby. So I really developed a strong arm that was better than ever.

Lennie and I continued to play for the Triangles in the summers through 1937. The team's schedule didn't begin until after school was out, so there was no conflict with high school sports. The Triangles passed the hat at the games, but usually the money that we collected went to expenses. There were some other teams that paid their players, and at that time it was fashionable for talented high school athletes to pick up some extra money by playing baseball summers and weekends.

In addition to playing in East Orange with the Triangles, I used to go up to Paterson East Side Park and play with the Paterson Smart Set, a ball club managed by Charlie Jamieson. Charlie was an ex-major leaguer, who had played in the 1920 World Series with the Cleveland Indians and finished his eighteen years in the majors with a lifetime .303 batting average. Paterson was about twenty-five miles away and we traveled in cars. Usually we had three or four thousand people there, sitting around watching the ball game. Sometimes we might have two black teams, or maybe a black team and a white team, but the games were always a big attraction.

At that time baseball was king. I played shortstop for Paterson and my buddy, Charlie Wright, was the catcher. He used to pick me up around ten o'clock in the morning, and by the time we got to Patterson, it would be about eleven-thirty. Then, by the time we got dressed and practiced and warmed up, the game would start at one o'clock. Around the second or third inning they would pass the hat to pay for uniforms and expenses. A few players would also get paid, and if they collected enough just about everybody would get a few dollars.

Things were definitely going good for me as far as my athletic career was concerned. The arm injury had caused me some apprehension for a while, but that was nothing compared to a couple of scares that I had while I was in high school.

The first one was when three of us who ran around together almost were run over by a train. My buddy had just gotten his driver's license, and we were going to a party in Plainfield, New Jersey. On the way, we saw this flashing light at a railroad crossing, but the gates weren't down. And we just kept right on going. We should have known to stop, but we were having a good time and weren't paying attention. We just went on across the track and, about ten seconds after we passed, we looked back and the train came rolling by at full speed. We didn't get afraid until we had already passed across the track. It frightened us so much that we quickly got out of the party mood and went on back home to Orange. We just forgot about the party.

But that was nowhere near as bad as the scare that I had during my senior year. When I say I had a scare, I mean I almost died. It happened during basketball season. We had played six or seven games and started off well. On my way home from school one day with my teammates, I was feeling real headachy. I had to sit down on the curb and wait until my head cleared before I could continue walking. I told my teammates to go on because I thought I would eventually be okay. I only lived about a mile and a half from the high school, but I had to stop and sit down three or four times before I finally made it home.

When I got to my house, I told my mother that I didn't feel so hot. "Well, here," she said, "take these aspirin and go to bed." I did, but I started to feel worse. It felt like there was a hammer pounding in my head. "Mom," I said, "I've got to go someplace. Call the doctor or do something. I can't stand this." So she called our family doctor, and he came over and examined me. He didn't know what to do, so he put me in the hospital.

When I arrived there, they gave me all kinds of tests to find out what disease I had. They suspected that I had Rocky Mountain spotted fever at first, but later the doctor told me I had contracted hemolytic streptococcus. He asked me all about where I had been and what I had been doing. We traced it down to when I was playing basketball. I probably contracted it when I got a scratch on my middle finger, and the infection traveled up my arm and settled in my chest. I had a heck of a time with it.

I really suffered for the first two days before they found out what was wrong. I never will forget a wonderful surgeon named Dr. Davis, a southerner from Virginia. On the third morning, he came in and said, "Monte, we're going to have to find out what's wrong with you today, one way or the other." He had about four or five student nurses, who were in training, and he had them crowd around the bed. Then he took out a needle, and it seemed to me like it was about two or three inches long. Then he inserted that needle straight down into my chest cavity. The first time he came out with the syringe full of blood. Then he moved it over a little bit, and the second time he came up with a syringe of pus.

Within five minutes, I was on the operating table. They made a big hole in my chest and a big hole under my arm so that the poison could drain. A year later they invented sulfur drugs, and if they had already been around, I would have had a very easy time. But since there was no cure for this at that time, the only thing the doctors could do was to operate and hope the poison would drain off.

Even after the operation my condition was still critical and could have been fatal. But I was lucky. I guess, in a way, I saved my own life. There were four beds in this ward, and I was the farthest from the window. It was February but the heat was coming up, and I was awfully hot. I felt like I was suffocating. I told the nurse, "Mrs. Martinetti, if you would put me over near the window where I can get some air, I know I'll get better."

During this ordeal, I had lost about twenty pounds. I couldn't eat and I couldn't do anything. Rather than move me over by the window, they put me in a private room and piled the covers over me and raised the window. In two days, I was off the critical list because I finally got some air. I could just lie there and breathe. And I could feel myself getting better by just from being able to breathe that good fresh air.

In the meantime, the doctors had kind of written me off and

thought I wouldn't get any better. They didn't think I could make it. In fact they had called my mother and told her to come to the hospital. They wanted to get permission from her to amputate my left arm. "No," she said emphatically. "No, I can't do that. He's an athlete. If he wakes up with no left arm, he'll die anyhow." Obviously I've always been grateful to her for not permitting them to do it.

Since my condition was so serious, and I was losing so much weight, I needed a lot of blood. Each member of my family came to the hospital and gave me the Type-O blood that I needed. I was using so much blood, they advertised in the paper for more. The newspaper stories said, "Monte Irvin needs blood. If anybody that has this same type, please come up and be a donor." I looked up from my bed the next day, and all the kids in my high school class were there donating blood. They were Italian, German, Irish, and black, so I've got all kind of blood in my veins. I guess that's another reason why I survived. All this blood along with the fresh air and the good care that Dr. Davis administered.

I was in the hospital for about six weeks and I was near death. My mother was a highly spiritual woman with great faith, and she told everyone that she had talked to a "Higher Doctor" and that I wasn't going to die. So I had spiritual help as well. Ministers were saying prayers and priests were lighting candles. A lot of people really didn't think I was going to make it. But with the help of the prayers of my mother and father and friends, through the grace of God, I was able to pull through.

So I got better, but I lost about thirty pounds. My mother told the doctor, "Don't worry about the weight. If I can get him back home, I can put the weight back on him." And sure enough, when I came home she cooked candied yams, fried corn, carrots, peas, and cobbler. All the things that I liked. I also drank very rich goat's milk and in a month I had gained most of the weight back.

That near-fatal illness happened in the winter, and the following spring I was ready to graduate. I went into the hospital the first of February and I didn't get out until March. After all that care and staying in to the hospital that length of time, the total bill was about nine hundred dollars. That was more money than I ever thought about or heard of. When they sent the bill home, my mother said, "I don't think it's our responsibility to worry about the bill, because he was playing for the school and we think it's their responsibility."

The school didn't have much money so the administration decided to give me a benefit to raise money to pay for the hospital plus put a few bucks in my pockets since I was getting out of school. They gave me a dance at the Orange Armory and asked me who my favorite band was. I told them, "Jimmy Lunceford." He was a famous orchestra leader at that time and his band played the best music that you ever want to hear. They got Jimmy to perform and we had one heck of a time. All the people from near and far came.

Afterward, I asked for an accounting. I asked the man in charge to come around to the house and talk about the funds. He said, "Well, we did pretty good except that we had to deduct for this and we had to deduct for that, and we had a couple of surprises and we had to deduct for that too." So I was eaten up by the "ducts" and I didn't get anything. The city paid the hospital bill, but I received nothing from the benefit dance.

On a positive note, my mother's good cooking and special care had me back on my feet much sooner than most people expected. In fact, I felt so good that I started to travel with the Eagles that summer. This was in 1938.

The team had an old bus that we affectionately referred to as the "Blue Goose." All the equipment was loaded onto the back seat, and all rookies, no matter how good they were, had to start there. The only rough part about it was, when I sat on the back seat of that bus, I would get jostled up and down as we rode along. It didn't hurt, but it just felt funny because my chest hadn't healed completely. But I was young and didn't mind. I was just happy to be playing baseball with the Eagles, and I spent a great summer that year.

The year before the Newark Eagles had picked me up from the Triangles, and to protect my amateur standing, I only played in out-of-town games where no one recognized me. I also played under an assumed name. After graduation from high school, the same situation existed when I was going off to college. So when I signed on with the Eagles in 1938, I was still playing under an assumed name. The name I assumed was "Jimmy Nelson."

The reason that I chose that name was because Jimmy Nelson, who was a catcher, was my buddy. He was like Roy Campanella, a natural catcher, and that's why I was particularly interested in catching. I liked the way he used to squat down, the way he could throw, and the way he handled himself. He was a fine-looking fellow with a good physique, and he looked good in his uniform.

Sometimes I wonder if he's still alive. We're about the same age, but I don't know what ever became of him. Wherever Jimmy is now, I still think about him. I was Jimmy Nelson when we would go out West to play the Grays, or out to Kansas City, or up to Rochester, Syracuse, or Buffalo. When we came home all I did was to work out with the team before the game started. Then I got dressed and sat in the stands or sometimes on the bench, if the umpire would permit it.

When September came, I went on to Lincoln University, where I received a four-year scholarship. Originally I was supposed to go to the University of Michigan. That was the only rough break I think I ever got. After playing four sports for all those years at East Orange High School, my coach didn't help me get the scholarship to Michigan as he had promised.

Coach Heinie Benkert, who was an alumnus of Rutgers University, was supposed to get me that scholarship. I needed to get a hundred dollars that summer to go out to Michigan and get set up. I asked Coach Benkert if he was going to arrange it and he said, "Yeah. Yeah, I'll take care of it. Between the two of us, you need about a hundred dollars." Now this was in 1938, right in the heart of the Depression. So I got a little job making about five dollars a week. It was a dollar a day and I didn't work every day.

When it was getting close to September, I checked with him and asked, "Well, Coach, are you going to be able to loan me that hundred dollars that you promised?" He said, "Well, Monte, it's been a bad summer for me, and I don't think I'll be able to let you have the hundred bucks. You'll have to do it on your own." "Well," I said, "I found a little job but I don't have a hundred dollars either." I knew then that I probably wouldn't be attending the University of Michigan.

That's when my family doctor, Dr. Walter Longshore, entered the picture. One day he told me, "If you want to go to school on a four-year scholarship with no money needed, you can go to my alma mater, Lincoln University. It's nearby, right down there in Oxford, Pennsylvania, about fifty miles south of Philadelphia and about fifty miles north of Baltimore on Route One. It's an all black school, except for one white student, a football player. It has a great faculty, the food is good, you don't need a lot of clothes, and you're close to home. It's small, with only about four hundred students, but it rates very high academically and is out in the country in just a wonderful setting for a college. I'm sure you'll strike up lifelong friendships with the guys you go to school with. You'll also know all about all the other guys because you'll play in the CIAA against teams from all these colleges in the East. I think you'll be very happy there." And he cited some examples of the guys who had gone there. So I accepted a four-year scholarship to Lincoln University.

When I got there the coaches wanted me to play football. I told them, "I don't think I've fully recovered yet, and I need a little more time." So the season started and when the team lost a few games, they kept pressuring me to play. Finally I said, "I don't know if I'm ready or not, but I'll give it a try." I worked out and when I got in a game, it was like I had never left it. So I played football for the remainder of the season, and when basketball season began, I started to play basketball.

Then in the spring, I started to throw the javelin and to play baseball. That's where I met Max Manning. He was a great pitcher from Pleasantville, New Jersey, and later we played together on the Newark Eagles. Max and I were in the same class and we became very close, and we're still very close today.

I went to Lincoln for a year and a half, but I was broke and I was tired of not having any money or recognition. One thing that I didn't figure on was that, with the college being so small, the athletic program was not as organized as I would have liked. If I wanted national publicity, I should have gone to Ohio State, Michigan State, the University of Michigan, Iowa, or some major college.

Another thing I found out after I got down there was that Lincoln's athletic director was not as knowledgeable as he should have been. His name was Manny Rivera and I wasn't getting along that well with him. He's retired now. He was a Cuban and wasn't used to being around black guys. He didn't know how to get the most out of us. We had eight or nine all-staters and had one hell of a team. But most of the guys who matriculated in 1938 didn't come back in 1939. Manny had his ways of doing things, and I had my idea about doing them. I never had any problem with any other coach or manager, but somehow the chemistry wasn't just right in this case.

At the break in February of my sophomore year, I thought seemingly I'm wasting my time here, and when I go home, I'm not coming back. So I quit school and went home to start playing baseball for the Newark Eagles. I signed a contract and come March, I went down to Daytona Beach, Florida, to spring training.

Again, at that time if you thought about playing professionally, you thought about playing baseball. I'm talking about black or white. Baseball was *the* game. Even though you didn't make much money, you made more money playing professional baseball than any other game. So I decided that's the route I'll go because I won't get hurt that much and I can last a longer time.

II

The Negro Leagues

5 Eagle on the Wing

I remember Monte's first year with the Eagles. He was just out of college, and I had missed the whole year before because I hurt my arm and couldn't pitch. I guess we both had something to prove that spring.

—Leon Day, Newark Eagles

MY FIRST SPRING training with the Newark Eagles was when I began to really concentrate on baseball and started to progress as a ball player. I was a full-time ball player now, and playing under my own name, since I no longer had to protect my amateur standing.

I'll always remember my first spring training camp because that's the year after Leon Day hurt his arm. He couldn't pitch the whole year of 1938 and just sat around the entire season, brooding about his future. Our owner, Abe Manley, kept him on the payroll because Abe knew Leon was a good pitcher and was young enough to overcome the sore arm. So Abe paid Day his regular salary for the entire year, which was unusual for owners to do at that time.

On the way down to Florida, I had said to Leon, "You've been to a lot of doctors and you've really taken care of yourself, but your arm has been sore for a long time. What are you going to do?" "Well," he said, "you know, I've been thinking about it all winter. Once we get to Daytona, I'm going to get out there and just throw the soreness out. If we get a hot day, I'll get out early and put on one of those rubber jackets, and throw as hard as I can for as long as I can. I'm going to find out if I'm still a pitcher, or if I ought to go on back home and get a job."

Sure enough, a few days after we arrived down there, we got a good hot day. It must have been about a hundred degrees. Leon put on a rubber jacket and went out and started to throw. He warmed up for maybe ten or fifteen minutes and then he just cut loose and zipped the ball. He hadn't done that in quite a long time. Leon threw as hard as he could for about six or seven minutes, and when he threw he would wince in pain. But he got the ball and just threw, and threw, and threw until he couldn't throw anymore. Then he went into the clubhouse and took a good hot shower, and went back home and went to bed.

After that Leon didn't touch a ball for a while. But in about four or five days, his arm started to come back. By the time spring training was over he was almost the same Leon Day that he had been before. His arm was as good as it had ever been. That was the most remarkable thing I had ever seen.

Leon had tried medication, manipulation, massages, and everything else, but nothing had worked. So he figured that he would get an answer to what his future was going to be, and I admired him for what he did. I knew what he was going through because the same thing happened to me in 1936 when I hurt my arm from pitching baseball and throwing the javelin.

But my arm was stronger than ever now. It felt so good, and I could throw so well that I used to put on exhibitions. Down at Ruppert Stadium, we sometimes had a throwing contest before the game. Charlie Biot, Gene Benson, Bill Wright, and other outfielders who had good arms would participate. We would get way out, about three hundred feet, and hop the ball in to see who could come the closest to home plate. In one contest, on my second throw, the ball hopped behind the pitcher's mound and hit the heart of home plate for a perfect strike. Biz Mackey was the catcher and he told the other guys, "There's not any use in you guys throwing. There's no way you can beat perfection." So I won that prize real easy. I think it was fifty dollars.

Later, when I went to Puerto Rico and played winter ball, the crowd would just *oooh* and *aaah* when I warmed up. And when I was in Mexico, I used to put on exhibitions between doubleheaders. They had never seen anybody throw the way I could. I was like Clemente, or Mays in his prime. I had a strong arm, could get rid of the ball quickly, and was very accurate. I used to get a big thrill out of just throwing.

While my fielding was raising eyebrows, I was also developing my hitting. I saw the ball well, even a curve ball, but I was hitting the ball to the right side too much. I had terrific power to right field but I wasn't happy because I knew that as a right-handed batter, I was supposed to hit the ball to left field.

One day, around 1941, I went to Yankee Stadium and watched Joe DiMaggio. I noticed his stance and the way he held a bat, and the fact that he didn't stride. I think one of my big problems was that I was lunging at the ball because I had already taken my stride before the ball left the pitcher's hand. So I opened up my stance with my feet staggered about a foot apart. I also noticed how Joe would lift his left foot up, and put it right back in the same place, and then hit with his wrists. With this great wrist action and timing, he could hit the ball four hundred, fifty feet without striding. So I said to myself, "When I go to spring training next year, I'm going to try the same thing."

That's when I began making the same progress as a hitter that I had made with my throwing. I didn't stride and I held the bat back. At that time pitchers wouldn't throw me changes because, if a guy hits to right field, you never want to change speeds on him. You crowd a guy that hits the ball to right. So pitchers would always throw the ball real hard and inside to me, and that was what I wanted with my new batting style.

The first guy that I tried out my new stance on was Terris McDuffie, a former teammate but now one of the Homestead Grays' top pitchers. That day, I must have hit two balls that easily went about four hundred and fifty feet each. They were outs at the park there at Bethune Cookman College, where we trained in Daytona Beach, but at least I was making good contact. Then I noticed that it was just a matter of getting my timing down. I could see the ball well and I could hit it hard, but in order to hit for a little more distance, all I needed was to have a little better timing.

By the time spring training was over, I was a completely new hitter. One day we were playing the Grays and Josh Gibson remarked, "Where did that big fellow learn how to hit?" I knew I was making progress when he said that. All I did was just keep on going. Consequently, in 1941, I must have hit about forty home runs, with a batting average around .400. Pitchers couldn't fool me. I knew, too, that I had to be a good clutch hitter, and I concentrated on hitting with men on base until I was particularly tough in the clutch. I felt good when the pressure was on, and that continued right on throughout all my baseball days. I learned how to hit just by watching DiMaggio.

In 1941, I was selected to play in the East-West All-Star game that was played annually at Comiskey Park in Chicago. This was my first All-Star appearance and there were over fifty thousand fans there from all over the country. I played third base the entire game, and batted between Buck Leonard and Roy Campanella in the lineup. Fortunately, I had two hits, including a double, and a stolen base in the 8-3 victory.

However, what I remember most was when Satchel made his appearance in the game. In the bottom of the seventh inning, the crowd started to yell, "We want Satchel. We want Satchel. We want Satchel Paige." So Satchel got up and started to warm up. Then, when the eighth inning started, he took that long, looping stride to the mound, as only he could.

I was sitting in the dugout between Lennie Pearson and Roy Campanella. I told Lennie, "You know, I feel sorry for you." He said, "Why?" "Well," I answered, "you're the first hitter and you know what he wants to do to the first hitter. He wants to strike him out. You know what a crowd pleaser he is." Lennie said, "You had to remind me, huh?" "Well, that's the way it is," I replied. Lennie went up to the plate and after taking three strikes, he came back to the dugout. I asked him, "How did he look?" "I don't know," he said, "I haven't seen the ball."

It was hot, over a hundred degrees on the field that day, and those little heat waves were dancing in front of our eyes. But that wasn't as bad as the heat from Satchel's fastball that was dancing past our bats. After Satchel struck out Lennie, the only hit we got off him in the two innings that he pitched, was a swinging bunt by Campy. And even though we beat them, Satchel Paige was the star of the show. Everyone was happy that Satchel had made his appearance, and he didn't disappoint anybody by the way he pitched. He was a real showman and almost never failed to please the crowd.

I played with the Eagles until the spring of 1942 and was constantly improving. I came up to the Eagles as a third baseman and played third base in the All-Star game, but my best position was center field. Willie Wells was responsible for that.

When I first joined the team, we were having an infield practice one day and I was working out at shortstop. Wells, who was one of the greatest of all shortstops, said to me, "Monte, this is my position." And he pointed to center field, "That's your position out there. With your arm and your power, that's where you belong. You go on out there and practice." I said, "Well, I don't care where I play as long as I play." And sure enough, I loved it out there. I enjoyed running down fly balls and I was very successful. I played center field in 1939, 1940 and 1941, but I could play anyplace. I still played some at third base and, after Wells left the team, sometimes at shortstop.

I had been with the Eagles almost from their beginning. The team first came into existence in 1936, when Abe Manley bought and consolidated two ailing franchises, the Newark Dodgers and the Brooklyn Eagles, and renamed them the Newark Eagles. Abe's wife, Effa, was active in the team's operations and handled the business affairs for the ball club. The Manleys were a very unusual combination.

Abe had the money, which he made in the numbers business. He had what was called a policy organization that operated much like the lottery. After he made a substantial amount of money as a numbers banker, he went legitimate and bought up a lot of real estate. I would say the Manleys had a couple of million dollars, and that was a lot of money at that time. So he could field a team and stand the losses, if there were any.

As far as sports were concerned, Abe was just a natural baseball fanatic. He loved everything about the game, especially being around the players. He would ride on the bus with us, play cards with us, and do things like that.

I remember one year we opened the season with the Homestead Grays. We had a capacity crowd because the Grays always drew well. But just before the game started, it started to rain. We waited and it rained, and we waited a while longer and it rained harder. Finally, the umpires called the game. Consequently, Abe had to refund most of the money to the fans. When the game was called, we dressed and got on the bus. We were waiting for Abe so we could go on back to the Grand Hotel on Market Street in Newark.

Now, the Inkspots had come out with a song called "Into Each Life Some Rain Must Fall," and it was an extremely popular song at the time. We had the radio on and the Inkspots were singing that song. And two or three guys started to sing along, "Into each life some rain must fall." Abe came out just at that time and told Bill White, the bus driver, "Cut that goddam radio off." "Cap," Bill said, "that's one of the most popular songs." Abe said, "I don't give a damn. Cut it off." "Okay," Bill replied, "but why?" "Into each life some rain must fall," Abe said. "Well, today, too goddam much fell in mine."

We died laughing. But nobody turned the radio back on because we knew he meant it. It was kind of funny to us because we weren't doing the paying, but it wasn't funny to him because he had to give all that money back. Sometimes he was a very funny guy. In general, however, he was a quiet and kindly man.

Effa was just the opposite. She was very fair and looked like a white lady. She was very proper, good-looking, built very well, and intelligent. She was quite a sexpot. When they first got married, everything was okay but later on, I understand Abe got sick somehow and wasn't able to satisfy her sexually. So Effa started to look for sex wherever she could find it. I hated to see a thing like that happen because Abe was such a nice guy.

Effa developed a fondness for our star pitcher, Terris McDuffie, and there's no way to keep a thing like that quiet. I guess everybody knew it a long time before Abe did. When he found out, he called a meeting and told McDuffie that he had been traded to the New York Black Yankees for two broken bats and an old pair of sliding pads. McDuffie was gone, but he was not really far enough away. He was only across the Hudson River, and trains run from New York to Newark all the time.

Then Effa started to date another fellow. His name was Ham Jones. He was a big, tall, handsome guy, who was a detective on the police force in Orange. She went with him a long time, and then along came Lennie Pearson.

Lennie was much younger than Effa, and a very popular player. In addition to baseball, he had played basketball and football. Lennie could also sing and he could do almost anything. Most especially, he had a way with women. Effa fell in love with Lennie and they went together for quite a long time.

During the forthcoming winter, he wanted to play in Puerto Rico but Effa forbade him from going and leaving her in Newark. But Lennie told her that he was going anyhow and left to play with

Roy Campanella, Bill Byrd, and Luis Olmo in Caguas. After Lennie defied her, it was an on-again, off-again affair. Effa still tried to keep him happy by giving him a watch and other expensive gifts, but never much money.

Meanwhile, the Manleys were putting together some good ball clubs. During the years that I was with the Eagles, we had some great ball players. I had already met many of them before my first full season with the team. Leon Day, Ray Dandridge, Willie Wells, Mule Suttles, and Ed Stone were all there in 1938, but I didn't really get to know some of them until I went to my first spring training camp.

When I first joined the Eagles, we had one of the best infields that I've ever seen. They were called the million-dollar infield, and consisted of Ray Dandridge at third base, Willie Wells at shortstop, Dick Seay at second base and Mule Suttles at first base. They were all coming back in 1939 except for Dandridge, who had jumped to Venezuela for more money.

Dandridge was one of the best ever at the hot corner. I've seen Brooks Robinson, Mike Schmidt, Red Rolfe, Graig Nettles, and the other great third basemen, but I've never seen anyone who could make the plays better than Dandridge. Billy Cox was the premier defensive third baseman in the National League when I was with the Giants, and he was a super fielder with a good arm. But Dandridge was a better hitter and just as good, or better, as a fielder.

Once you saw Ray you'd never forget him. They called him "Squatty" because he was short and bowlegged, but he was quick as a cat. He was the best I've ever seen at coming in and getting a swinging bunt down the third base line, because he was already short and close to the ground. He'd come in at full speed, take the ball and flip it underhand and just get the runner. It was a thing of beauty just to see him make that play without even slowing down. That was the darnedest thing I've ever seen. He had an adequate arm but he would always time it so that his throw would just beat the runner. Whether he had to hurry his throw, or if the ball got to him real quick and he had plenty of time, it was the same way, the throw would just beat the runner by a half-step. Dandridge could get the ball over to first base better than anybody I've ever seen.

I saw him play and I have so much respect for him. He was very spectacular but certainly not a showman in the field the way Willie Mays was with his basket catch. It's hard to describe Ray's style of fielding, but there was something about the way he moved that set him apart from the rest of the third basemen. The way he went after a ball, the way he would backhand a ball with that big glove of his, the way he would come up with a hard hit ball, and the way he'd take the ball and shake it before he'd throw it to first base. You just had to see him play to believe it. Dandridge was really something. People would have paid their way into a game just to see him play third base.

Ray was with me down in Mexico and they really loved him there. They thought he was the best third baseman in the world, and they still talk about him. It was the same way in Cuba. Ray was about forty years old when Tommy Lasorda first saw him play there and, even at that age, Lasorda said he had never seen a better fielding third baseman than Ray Dandridge.

At Minneapolis, even though he was near the end of his career, Ray was still bringing people out to the ball park. The fellows in the minor leagues who saw him playing there thought it was a crime that he never got to play in the major leagues. They said that even though he was forty years old, the man should have been given a chance. The Giants said that he was too old, but all we knew was if they had brought him up in 1950, we could have won the pennant. Durocher would have played anybody, but Dandridge never did get a chance. Ray told me one day, "All I want to do is just get dressed and go out on a major-league field and play one game. Then I would be the happiest man in the world."

Dandridge and Wells were two of the finest infielders I've ever seen. I'm talking about bar none. One year they put Dandridge at second and Wells at shortstop and you should have seen them. What a combination that was. They were unbelievable. You had to shoot a ball through the infield to get it through the middle.

One time they made a play that I had never seen before. Wells was at shortstop, and the ball was hit to his left. He went over and fielded it and then gave it to Dandridge, who threw the ball to first to get the runner. There was no double play, they worked that play to just get the batter out at first.

Willie Wells was one of the greatest shortstops of all time, and was the hub of our infield. He was also our captain and later managed the team. Wells had great hands and was a clutch player. He always came up with the big play in the field or the big hit at the plate. Earlier in his career, he had a very strong arm, but hurt it trying to pitch and, to compensate, developed a knack for getting rid of the ball quickly. Even when he had to backhand the ball and get it to first base, he'd still get the batter out. Since his arm wasn't as strong, he played real shallow, but was great going back on pop flies and Texas leaguers.

Wells was also a very smart ball player and knew how to play the hitters. Very rarely would anyone hit a ball that he couldn't get to. In Mexico his nickname was *El Diablo*, which means *The Devil* in Spanish. The players used to say, "Don't hit the ball to shortstop, the Devil's out there today."

He had good speed and was an excellent baserunner. Willie was one of the best curveball hitters I ever saw and, although he wasn't big, he had good power and could adapt his hitting to the ball park. Wells was a much better hitter than Pee Wee Reese and just as good in the field. Pee Wee is in the Hall of Fame and Wells definitely deserves to be there, too. His name has been mentioned for several years and I think that there's a chance that he will get in someday. In comparing Wells to Ozzie Smith, Ozzie could field with him, but no way could Ozzie hit like him.

Wells and Dandridge were complete ball players. They could do everything. The other half of that great infield, Mule Suttles and Dick Seay, were good players but not complete ball players. Seay was a very smooth second baseman and could pick the ball, but he wasn't much of a hitter. He could bunt and hit-and-run, but didn't hit with power or for a high average. However, he was a great team player and everybody liked him, including his opponents. He played winters in Puerto Rico and was very popular down there.

While Seay was a good-field, no-hit type of ball player, Suttles was just the opposite. He could hit the ball as far as anyone, but he was not noted for his fielding. Mule's home runs were usually towering fly balls and he won a couple of All Star games hitting them in crucial situations. I understand that when he was younger, he hit for a pretty good average, but when I saw him, he was most noted for his power. A pitcher might get him out with a high-inside fastball, but Suttles was deadly when they threw him a curve or a drop. He beat Martin Dihigo in the 1935 East-West game, after Dihigo got two strikes on him and thought he could sneak a curveball past Mule. Suttles hit it in the upper deck in left field to win the game and MVP honors.

The Eagles also had a good pitching staff and Leon Day was our ace. But he could do more than just pitch. I remember one game when we were playing against Satchel Paige. Leon said, "Get me a run." But Satchel had us shut out that day and we couldn't do anything. So, Leon hit a home run and won his own game. That's the kind of player he was.

I wish you could have seen this man when he was in his prime. Day was probably the finest all-around player I've ever seen. He had the heart of a lion and threw as hard as Bob Gibson. In addition to his real good fastball, he had a small but sharp-breaking curve and had control of it. When Dwight Gooden was at the top of his game, he was the same kind of pitcher as Leon Day.

Day could field his position, and he also played second base, third base or in the outfield. He was good batter and was sometimes used as a pinch hitter. And he could outrun me. When the going got tough, you wanted Leon Day on your side. We always said that if we had one game to win, we wanted Leon to pitch.

Another pitcher that the Manleys had before the war was a little left-hander named Jimmy Hill. He was originally from Lakeland, Florida, but Manley found him pitching up in Schnectady, New York. Hill was small, but very strong and powerful. He had a great fastball, a real good curve, and kind of reminded me of Ron Guidry.

Around the time that I left for Mexico, the Manleys acquired another player, Johnny Davis, from that same area. He was in prison for a felony, but Abe went up and got him out and put him on the team. He could pitch and play the outfield, and was a pretty good hitter. Johnny was a great acquisition and he became a star on the Eagles. But because of his prison record, someone had to be responsible for him if he left the state.

That was not the first time that Abe had gotten a player out of prison to play for the Eagles. Even before he signed Johnny Davis, he got another player from prison to play with us. His name was Fred Wilson, who was with us in 1939, and he was the most unforgettable player I ever met.

6 The Meanest Man in Baseball

Fred Wilson was a mean player. Didn't nobody like him. He was a tough man and was hard to get along with. Monte was about the only person who could get along with him, because Monte is the kind of person who can get along with anybody.

—Buck Leonard, Homestead Grays

FRED WILSON PLAYED with us in my first full season with the Eagles. He was what we called "evil" and he stayed that way all the time. He was also called a "real bad dude," a "real mean hombre," and other things that can't be put in print. Without a doubt, he was one of the most unusual characters I've ever run across anywhere or anytime.

He came to us from Miami, where he was in jail at a federal penitentiary. The warden there wrote to Abe Manley and told him that he had an extraordinary baseball player, and all that was needed for his release was somebody to be responsible for him. Abe went down to Florida, saw Fred and liked him, and brought him back to Newark. That was in 1938. He played with us some that year and all of the 1939 season in right field.

Fred Wilson was the meanest man I had ever seen in my whole life. He was so mean that he would sit in the bus and just grit his teeth. He always carried a big switchblade in his pocket and wanted to "cut something up." He wanted to see some blood - to see somebody bleed. We used to say, "Fred, have you got your knife?" And he would say, "I've got my pants on, ain't I?"

Fred was a good left-handed hitter and became our number-three batter in the lineup. Since he was attracting a lot of attention and getting a lot of base hits, pitchers started to throw at him. But he was so stubborn that he refused to duck from a baseball headed right for his skull. One day I told him, "Fred you've got to learn to duck, man. I know your head is hard, but it's not as hard as that baseball. You're going to have to learn how to get out of the way." But he had that stubborn, mean streak and he'd say, "Let the sonofabitch learn some control."

One day he got hit by a fastball. Big Edsall Walker, a left-hander for the Homestead Grays, sidearmed it and zipped him right in the side of his head, and Fred went down. I went over to him and asked, "Fred, where does it hurt?" He said, "Hurt nowhere." "Aren't you going to rub?" I asked. "Hell, no!", he said. "I ain't going to let that sonofabitch think he hurt me." I said, "Fred, if it hurt, rub. Don't be too proud to rub." But Fred was too mean to duck and too ornery to rub. That's the kind of person he was.

Fred also had awfully bad feet, the kind that was always acting up, and they caused him so much misery that he trudged along like he was walking on hot coals. Needless to say, he didn't like to run. He *could* run but he didn't like to.

One time we were playing Roy Campanella's team, the Baltimore Elite Giants, up in Buffalo. Fred was hitting in the number-three spot in the lineup and I was batting cleanup. The first time up, Fred worked the pitcher for a walk and I doubled. Fred really had to let it all hang out going around the base paths in order to score. The second time up he doubled and I singled sharply to left field. Again Fred had to hustle all out to make it home safely. The third time up, Fred singled and I immediately doubled him home, and he had to really go all out again to score. The final time up, Fred was on base again and I hit a long triple. Once more he had to circle the bases, bad feet and all.

I had almost caught up with him, as he was rounding third. Dick Lundy, our manager, was coaching at third base and he was waving him on. "Come on, Fred," Lundy yelled. But Fred rounded the bag and then just stopped and started to walk toward home plate. "God-damit," he said, "I'm not going to run any further." After he was tagged out by the catcher, he started to the dugout but stormed over to Lundy and said, "And I'll tell you another goddam thing. From now on get me from in front of that young sonofabitch, because he's about to run me to death. Let him hit number three and I'll hit number four so I can run his ass all over town."

That was in the first game of the series, and we all had a big laugh about it. Then in the next game, we were treated to another one of his escapades. Sometime in the past, Fred had encountered some trouble with the law up around Buffalo. He had shot somebody up there, and the police were still on the lookout for him. So, when we went up there, Fred had to change his name.

The next night, the game was close and the score was tied as Fred was coming to bat. Dick Lundy really got excited and instead of calling Fred by his make-believe name, he shouted, "Come on, Fred!" So Fred called time and said, "Hey, Dick Lundy, come here." The dugout was on the third-base side. So Dick walked halfway toward home plate and Fred went out to meet him. "I told you, goddamit, my name ain't no Fred Wilson," he said. "My name is Jimmy Little. And don't you forget it." We had to stop the game because everybody in the dugout was laughing so hard.

After we left Buffalo we were playing one of those teams out on Long Island. Our pitchers were overworked and their arms needed some rest. Dick Lundy said, "Who can fill in for a few innings?" Fred said, "I'll pitch." So Fred started to pitch and Leon Ruffin was catching. Every time Ruffin got down to give a sign, he would put two fingers down for a curveball. Fred didn't have that good of a fastball and Ruffin was thinking if he threw nothing but fastballs, the third baseman might get killed. But if Fred threw a curve, the batter might miss it.

Fred called time out and said, "Hey, Ruffin, you come out here." They had a conference about halfway between home plate and the mound. "Every time, goddam it, I look in for the sign," said Fred, "I see two black fingers down. Why do you always put two black fingers down? Put one black finger down sometimes." "What?" Ruffin said. "And get somebody killed? If you throw that little dinky curve in here, maybe the guy will swing and miss it and nobody will get killed. I'm going to stay with my two black fingers."

We all laughed and Ruffin went back behind the plate. Then all of a sudden the sleeve on Fred's sweatshirt was dangling, and the umpire called time and stopped the game. He told Fred that he had to go in the clubhouse and change that sweatshirt. Ruffin merely went out, took the switchblade out of his back pocket, and cut the damn thing off. Now both of them were real mad.

The next night, we were at Slaughter's Hotel in Richmond, and

Fred and Ruffin roomed together at that time. A few of us went back to their room, and there was Fred sitting on one side of the bed with his knife and Ruffin sitting on the other side with his knife. We said, "What the hell's wrong with you guys? Why don't you go on to sleep?" "What?" Ruffin said. "Go to sleep and let this damn fool cut my throat? No way." Both of them still had their blades out and were sitting on the opposite sides of the bed nodding. Each one was afraid to go to sleep before the other one did. So we went over and took their knives away and told them, "Go ahead to sleep. We'll keep the knives for you until tomorrow and we'll give them back to you at breakfast." That's the only way they got some sleep that night.

Fred was awfully mean and his reputation made all the other players give him a wide berth at all times. When he came to the club, nobody wanted to room with him. Since I had a sense of humor and was rather mild-mannered, they put him with me. He was also assigned as my seatmate on the team bus. For some peculiar reason Fred took a liking to me right from the start, and he didn't want me to be mad at him. The way I handled him was just to automatically agree with whatever he said to avoid an argument.

For some reason Fred had a dislike for Willie Wells, and they got into arguments all the time. Everytime he and Wilie would get into an argument, Fred would almost invariably conclude his argument by turning to me to get support for his point of view. He'd ask,"Now, ain't that right, Monte?" I'd always respond, "Yeah, that's right, Fred." And that would be the end of it.

One day we were on the bus and something came up, and Fred got in another argument with Willie Wells. As always, to make his point, he said, "Ain't that right, Monte?" And as always, I sided with Fred, "That's right, Fred, you're right." For some reason, that set him off. He told me, "Goddam it, I'm sick and tired of hearing that all the time." "What are you talking about?" I replied, "I'm agreeing with you." "Well, damn it, I'm sick and tired of you agreeing with me all the time," he said. "I don't want any *yes man*. Disagree with me sometime. From now on, whenever I ask you something, don't always say *yes*. Say *no* sometimes." Without even thinking, I automatically responded "Okay, Fred, you're right." We both fell out laughing.

But Fred still hated Willie Wells. One day I told him, "Fred, he's the captain of our team." "I don't give a goddam," he said. "Everytime something comes up that sonofabitch knows more than anybody else." "That's all right," I said. "Maybe when you get to be captain, you can do that." Fred said, "Well, I just want to stick him. I just want to see what color his blood is." I said, "Fred, don't you do anything to that man." He said, "Well, one of these days, I'm going to stick him just to hear him holler."

"And I'll stick you, too," he added. "Now listen," I said, "I've kind of gone along with you on things before, and we're seatmates and I'm for you. But if you get that knife out on your roomie, one of these days, I'll get a bat out and make you eat that damn knife. You just remember that." Then he laughed and reached over and said, "Kiss me, roomie." He didn't want me mad at him. After that everything was okay between us, but he still had problems with almost everybody else.

When Fred lost his skills, Abe traded him to the New York Cubans. After he was with them for a while, he got in an argument with Dave "Skinny" Barnhill, their star pitcher, and stabbed Skinny in the side. Barnhill was out for a month and a half from where this crazy man stabbed him. The Cubans turned him loose, and I think he went back to the Indianapolis Clowns for a while. His behavior was still erratic and they eventually released him, too.

Fred went back down to Miami and after about two weeks, he got in an argument with a guy in a bar and the guy stabbed him to death. Fred Wilson was something else. He was *really* mean. He was the meanest man I've ever seen.

I've seen a lot of evil people, like Henry Kimbro, Ed Stone, Bubber Huber, and a few others. Bubber used to pitch for the Birmingham Black Barons and Baltimore Elite Giants, and he and Fred liked to hang out together. I think both of them were in jail together, and they both looked the same, and that was *bad* and *mean.* They would drink but they couldn't hold their liquor. After two beers they would be drunk as could be. But drunk or sober, Fred was bad news and an unforgettable character. He was simply unbelievable. If you could survive on a team with Fred Wilson, you had to be doing something right.

7 Josh and Buck

The first time that I saw Monte was when me and Josh watched him taking batting practice one day. We said that he had good size and that he looked like he would develop into a good hitter. And he did.

—Buck Leonard, Homestead Grays

FROM THE TIME that I joined the Eagles until I went into the service, the best team in the league was the Homestead Grays, who won every pennant from 1937 through 1942. Then, while I was in the army, they won three more to give them nine in a row.

Their best player was Josh Gibson. He, without a doubt, was the greatest hitter I ever saw, black or white. I think he would have broken Babe Ruth's single season home run record if he had been given the chance to play in the major leagues. The fans saw the Babe from the left side, and they would have seen Josh from the right side. By now, most people have heard about Josh as a hitter, but they still don't know about him as a person.

Josh was one of the most imposing men that I have ever met. He was big and strong and boyish. And he had charisma. He could walk into a room and light it up. I understand that Babe Ruth was like that. And I understand that it was the same way when Joe DiMaggio, Mickey Mantle or some of those other superstars walked in a room. That's the kind of guy that Josh was.

More than anything else, when you looked at him, he was impressive with his physique. He had big broad shoulders and might have had a 32-inch waist, when he was in his prime. And he always had a happy smile and had a funny little laugh that would always warm the cockles of your heart. He looked the part and he played the part. I think he knew he was the best when he got out there on the field, and it carried over to after the game.

In the hotel, in the restaurants, or at a bar everybody wanted to meet Josh Gibson. He would always accommodate everybody and was very friendly and sociable. He could handle the attention that came with his celebrity status. Josh never did get a swelled head. He had that kind of quiet confidence. Naturally, the ladies were all crazy about him because he looked so boyish.

I remember, in 1941, when the Homestead Grays came into Newark for the first time that season to play the Eagles. They arrived around four o'clock and I happened to be sitting on the front steps of the Grand Hotel when their bus rolled up. Josh said to me,"Hello, Monte. How are you doing?" I said," Fine." And he asked, "Where are all the girls?" "You know where all the girls are," I told him. "Lennie has them up there in Orange." "Well, then let's go find Lennie," he said. So we went up there to a little place called the 42nd Street Club.

It was about twenty minutes away and, sure enough, Lennie was sitting there at the bar having a beer with one of his lady friends. When Josh walked in he greeted Lennie, "What you say, lover boy? I understand you've got all the girls up here. How about letting me have just *one*?" "Hell, no," Lennie replied. "I'm not going to let you have any of my girls. You have to get your own." "Oh, Lennie, just *one*," Josh said. "That's all I want. Just *one*."

After talking to Josh for a while, Lennie got on the phone and called a fine young lady by the name of Anna May. I can't remember her last name, but she had been living in Orange for some time and was a lovely, voluptuous-looking thing. The five of us sat there and I had another beer. Then I said, "Well, since Roy Partlow and Raymond Brown are pitching tomorrow, I think I'll go home and get a good night's sleep." As I started to leave, Josh said, "I'm going to leave, too, and take Anna May with me if Lennie lets her." "I can't tell that lady what to do," Lennie said. "She's old enough to have to make up her own mind."

The next day the game started at one o'clock in the afternoon. Wells and Dandridge both singled and Lennie came to the plate. He was the third hitter and I was over in the on deck circle. Josh liked to kid around a lot, and he was talking to Lennie through me. "Hey,

Monte, I want you to tell Lennie something for me." I said, "There he is, you tell him." "No, I want you to tell him for me," Josh said. "What do you want me to tell him?" I asked. "Tell him I screwed his girl last night," he answered. And he laughed that little funny laugh that he had.

While Josh was talking, the pitcher got two strikes on Lennie. Then Josh said, "And I want you to tell him something else." "What's that?" I asked. "Tell him I'm going to screw her again tonight," he responded. And with that Lennie struck out. He went zero for nine in the doubleheader, and swore he was going to kill Josh after the game was over. I told Lennie to cool down and reminded him, "If Josh gets mad, he'll pinch your head off. So just forget about it." Fortunately he did, because as strong as Josh was, you didn't want to tangle with him.

Josh was some kind of character. If you saw him play you would never forget him. Every move was natural. Like Willie Mays, he had natural moves on the field. If you saw him catch or if you saw him hit, everything in his actions was natural. The way he got down and gave the signal, and the way he would prance behind home plate. Even the things he would say.

I remember we were playing a game in Newark in 1938, the last year that Jimmie Crutchfield was with us. It was in the bottom of the sixteenth inning and Crutchfield was sitting on the bench. Josh yelled over to him, "Hey, Crutch! Next inning, I'm going to hit one. You're sitting on the wrong side." But big Mule Suttles came up for us with two outs and hit one over the center field fence, and we won the ball game. So Crutch yelled across the field, "Hey, Josh, I was sitting on the right side." That was really comical. That was one of the few times that Crutch got the best of Josh.

Josh and Buck Leonard were always together. They were the big home run hitters on the Grays, and they would intimidate the opposing pitchers. They would come out before a game and the young pitchers would be sitting around. Josh would ask Buck, "Who won last night?" He'd say, "We did." Josh would say, "Well, the same team that won last night is going to win again tonight." And he'd go up and down and talk to the young pitchers. "You know about me?" he'd ask. They would say, "Yes sir, Mr. Gibson, I heard about you." He'd tell them, "Since the fact that you know about me and acknowledge me, I'm only going to hit two off you today instead of three."

I think Josh got that from Satchel Paige. Because Satchel would come over to the visitor's dugout before a game and introduce himself to the pitchers and ask, "Who's going to go against me today?" Then he'd tell the pitcher that answered, "Well, you ain't going to take out nothing."

Then Satchel would talk to the batters. He might say to Pat Patterson, "Pat, I'm going to get you three times today." Or he'd say, "Pearson, you're a pretty nice guy, I'm only going to get you twice." That's the kind of strategy some of these guys used to intimidate the opposition.

The Eagles went out west on a three-week tour with the Grays in 1941. We beat them the first game of a doubleheader in Columbus, Ohio, and our regular second baseman got hurt. In the second game we had to put Leon Day at second base, because he could play almost anywhere. I was at shortstop in that game, and in a key situation, Leon went behind the bag and shoveled the ball to me, and I got the man at first for a game-ending double play.

After we beat them the doubleheader, we played them again that same night in Dayton, Ohio, sixty miles away. That was the hometown of the Grays' ace Raymond Brown and he naturally wanted to look good in front of the home folks. But Len Hooker, with that knuckeball of his, shut them out 6-0 to beat Brown.

After the game Day said, "Monte, we'll have to find us another team. I'm tired of beating these 'sockamayocks' anyway. We beat them three today and that should be enough. Let's look for another team to play." He suggested this within earshot of Josh and Buck because he wanted to get a reaction out of them. They didn't say anything then but all we did was wake them up and make them mad.

When Buck Leonard was inducted into the Hall of Fame in 1972, I told the commissioner, Bowie Kuhn, the story. "Commish," I said, "we beat Buck and the Grays three in one day, way back in 1941." And Buck kind of perked up and said, "Commissioner, did he tell you that was the last time they won in three weeks?"

Buck could aways find something to laugh about. He was full of fun, but didn't drink and was classy. We admired him because he was a decent kind of guy. It was rare in those days to have an intelligent and compassionate guy like that. He didn't hit the ball as far as Josh

Gibson but he hit it almost as often. Josh hit towering fly balls, and Buck hit line drives. Josh was a better curveball hitter but Buck feasted on fastballs. Trying to sneak a fastball past him was like trying to sneak a sunrise past a rooster.

Leon Day, our ace pitcher, had a fastball like Bob Gibson's and he was confident that he could throw it by anybody. I remember one night game in 1941, when Day was pitching and he said, "They tell me that Buck is a real good fastball hitter. If we get way ahead, I'm going to test him." So we got four or five runs ahead and Leon tried to throw the fastball by him. Buck hit the ball right down the line and almost hit those oil tanks out beyond the right field fence at Ruppert Stadium.

"Well, maybe he was lucky," Leon said. "I think I'll try him one more time." The next time Buck came up, Leon "showered down" on him and got two strikes. He was working him inside and then Leon went outside, and Buck hit the ball *over* the tanks. When Leon came in the dugout after the end of the inning, he said, "Well, he convinced me. He'll never get another fastball from me." From that time on, Leon threw changeups to Buck, and nothing else.

Buck and Josh were a great power combination and were called the *Thunder Twins* by the press. Either one of them could beat you. I remember a game against the Grays in 1942 that also involved Day, but this time it was Josh who was the batter. We were leading two to nothing in the top of the ninth inning with two outs. Jimmy Hill, a left-hander, was our pitcher. He got wild and walked Sam Bankhead, with Buck and Josh coming up. Buck was a left-handed hitter, so we figured we'd leave Hill in there to pitch to Buck. But, just in case Hill didn't get Buck out, we told Day to get warm real quick so he could come in to face Josh.

So, when Hill walked Buck, Day came in and got two quick strikes on Josh. Instead of wasting one or two pitches, Leon figured to get him in three pitches. The next pitch was a low fastball that he got just a little too good on the outside part of the plate, and Josh hit it into the center field stands to win the game 3-2.

After the game we got dressed and Buck and Josh came out. As they were getting ready to get on their bus, Mrs. Manley came out and said, "Josh, you should be ashamed of yourself. You spoiled our day. We had this wonderful crowd and you just spoiled it for us." "Mrs. Manley," Josh said, "I've been known to spoil a lot of days for a lot of people." We all laughed and got on our bus. But it was true, Josh *did* spoil a lot of days for a lot of people, especially pitchers.

It's just too bad, that most major-league fans never got a chance to see Josh play. The local fans all knew about Josh. A lot of white fans, particularly around Pittsburgh, came to see the Grays play and they knew about him. They also knew about him in Washington because the Grays played many of their games in Griffith Stadium. Of course, they knew about him on the Islands where he had played in Cuba, Puerto Rico, and Santo Domingo. And they also knew about him in Venezuela and Mexico.

Josh was remembered everywhere he played because he was always at the top of the league in batting and he always hit more home runs than anybody else. Not only was he a home run hitter but he also hit for a high average all the time. A pitcher might strike him out the first three times, but then Josh might go ten for ten. That's the kind of hitter he was. He was as good as he wanted to be.

If Babe Ruth would hit a pair of home runs and it was in the papers, Josh would say, "Well, I see where Babe hit two today. Maybe I'd better go out there and hit three." That was Josh's way of saying, "I'm pretty good too. I wish they'd give me a chance."

He had this wonderful sense of humor. I'll always remember Easter Sunday in 1942, when we played the Grays at Griffith Stadium in Washington D.C. In the first game we beat them something like 9-3, and the second game we beat them about 10-2. Whatever the final scores were, we scored a lot of runs in both games. So after the last run crossed the plate in this doubleheader, I never will forget Josh saying, "Well, I'll tell you one damn thing, you guys will be tireder tomorrow than we are - from running around the bases." That was a typical remark by Josh. He could always find something funny to say about anything.

Josh knew that Terris McDuffie couldn't read very well, so he was always on McDuffie. "Hey, Mac, here's a newspaper. Come read me the sports page. See what it says over here, Mac. I don't understand it. Come read it to me." He kept up that kind of thing. He would ride you to death if he knew it got under your skin. But you couldn't stay mad at him.

One of the funniest things that ever happened to me in baseball occurred while we were on a bus going from Butler, Pennsylvania, to McKeesport, Pennsylvania. Eric Illidge, our traveling secretary, said to McDuffie, "McDuffie, why don't you be quiet? You're always talking but you don't know anything. In fact I believe you're dumb. In fact you *are* dumb. I'll tell you what you do. Can you spell fifteen? I'll bet you five dollars that you can't spell fifteen." McDuffie said, "Fifteen? Anybody can spell fifteen." "We'll let Irvin hold the money," Illidge answered, and both of them gave me five dollars. If McDuffie spelled fifteen, he knew I was going to give him the money.

"Any time you want to start, go ahead," Illidge urged. We must have ridden about two miles and he said, "What the hell are you waiting for? Spell it or I'll pick up the money." "Just a minute," McDuffie said, "I'm warming up." "Well, go ahead whenever you're ready," Illidge replied. We rode along a little farther and finally McDuffie said, "Well, I'm ready. F.I.V.E., five. T.E.N., ten. Now give me my goddam money." Everybody on the bus died laughing.

"No, that's not the way you spell it," Illidge said. "Spell it for him, Monte." So I spelled it for him, and McDuffie said, "Just because he's in college, that doesn't mean he knows how to spell it." At that, McDuffie took a switchblade out of his back pocket and said, "The way I spelled it is the way it is." I told him, "McDuffie, the money is yours." For the rest of the season, everybody was asking McDuffie to spell fifteen for them. It took him a long time to live it down.

It seems like McDuffie was always involved in some kind of incident. One year in Cuba, he came into the clubhouse and Adolph Luque, the great Cuban pitcher and manager, came over to him and said, "Mac, you've got to do me a favor. Our scheduled pitcher has a sore arm and can't go tonight. You've had more rest than anybody else, so I'm going to give the ball to you."

McDuffie said, "Hell, no. I just pitched two days ago." "Please," said Luque, "this is an important game, so do me a favor and try it." At that, Luque went away for about a minute. In the meantime McDuffie sat on his stool and started to get dressed. When he looked up, Luque was standing over him with a forty-five. Luque reiterated, "McDuffie, I said, you're the pitcher." McDuffie looked at the pistol and said, "All you gotta do is give me the ball." Then he went out and shut out the opposing team 2-0. That's the kind of influence that Luque had over some of his players while they were playing down in the Cuban winter league.

Another incident involving McDuffie happened when we were playing Josh and the Grays during the late thirties. McDuffie had good stuff that night, and Josh came up to the plate in a key situation. McDuffie got two strikes on him and threw him a good fastball, and Josh fouled it off. Then he threw Josh three curveballs and Josh fouled them off, too. So McDuffie tugged at his pants, looked in, and took the sign. Then he threw a pitch right down the middle, which Josh took because he was so surprised.

When Josh took the pitch for a called strike three, McDuffie boogied from the mound to the dugout. "Don't mess with me," he said. "I'm the great McDuffie. I've got more heart than anybody else. Don't mess with McDuffie, when the going gets tough, 'cause when the going gets tough, McDuffie gets going." And everybody died laughing because just to see him boogie from the mound to the dugout was a sight I'll never forget. Josh just laughed and every time he saw McDuffie after that he said, "Hey, Mac! Do that boogie for me again." He always had a repartee for whatever happened.

8 An Historical Perspective

They said we weren't organized. We were organized, we just weren't recognized. We had two leagues, and we had a World Series and an All Star game every year. We loved the game and we felt like we were making a contribution to baseball, too.

—Buck Leonard, Homestead Grays

THE LORE OF black baseball is rich in anecdotes and tradition, yet most people know very little about the Negro leagues. In recent years there has been a growing interest in the style of baseball that we played, and people are trying to learn more about the history and conditions that existed. I think, in order to fully appreciate the special qualities that were embodied in black baseball, it would help to understand the circumstances surrounding the organizational aspects of the leagues and the conditions under which they had to operate.

During the years that I played, we structured our leagues along the same lines as the white leagues. Our top two leagues were considered major leagues and all others were the minors. My team, the Newark Eagles, was in the Negro National League, which was comprised of ball clubs located in the East. The other teams in our league were the Homestead Grays, Baltimore Elite Giants, Philadelphia Stars, New York Cubans, and New York Black Yankees.

The other black major league was the Negro American League, and their teams were located in the Midwest and South. Some of their weaker franchises only lasted a year or two, but the league usually consisted of the Kansas City Monarchs, Chicago American Giants, Birmingham Black Barons, Memphis Red Sox, Cleveland Buckeyes and Indianapolis Clowns.

Beginning in 1942, we played a World Series, with the pennant winners of each league playing for the championship. That continued on through 1948, when the Negro National League folded after the end of the season. We had some good teams in the Negro leagues. I wouldn't say that the teams intact were major-league caliber, but they could *play*. Each team would have two or three outstanding stars, and at least two or three excellent pitchers. The raw talent of the players was generally major-league caliber, but in other ways, the leagues were not at that level. The owners had a loosely formed league and they stayed together, but they were not very well organized.

In the East, all the owners were black, except Eddie Gottlieb who was part owner of the Philadelphia Stars. There were other white owners in the West. J. L. Wilkinson in Kansas City, Syd Pollock of the Clowns, and Abe Saperstein, who had a partial ownership of a franchise, were the main ones. In earlier years, there were a few other white owners. At the time when I was playing, most of the owners were in the numbers business, because that was the only way a black man could garner enough money to field a team.

The owners in the Negro leagues were unusual. They could have wielded a lot of power but one thing that limited them was that they didn't control their ball parks. Black owners were always at the mercy of the major-league or minor-league teams that owned the stadiums. Sometimes we played in major-league parks, but mostly we played on minor-league fields. For the Eagles, Ruppert Stadium served as our home field when the Newark Bears of the International League were away. Likewise, the New York Black Yankees played at Yankee Stadium when the Yankees were on the road, and the New York Cubans played in the Polo Grounds when the Giants were away. So, when we played one of those two teams, we played in a major-league park.

Major-league owners did that because they gained additional revenue from renting their ball parks to black teams. But they wouldn't let the teams rent directly, so the black owners had to go through a booking agent. Bill Leuschner, who took over in the New York area after Nat Strong died, was one of the booking agents. Another one was the man from Philadelphia, Eddie Gottlieb. I think they would get fifteen to twenty percent off the top. They would buy up the key dates and control them. If you wanted to play on those dates, you would have to go through them. I think Abe Saperstein, who owned the Harlem Globetrotters, was involved in some way with booking games, too.

Mrs. Manley was a very astute businesswoman and she became very knowledgeable about baseball affairs. This practice of having to go through booking agents was one of the things that stuck in her craw. I think she tried to get the other owners to organize and fight this practice somehow, but she was not successful. It was that way throughout the country, except for the ball parks that were owned by the black owners.

Years earlier, in Pittsburgh, Gus Greenlee built his own stadium, but I don't think Greenlee Field was a very good park. He never did put in a proper grandstand, and it wasn't constructed according to major-league standards. I can remember seeing it from the outside, but I never did play there. Another black ball park was Martin Field in Memphis, Tennessee. There may have been one or two others but, for the most part, we played in the white baseball parks.

Since each team didn't have control of their own home park, scheduling was not uniform and league operations were not consistent. This caused some people to consider Negro baseball a second-rate operation. Teams didn't play a balanced schedule and, if a game was rained out, it might never be played. The league was not very well organized and they had trouble getting umpires. There was a lot of internal squabbling going on among the owners and league officials, and it's too bad that those conditions existed. But that doesn't take anything away from the individual players, who had real ability.

Probably the best place to showcase all the talent that was in our leagues was the East-West All-Star game. That was the biggest attraction in black baseball. It was started in 1933, the same year as the major league's inaugural All-Star game. Gus Greenlee was the person most responsible for organizing the East-West game, and it became an annual classic. Fans voted for the starting players in a poll conducted by the leading black newspapers across the country. When they filled out the rest of the roster, each club had to be represented and they tried to pick one or two players who had performed well for each club.

I played in four of these All-Star games and missed four others because of playing in Mexico and serving in World War II. By comparison, the major-league All-Star games weren't nearly as much fun. The East-West games were played in Chicago at Comiskey Park and each one was always a joyful experience. The park would be decorated with red, white, and blue banners that had been put up everywhere, and a jazz band would play between innings. The whole scene was festive and fun. People like Count Basie, Ella Fitzgerald, and Billie Holiday would always make it their business to be in town for the East-West game, and we'd be sure to check them out at the jazz clubs. You didn't go to Chicago to sleep.

I remember my first East-West game. When we were selected, we would leave on a Friday and get to Chicago either Friday night or Saturday morning. I was twenty-two years old and I couldn't wait to get to Comiskey Park. Count Basie had written a song called "Goin' to Chicago Blues," and it was a very popular song in 1941. They were playing it on the radio during our train ride, and everybody in our car was singing along, "Goin' to Chicago, sorry I can't take you." We finally pulled into Chicago late Friday night and checked into the Grand Hotel.

The game was played on a Sunday afternoon. At that time I think Comiskey Park's capacity was about fifty thousand but sometimes they would have as many as fifty-five thousand in attendance because the promoters could always do business with the fire department and they would let fans sit in the aisles.

People would come from all over the country to be part of this spectacle. They came all the way from Misssisippi, New Orleans, Birmingham, Mobile, Kansas City, Detroit, and from all over just to see the big stars. There were a few whites scattered throughout the ball park, but mostly it was blacks of all backgrounds, all shapes and sizes, men and women and children. Black people used to love baseball. I wish I knew what happened to that love for the game. Maybe it has become an economic hardship. But people had to scrape to get by in the old days, even more than now.

But the fans really turned out for the East-West game and they always saw a good game and great players. If you picked an All-Star team from the two squads, it surely could have rivaled any white major-league all star team of the time. That team would have been as good as any All-Star team that's ever played.

Playing in these games was a way for us to promote the Negro leagues and to pave the way for the present-day black ball players. But more than anything else, our games gave black Americans hope all across the country. The same thing was true of our regular season games, everywhere we traveled. When we would play down South, out West, or here in the East, black people got a chance to come out and see these great players perform on the baseball field and it gave them hope.

They said, "If these ball players can succeed under these very difficult conditions, then maybe we can too." Maybe many of the people who came out to the ball park caught hell all week. If they had a job, it was usually a menial one, and they were not getting any encouragement at the workplace. But on Saturday or Sunday, they went to a game and saw players the same color performing well on the baseball diamond. That made them feel pretty good and just generally uplifted their spirit.

9 Days That Used To Be

We would sing and joke and talk on the bus. We called Monte "Bring me Back" because just as soon as anybody got out, he would say, "Bring me back a coke" or "bring me back a sandwich" or "bring me back something else."

—Leon Day, Newark Eagles

THE LIFE-STYLE OF a baseball player in the Negro leagues is almost forgotten. It was an arduous existence, which consisted of "long rides, low pay, and a game almost every day." The traveling conditions were almost unbelievable. That was the tragic part about traveling, particularly in the South, where we couldn't even stay in the third- or fourth-rate hotels. The only places we could stay were rooming houses. We had to find a black family that would rent a room to us. When we came into a town and that was the situation, Abe would have made arrangements so a certain number of us could dress in one house and others in another house. That was in towns where there were no black hotels.

When we would go to Syracuse, Rochester, or places like that, most of the time there was a black hotel. Later on, we were able to stay in a third- or fourth-rate white hotel, but we couldn't stay in any of the league hotels. It was even that way in Pittsburgh and Chicago, but it was no problem because there were plenty of black hotels in those cities.

But small towns were where we'd run into all kind of problems. We couldn't get anything to eat because we couldn't eat in the restaurants. We'd have to send in and get a can of sardines or Vienna sausage, and some soda crackers. Or we'd get a candy bar and a bottle of soda, and then wait until we got to a big city where they would serve us. It didn't matter how hungry we were, these restaurants wouldn't serve us.

I remember one time when we pulled up to a cafe that had a gas station. We were going to get filled up, which would have cost about twenty-five dollars. Back then, that was a lot of money to spend on gas. So, we asked the guy, "Can we get a hamburger?" He said, "No I'm sorry, I can't give you no hamburger." We said, "You mean to tell us, we can't have a hamburger, after we're buying all this gas?" He said, "No." He was in the process of filling up, so we told him, "That's enough. That's all the gas we want." And we left, just like that.

When these things happened, we couldn't get too mad because we never knew what they would tell the law. And they *were* the law. We were completely at the mercy of the local people. If they really wanted to do something to us, they could. And there wouldn't be a darn thing done about it. Fortunately, we used to avoid situations like this by having a sense of humor about it. We told them, "We're baseball players. We don't hate anybody. All we want to do is play baseball and make somebody happy." We'd try to handle it like that. We would make a joke out of it and humor them along until we could leave.

I remember in 1946 Mrs. Manley bought a brand-new, air-conditioned bus. It was the latest thing and was wonderful. We were in one of the southern states riding along the highway, and along came a bunch of farmers in a truck. They had been in the field and they came by and looked at us in this nice air-conditioned bus, all laid back. And they said, "Golly, look at the jig-a-boos." Just like that. Lennie Pearson, who was hot-headed anyway, yelled, "Your mother!" We almost killed him.

Biz Mackey was the one who got on Lennie the most. He said, "Don't you ever say a thing like that. Are you crazy? Aren't you used to being taunted down here? Leave these people alone. Let them say anything they want to say." We finally passed the farmers and Biz looked over at them, waved and shouted, "Okay, anything you say." He was trying to make things all right because these people could call ahead and when we got into town, the state troopers would be waiting on us. Or maybe the Klan would be waiting.

One time in Meridian, Mississippi, we pulled into a service station to change the oil, and they took out all our transmission fluid. We didn't know what they had done, and drove a little way down the road before we found out. And we had to call a repair truck to tow us back to town to get the damn bus fixed.

Another time we were going from Montgomery to Birmingham one hot afternoon, and we saw a cafe built up on a terrace. We pulled the bus off the road right at the foot of the terrace, and Leon Day, Lennie Pearson, Len Hooker, and I got out. We walked up some stairs and, a little farther on we had to walk up some more and, finally, we reached the top.

There was a lady serving people and, when she saw us, she started shaking her head. I said, "Miss, how can you shake your head when you don't even know what we want?" She said, "Whatever it is, the answer is 'no'." "Oh, that's too bad because all we wanted was a hamburger or a hot dog or something," I said. "But mainly, we just wanted a cool glass of water."

"Well, I'm not going to sell you anything," she said. "If you want some water, its back there in the well." I said, "Well, how are we going to get it." She said, "You can draw it. You know how to get the water. You throw the bucket down in the well and you hoist it up." We did that and got a bucket of water. They had one of those gourds to use for drinking, so we drank out of the gourd. Then we walked back down the steps and were getting in the bus to continue the trip. When we looked around, she was breaking this gourd into little pieces. We said, "How can she hate us when she doesn't know us? We're just baseball players trying to get along and that's all."

There were times when people indicated they would like to help if the laws were different. But they were afraid they would lose business. On that same trip, we pulled into another gas station late at night. The colored restroom was way in the back, and it was dark back there. So, we asked the attendant, "If you don't mind, let us use this one right here. Let us use the white restroom. It's nicer. It's not way in the back there. It's lighted and clean. Who the hell would know the difference?" He said, "Yeah, go ahead."

We were buying plenty of gas anyhow, and we also bought some peanuts and soda. In the meantime, some guys pulled up in a truck and got out to use the restroom. So, the attendant realized what was going on. He hollered "Hey, what are you niggers doing? I told you, goddam it, the colored restroom is in the back. Get your asses on back there." So we did. When we came back, we patted him on the back and said, "It's okay fellow, we understand. You tried and we appreciate it."

It was just like that, too, in 1941 when we were training at Virginia Union College. Willie Wells had a brand-new 1941 Buick, and we were on our way to play the Grays that Sunday in Washington. We stopped at a gas station and a guy came up, looked at the car and wouldn't even sell us any gas. Willie said, "What the hell are we going to do?" "Well, if he doesn't want to sell to us, that's fine," I answered. "If we keep riding, maybe we'll find somebody who will sell to us."

We got in the car and drove a mile or two and saw another gas station. We went in and the guy couldn't have been nicer. "You want some gas?" he said. "Sure. How much do you want?" While he was pumping the gas, we asked, "What's the matter with the fellow down the road?" "Oh, that sonofabitch is crazy," he said. "We get a lot of complaints about him. Well, you know, you find one in every crowd." We tipped him a dollar for being so nice.

It was a similar situation when we played exhibition games against white teams. Sometimes the fans would say something but most of the time they were complimentary. They'd say, "Well, you boys sure can play ball." And we'd answer, "Well, keep coming out, we like to please you." Some of the fans would say something derogatory, but it wasn't in a vicious way. They might say, "Well you darkies sure can run," or something like that.

Most of the white players were very fair. Every once in a while we might run into a guy who would give us a hard time or try to take unfair advantage. But for the most part, while we were playing, there were no problems with the opposing players. Their pitchers would brush you back, but that was all right because black pitchers did the same thing. That's part of the game.

The East Orange Baseball Club was an aggregation of marginal major-league talent on the way up or on the way down. The rivalry between the Newark Eagles and East Orange in the late thirties was big, and the games sometimes attracted crowds as large as five thousand.

We used to play in East Orange on Saturdays and in Newark on Sundays. We loved that because the Saturday game started at one o'clock in the afternoon and after the game was over, we had a chance to get something to eat and have a few beers before having to play a doubleheader the next day in Newark. It was only ten or fifteen miles away, so we didn't have far to travel. It was almost like a day off. So we loved to play in East Orange.

I remember once, when we were playing a key game against them, we were ahead 3-2 but they had the bases loaded with two outs in the bottom of the ninth inning. The last batter of the game hit a flyball to our center fielder, Jimmy Crutchfield, and he caught it behind his back for the final out. That's what a great talent he was. When he came off the field, Mrs. Manley told him, "Jimmy if you ever do that again, it'll cost you two hundred dollars." "Aw, I just wanted to give the fans a thrill," he said. "Besides, you've already advanced me next month's salary, go ahead and fine me."

Sometimes the East Orange contingent wanted to win so badly that they would engage in nefarious means. One time they put the baseballs in the refrigerator the night before the game. Of course the frozen baseballs wouldn't carry nearly as far as a regular baseball. So, when the Eagles batted, they used the frozen balls and, when East Orange batted, they used the regular balls. Other times they would enlist the aid of the umpires to give us a dose of home cooking with a key call at a crucial time in the game.

One day in East Orange Willie Wells, our captain, said, "I'm going to try something different today." So, when he went out to get the ground rules from the umpires before the game, all of a sudden he looked up at both of them and asked, "Are you prejudiced?" The plate umpire said, "No" and the other one agreed, "No, we're not prejudiced." "Well, I'm glad to hear that," Willie said. "Don't get us in a crack and squeeze us. We don't expect you to give us anything, but neither do we expect you to take anything away from us. Let's have a good game. Just call it like it is, that's all." And he turned around and walked away.

Usually in those kind of games, if the score was close and the count was three and two, you could throw a fastball right across the middle of the plate and it would be ball four. If it meant going ahead or tying the game up and the batter didn't swing, he was almost automatically on first base. That was what Wells meant. Sure enough, the game that day was close, and we wanted to win so badly that we relieved with Leon Day. Late in the game, Leon got a batter three and two and threw a fastball right over the plate. The batter took it, and the umpire called it strike three. But if Wells hadn't said what he did, it probably would have been ball four. He had found out from experience what you had to do to win.

The umpires in those exhibition games were white, but home cooking was not exclusive to exhibition games or white umpires. In Negro league games, the home team would furnish the umpires, and sometimes they were not always impartial. We usually had black umpires in league games, but sometimes they wouldn't show up. When this happened, there would be a white umpire on call and he would work the game, which was fine with us.

In earlier years, especially in the Eastern Colored League, they had mostly white umpires. But with the Eagles, we used black umpires. There were four or five pretty good umpires around Newark. Most of the time we would have Fred McCreary, one of the best umpires, Phil Cockrell, an old submarine, spitball pitcher, and another guy in Newark by the name of Hub Crawford.

Another of the better umpires was John Craig, from Pittsburgh. There were some other good umps from around that area but if you ever got out there, they would always favor the Homestead Grays. If a critical play came up you could almost bet that the Grays would get the benefit of the call. It was the same way in Philadelphia and other towns. One time Craig and the other umpires came out on the field before a game and little Jimmy Hill said, "Well, here comes Jesse James and the Dalton boys." The umpires wanted to eject him before the game started but the league officials in attendance wouldn't let them.

Players and fans in the Negro leagues got on umpires worse than they did in the white major leagues. It got so bad that a couple of the umpires carried pistols. Big Fred McCreary started carrying a pistol in his pocket, and Phil Cockrell had a gun, too, because somebody was always threatening him. They had to protect themselves because some players would come after them with a bat. And those guys would hit anybody.

The worst incident I ever saw was when the Eagles were playing the Grays at Griffith Stadium in Washington, D.C. We had an umpire in the league by the name of Pop Turner, who was a graduate of North Carolina Central University in Durham, North Carolina, and he was umpiring the game. Boojum Wilson came up to bat for the Grays in the ninth inning, with the bases loaded and the winning run on base. Turner called Boojum out on strikes on a questionable pitch for the last out.

Both teams and the umps were dressing in the same clubhouse. After the game, Pop was over in a corner of the clubhouse getting dressed. Boojum came in and confronted him. "Why didn't you call the goddamed play right, you blind sonofabitch?" Then Boojum picked up a bat and said, "I ought to take this bat and bust your goddam brains out." And he drew back with the club end of the bat and was going to hit Pop with the butt of it. Pop Turner just happened to have the presence of mind to duck under it, and the bat splattered all the plaster off the wall.

If Boojum had hit the man he would have killed him. We all grabbed Boojum and tried to cool him down. And somebody brought the cops into the locker room and escorted Turner out. That shows how dangerous it was sometimes. Some of the guys were really crazy and that's why some of the umpires got in a habit of carrying a small gun in their pockets to protect themselves from some of those big bastards.

Boojum was a tough character. I've heard a lot of stories about him hitting players, fans, umpires, and even cops. He was bad, but he wasn't as bad as Fred Wilson because you could kid with Boojum. You could cajole him a little bit better than you could Fred. But Boojum was no piece of cake. On the field he was poetry in motion as a hitter. He was smooth and he could really hit that ball. He was not much of a third baseman, but he sure could hit. He was a left-handed batter, but he didn't care anything about left-handers or right-handers. He could hit *any* kind of pitching. *And* he was a fierce competitor.

Another player on the Grays who was rough on umpires and opposing players was Vic Harris, God rest his soul. I remember one game, I was playing shortstop and I was waiting for the ball on a play at second base. Vic was the base runner and he jumped and spiked me on the arm and on the knee. I was so mad I said, "You sonofabitch, if you ever do a thing like that again to me I'll take this ball and hit you right between the eyes. Why don't you play fair, you old bastard? You're too old to pull a stunt like that. And furthermore, I'll get you. Somewhere down the line, I'll get you."

Later in the year we were playing the Grays again and Harris was on first base. The ball was hit to the second baseman, who threw it to me to start a double play. I got the ball and Vic Harris was running between first and second base, and I had meant to hit him right between the eyes with the ball. I drew back, but I couldn't do it because if I had hit him in the head, I could have killed him. I just couldn't bring myself to hit him, so I threw the ball by him on to first base. He knew what I had in mind and that I could have done it.

Vic and I became good friends after that and we used to talk about that incident after he moved to California. I told him, "You came awfully close. I started to hit you right between the eyes for what you did to me." He said, "Well, let's let bygones be bygones." I said, "Okay," and I did just that.

There were a lot of players with short fuses who would explode under the right circumstances. A near riot occurred on opening day in 1946 when Leon Day pitched a no-hitter against the Philadelphia Stars. It was triggered by a close play at the plate, where Larry Doby was called safe. Bill Cash, the Stars catcher, knocked the umpire down. Cash still maintains it was an accident but, regardless of whether it was intentional or not, the ump went down. Their manager, Goose Curry, came running in from his spot in right field and got involved in the fracus while the umpire was still on the ground. Then the players rushed out on the field and fans came out of the stands. The police had to come on the field with their horses to break it up. I guess the most interesting thing about that incident was that Leon Day just sat calmly in the dugout watching the whole thing until it was over. Then he went back out and finished his no-hitter.

I remember another time when an altercation was narrowly averted in a four-team doubleheader at Yankee Stadium. The Grays were playing the Baltimore Elite Giants and the Eagles were playing the New York Black Yankees. As a promotion, they arranged a race between the fastest men on each team, with the winner taking a prize of one hundred dollars.

Everybody knew that Wild Bill Wright was the fastest man in the contest, but the Grays got together and decided to pull a fast one. They were going to have two of their players box Bill Wright in so that Jelly Jackson could win the one hundred dollars and then they would split the money three ways. And that's precisely what they did. Roy Partlow and David Whatley hemmed Wright in and wouldn't let him through. When he got free, you should have seen that big S.O.B. run. He was like Jesse Owens. But Jelly Jackson just nipped him.

Right after the race was over, Bill Wright went over to Jelly Jackson and said, "You no-good sonofabitch. Why don't you play fair?" Then here came Josh Gibson, big Tom Parker, and all those other big guys from the Grays to help Jelly. Everybody got their bats, and the cops had to come on the field to separate them. It got real serious and they had to hold the game up for a half an hour because of this big hulabaloo.

That's the way it was back then, there was always something going on. The playing and traveling conditions were bad in the Negro leagues, but the thing that bothered us most was that we could not play in the major leagues. We couldn't achieve the pinnacle of success in our field. We didn't like it, but at that time, we couldn't do anything about it, so we didn't let it really bother us. There is no need to be bitter about the slights and injustices that we encountered, either on or off the playing field.

It was a sign of the times. Segregation was a known thing and the rule of the day. They just didn't believe in any kind of experiment. It's easy to sit back now and criticize, but that's just the way it was. I can't understand why it *was* that way, but at that time they simply didn't want blacks to play in the big leagues.

10 A Comparison

I knew the Indians weren't the Monarchs, but I'd still be out there with a ball in my hand and the fellow at the plate'd have a bat in his hand.

—Satchel Paige, Cleveland Indians

I CONSIDER MYSELF fortunate to have been able to play in both the Negro leagues and the major leagues. We played with a round ball and a round bat and the bases were still ninety feet apart, but there were several differences between the brand of baseball in the two leagues. The main differences between the two styles of play were in the approach to the game, the degree of organization, and the depth of the rosters.

I think that in many ways these differences made for a more exciting style of ball being played, game after game, in the Negro leagues. There was so much raw talent available that it showed up in many different ways. Bunting, base-stealing, sensational pitching, flashy plays in both the infield and outfield, and daring plays of all kinds occurred daily. We played for the love of the game and I think that was reflected in our style of play.

In the Negro leagues, most of us were young, had some talent, but were very inexperienced. We hadn't done much. We hadn't made any money, done any traveling, or really enjoyed any success. But it was fun because, when you're young, you don't have any responsibilities. Few of us were married at that time, and everything we did was fun. It didn't matter if we were playing in Buffalo, Syracuse, or Pittsburgh. Wherever we went, I had never been there before so everything was a brand-new experience. I can truthfully say that almost every moment that I spent in the Negro leagues was happy.

The average worker then was only making around fifteen or twenty dollars a week. I started out with the Eagles making a hundred dollars a month plus a dollar-a-day meal money. At that time you could do a lot with a buck. Gas cost ten cents a gallon, a pack of cigarettes eleven cents, potatoes were five pounds for a dime, and bacon and hamburgers were very inexpensive. Everything was unbelievably cheap. Five dollars would feed a family of six for a week. By other standards, ballplayers really didn't make any money to speak of, but we stuck with it because it was better than working at a regular job. If I made fifty dollars a week, as I did in later years, I was way ahead of the game.

Looking at the contrast in salaries between my day and today, I say, "I wish my momma had better timing." Of course, I'm only joking. If I was playing today, I could get as much as the highest paid player. I would be making as much as Barry Bonds, or more. I might even ask for a piece of the team. I made more money when I was in the majors, and the caliber of baseball and the playing conditions were better, but I had more *fun* in the Negro leagues. And I also have memories that can't be bought for money.

The years that I spent in the Negro National League as a member of the Newark Eagles prior to going to the major leagues served me well. I was a fairly complete ball player by the time I reached the majors, and I'm pretty sure the same holds true for the other black players who made the transition.

One of the pleasing differences that we found after making that transition was the presence of a trainer and a clubhouse manager. In the Negro leagues we handled our own bags and were responsible for our own equipment. We had to make sure that our clothes were dry, and had to shine our own shoes. A player had to do all that. In the majors, everything was taken care of for us. When we arrived at the clubhouse, we had a clean uniform hanging in our lockers every day waiting for us.

In the majors, we also had a trainer who spent a lot of time with players, giving proper attention to injuries, prescribing special exercises, and giving rubdowns every day. It was different in the Negro leagues. We used to have to rub each other. If we were injured and it was bad enough, Mrs. Manley would send us to a doctor. Usually we reported our injuries to the manager and he would recommend certain care. Near the end, just before the league broke up, we started to have trainers who would come in and give us a rubdown. But this didn't happen until after World War II. Until then we were our own trainer.

There was also a difference in the atmosphere and in the approach to the game in the Negro leagues. With the Eagles, we didn't stay in the clubhouse that long. We usually dressed quickly and got on the field early to look at the opposition. Because sometimes we would play a team one week, and then we might not see them for the rest of the year. We wanted to see how these guys played and get to know them. And before a game, we really didn't know what the routine was. We would just sit around until the manager said, "Okay, it's time for infield," or "it's time for batting practice."

In the major leagues everything was on schedule. We knew exactly what we would be doing before a game, and when we would be doing it. There was time for infield, time for batting practice - first the scrubinis would hit and then the regulars would hit - and everything was timed. We knew what the routine was before a game.

After you made the major-league circuit once, you knew what to expect in each town. You could also look at the schedule and know you'd be back again in about three weeks. Everything was very organized. We loved to get dressed and go out and talk to the fans, and we were happy to have somebody ask for an autograph. At that time, there was not that much autographing in the Negro leagues, but in the majors, we'd go out and try to make ourselves available. Particularly, if a kid came over and asked for an autograph, we'd be happy to give it to him. We'd say, "No problem. Glad you asked me."

We'd have a dialogue going with the fans. They would ask, "What do you think about this pitcher?" And we'd say, "Oh, he's pretty good." They'd say, "Well, what are you guys gonna do today?" And we'd answer, "Well, we're going to do the best we can." They'd ask, "You gonna win?" We'd say, "We'll let you know after the game." It was that kind of thing with the fans.

When I was with the New York Giants in 1949 and 1950, I suppose the main contrast that I found in the quality of play was that, in the major leagues, I had to confront top-notch pitching day in and day out, week after week, month after month. In a four-game series,

I would most likely face the very best pitching in three of those games. And the remaining hurlers generally ranked only a notch or two below the top aces.

In the Negro leagues, for the most part, it would be a matter of having to face a superior pitcher only on Sundays and holidays with the prospect of a big crowd. The average pitcher on a black team was good, but in the major leagues, we were constantly face to face with the very best pitchers in the country, not just good ones. There simply were too many minor-league clubs ready to take back pitchers who became just average hurlers in the majors.

Another difference between the Eagles and the Giants was the fact that you knew that the games counted. In the Negro leagues many games were considered exhibitions and weren't counted in the standings. In the majors you knew that it was a league game, and there would be from ten to fifty thousand people in the stands who expected you to play well.

So more was expected of you with the Giants. If you made an error with the Eagles, there was no big deal. Nobody really cared, so to speak. You'd just say, "Well, that's what the E on the scoreboard is for." But in the major leagues, you tried to be more precise. There were certain plays that you had to make and you wanted to make those plays. You wanted to catch the line drives and hit in the clutch to keep a rally going. You wanted to play well, to make contributions, and to keep your mistakes to a minimum. So you just got accustomed to playing good baseball. I think that's still true in the major leagues today. The fewer mistakes you make, the better chance you have to win.

There was also a stronger disciplinary presence in the major leagues. In the Negro leagues sometimes a player might smoke in the dugout during the game, and maybe not really pay attention to the game situation. In the majors there was no smoking on the bench. If anyone smoked, he had better go down the runway and into the toilet. We also had to pay attention during the game because the manager might look over and say, "What's the count, Monte?" And I had to be able to tell him. Or he might ask something else just to see if we were on our toes. Players were more alert in the majors. We wanted to sit there, study the pitcher's pattern, and learn. I'm sure it's still that way.

Sometimes the major-league fans would be a little rougher on a player than they should have been. Particularly if he struck out in a key situation, they might get on him more than usual. They would say, "You'll wind up back in Jersey City," or something like that. Some fans are more sympathetic and say, "Get 'em next time" and that kind of thing. But even in the minors the fans could be really rough. They would yell, "You'll never make it." In the Negro leagues the fans would get on you too. But a player couldn't go down. Where would he go? If you went down, you were out of baseball. That was the big difference in that regard.

There was a lot of controversy in the Negro leagues. The umpires were not consistent. It got so bad that there were a lot of fights and, as I said, some umps started carrying pistols because they had been attacked by some of the players. We knew when those kind of things occurred, nothing was going to happen unless somebody brought a civil suit against you. But in the majors we knew that we could be fined, suspended, or thrown out of baseball. There were certain things a player did and said, and certain things that a player wouldn't do or say. We were much more conscious of our behavior.

For instance, in the Negro leagues, as soon as there was a dispute we'd leave the dugouts with bats. We would grab a fungo or a light bat that we could wield very handily to protect ourselves. That was the big difference there. If you did that in the major leagues, you would certainly leave yourself open for a big fine or a suspension.

Once when I was with the Giants, we were playing in Philadelphia and got in a free-for-all with the Phillies. They were after Durocher so as soon as the fight started, I grabbed a fungo and went out on the field. When I got out there, I was the only big S.O.B. with a bat. So I gave it to the batboy, rather sheepishly, and told him to take it on back and put it in the bat rack. Then I went to work with my fists and started pulling guys off teammates and warding other guys off. When I grabbed a bat, that was just what I was used to. I wasn't going to hit anybody with the bat, but neither was I going to let anybody hit me. After the incident had passed, I had to laugh because I thought about the old Negro leagues.

There was always some kind of excitement on the field at our games back then, and often some controversy off the field as well. Part of these problems were due to the fact that the Negro league owners couldn't control their players the way the major-league owners did. Players would often jump teams in the middle of the season if another team offered more money. Sometimes they would change teams two or three times in a year. Some teams would miss two or three paydays, and when owners didn't pay them in accordance with their contract, players felt that they were not bound to honor an agreement. That's why some of the guys would jump from one team to another like they did. When a team started to pay the players on schedule again, they could exercise at least a little bit of control over them.

Satchel Paige was probably the most noted for leaving one team and going to another. In 1937 he was playing with Gus Greenlee's Pittsburgh Crawfords, and Rafael Trujillo, the dictator in the Dominican Republic, offered him a contract. So Satchel, Josh Gibson, and some other stars went down there and played the rest of the Dominican season. That's the way it was.

11 Puerto Rico and Satchel

I played with Monte at Newark and I played against him in Puerto Rico. That's the year he went down there and started playing good ball. He was hitting real good and he was throwing more accurate. And when he came back, he was tearing the ball up.

—Leon Day, Newark Eagles

WHEN WE PLAYED in the Latin American leagues, we played with white players and learned that we could play as good as they could. Playing winter ball in Puerto Rico early in my career helped me develop as a ball player, and it also helped me get back my timing after I returned from the army. During my years there, I had some good experiences on the ball field and some good laughs off the field.

A lot of those laughs centered around Satchel Paige. There are a lot of stories about Satchel, and most of them are true. Everybody has one. And there are probably a lot more that have never been told, because nobody could really keep up with Satchel.

When I first got to know Satchel, he had a wife whose nickname was Toad. She was a barmaid at the Grand Hotel in Chicago, and when we played the Chicago American Giants, we would go there after the game. We'd say, "Hey, Toad! Where's Satchel?" "You asking *me* where Satchel is?" she'd say. "I should be asking *you*. I haven't seen him in weeks. If you see him, tell him to give me a call." That's the kind of personality she had. She was just lovely and a happy-go-lucky type of person. She was very pleasant and a very efficient barmaid. They eventually separated or divorced, so Toad didn't have that problem anymore.

I remember one year in Puerto Rico, when Satchel struck me out four times in one game. I used to hold my bat rather high and by the time I tried to get it down and catch up with one of his fastballs, the ball was by me. For some reason Satchel kind of took a liking to me and, at that time, he used to call me "Big 'Un." One day he said, "Big 'Un, after the game, I want you to go somewhere with me." "Sure, I'd be happy to go with you," I said, "even though you treated me like a dog during the game. Where are we going?"

"I met a girl and she's one of the nicest persons you'll ever meet," he said. "She lives a little farther out in the country." "Fine," I replied, and we got in the car and drove out in the country a little way. When we got pretty close to where we were going, he pointed and said, "Now, see that house over there?" I looked and there was a kind of a rural type house. On the front porch was a rocking chair, and in the rocking chair was a goat. And this goat was rocking back and forth. "Look there," Satchel said. "Have you ever seen anything like that?" "No," I answered, "this is the very first time." And he said, "Anytime you can train a goat to do that, you know these must be pretty nice people. And as pretty as she is, I'm going to marry that girl."

Don't you know, he took her back to Kansas City and they were married. Her name was Lucy Figueroa, and they stayed together for four or five years, until he met someone else. Satchel was gone so much that Lucy got tired of being at home by herself and went back to Puerto Rico. I don't know what she did after that.

After we left Lucy's house that day in Puerto Rico, Satchel asked me, "Do you want a beer?" "Yeah," I said. "I'd be happy to have a beer." So we stopped and while we were drinking our beers, Satchel started talking. "I've got a few things I want to tell you," he said, "and some things I want to show you. Because you'll never hit me." "What do you mean, I'll never hit you?" I said. "Sooner or later, I'll catch up to you."

"No, no. I'm going to have to teach you how to hit Satchel," he told me. "Hold your bat the way you did today." So I did, and he said, "You're holding your bat too high. When you've got that bat way up there, what I do is pitch you inside. By the time you get your bat down and around, old Satch is by you and gone. That's why I got you four times today." "Well, I'm going to have to make an adjustment," I said, "because what you did to me today was embarrassing."

The next time I faced him, I lowered my bat and tried to swing fast. So instead of four times, he only got me twice. Satchel said, "Just keep trying, and sooner or later you'll get a base hit." Well, eventually I did, but it took awhile.

Satchel loved guns and cameras, and he had a lot of both of them. When we traveled from one place to another in a car, he played with his guns and had this habit of shooting out the window. One day he had a .45 pistol, and saw a hawk circling around in the sky. "Stop the car!" he insisted. "Stop the car!" Then he got out, aimed the gun, and zoom - he hit that hawk and knocked it out of the sky. "Okay," he said. "We can go now. I got him on the first shot like I always do."

Satchel had a saying he always used: "Ain't no maybe so about it." After he got the hawk, that's what he said. "Ain't no maybe so about it. I am the best shot with a revolver that you have ever seen. And I don't do too bad with a rifle either. Ain't no maybe so about the way I can handle a gun." I don't think too many people disagreed with him either. But when he said, "Ain't no maybe so," it struck me kind of funny because he always used that expression. When he said that, he was dead serious. He was second to none and wasn't bashful talking about it. He'd say, "Ain't no maybe so about it, I'm the best." And he *was*.

Satchel played on a team in Guayama, a city in Puerto Rico directly on the other side of the island from San Juan, where I was playing. At that time we played one game on Saturday and two on Sunday. We would go home after the first Sunday game and maybe get a sandwich and a cup of soup. Then we'd go back to the ball park and get ready for the second game. Most of the time we didn't even take off our uniforms.

One Sunday afternoon Guayama came over to play us and Satchel was supposed to pitch the second game. We went to the hotel between games to eat, and it was getting late. So I said, "Come on. The game is going to start at two o'clock. We've got to go." Satchel said, "Now just take it easy." "What do you mean take it easy?" I asked. "I don't want to be late." "Well, I'm pitching the second game," Satchel explained, "and if I'm pitching, nothing can happen until I get there. Right?" "Well, yeah," I answered. So he said, "Sit and enjoy your sandwich, and then we'll go." And that's what he did. He was in no hurry. The game was held up for about fifteen or twenty minutes until he got there. But I wasn't worried because I was with Satchel, and I knew the game didn't start until he got there. And sure enough that's the way it was.

Another real funny story developed the next morning. Whenever they came over to play us, Satchel usually wanted to stay over a couple of days afterward and do some shopping because Guayama was a country sort of town and there was nothing to do over there. So he stayed overnight with Verdell Mathis and me at our hotel. We got up the next morning, had some breakfast, and then started to play Tonk, a game like 500 rummy only it's played with five cards.

We asked Satchel if he wanted to play with us but he said, "No I don't want to play cards today. I think I'll go to the movies. Where is the movie around here?" We said, "Well, there's a movie up the street and there's another one farther down the street. Or you can get on a bus and go to Santurce. There are some movies there." So he asked, "What's playing up the street?" "We don't know," we said. "Take a walk up there and find out."

So Satchel left but, in about an hour, he came back. We said, "We thought you were going to the movie." He said, "No, I decided I wouldn't go." "Why?" we asked. "Well, I'll tell you what happened," he explained. "I went up the street and *Hoy* was playing there. And when I went to the other movie, *Hoy* was playing there, too. And so I decided to get on a bus and go over to Santurce and see what was playing over there. And, I'm a son of a gun, when I got there, *Hoy* was playing over there, too. In fact, *Hoy* was playing all over town. And I noticed on the bus coming back, *Hoy* is playing all over Puerto Rico."

Both of us laughed like crazy. Of course, in Spanish, *Hoy* means *today*. And the marquee signs just meant the movie, whatever the title, was showing today. We said, "Don't you know what *Hoy* means?" He said, "No, what does *Hoy* mean?" We told him what it meant and he said, "Why, hell, I didn't know that. Why didn't someone tell me?" And everybody laughed again.

Another story that I like so much is about Josh Gibson and Spoony Palm. They used to have a tournament at the end of the season in Puerto Rico, where teams from Cuba and Santo Domingo came to San Juan and played round robin. Spoony Palm was the catcher for one of the clubs and Josh Gibson was the catcher for another club. If your team lost a ball game you were out of the tournament and had to get on a boat and go back home to that cold weather.

In one game Palm's team jumped off to a big lead, about 8 to 3, in the seventh inning. Spoony hollered over to Josh, "Hey, Josh. I was going to mail my wife a letter, but since you're going back, I'll get you to deliver it for me." Spoony laughed and added, "I hate to see you going back to that cold weather."

In the ninth inning, Josh's team came up with about a half dozen runs to win the game. When they got the last run, Palm hollered over to Josh, "Hey, Josh. Never mind. I'll take the letter my goddam self." Everybody laughed like hell. Because Spoony's team was eliminated and he had to go back to the cold weather. So, he delivered the letter himself.

Palm was a naturally funny guy anyhow. Anytime he had a good day at the ball park, he would get up early the next morning and go to the club offices. We asked him, "Why do you do that every time you have a pretty good day?" "I went down there and asked for more money," he explained. "Because I hit two home runs and a double yesterday, and I want them to know that. And while it's fresh in their minds, I want my raise and expect to get it." "Well," we asked, "what's going to happen when you strike out a couple of times and don't drive in any runs?" He said, "Then I keep my black ass at home."

Spoony Palm was real dark. When he would get down to give a signal, it was difficult to see. Particularly, when the sun was going down. So, the pitcher couldn't tell whether it was number one, number two, or number three because of the shadows and from the fact that he was so dark. One time Satchel told him, "When you're catching me today, put some tape around your fingers so I can see how many are there."

Another funny thing happened one year in Puerto Rico, when I was playing with San Juan and Roy Campanella was with Caguas. He got off to a fast start, but I wasn't hitting very well. The only way I was staying in Puerto Rico was because the management knew that when you first got down there, it took awhile to get used to the food, the climate, and to make other adjustments.

We went over to play Caguas at their park and Campy said to me,

"Dude, I see you're in a slump." I said, "Yeah." "Well, if we get a big lead," he told me, "I'll let you know what's coming." I just looked at him because I didn't think he was telling me the truth. But they jumped out to a quick 6-2 lead and, when I came up, I looked back at him and he was softly saying, "Fastball." It was just loud enough for me to hear, but not the umpire. The next pitch was a fastball, but I took it because I didn't believe him. On the next pitch he said, "Curveball," and I took that one, too. I took the two pitches for called strikes.

Campy was jumping around back there wondering what the hell was the matter with me and why I didn't swing? So I saw that he was for real. When he got down again, he said, "Fastball," and I hit it for a home run. He did the same thing the next time I came up. But when I came up for the third time, he said, "Well, Dude, since the game is close, now you're on your own." Campy's team beat us, but my team realized that I could hit a home run. That's what kept me there instead of catching a boat back to the cold weather in New York.

Later that season, Campy got in a slump. When I saw him I told him, "Well, what you need is to come over to San Juan and get away from the kids for a while. We'll go out and do a little dancing." He had his chauffeur drive him over from Caguas, and we went to this club where they played a lot of lively music.

At that time, he used to love to drink a lot of Coca-Colas. Every time he would get up to dance, I would put a little rum in his Coke. After about the third time, he came back to the table after dancing and said, "I don't know why I feel so good." I said, "See, I told you all you had to do was to get away from Caguas out there in the country, and come over here where everything is happening." So, it got to be about one o'clock, and Campy said, "I've got a practice tomorrow, and I'd better get on back. But let me tell you one thing. You thought you were fooling me, but I knew what you were doing. I knew you were putting that rum in my Coke. But please invite me back again and do the same thing." But I never did, because he got squared away in his hitting. From that day on, whenever he drank something, his favorite drink was rum and Coke.

12 Mexico

I told Mrs. Manley if she could match what Mexico was paying me to come down there, that I would stay. But she didn't agree on it, so I left and I went back to Mexico. That was the reason a whole lot of players left. In Mexico the money was good, the playing conditions were good, and the living conditions were the most beautiful of all.

—Ray Dandridge, Newark Eagles

I PLAYED AGAINST Campy in Mexico, too, but it happened under improbable circumstances. At the beginning of the 1942 season, we both were still playing in the Negro leagues. He was with the Baltimore Elite Giants and I was with the Newark Eagles. However, before the year was out we both ended up in Mexico. World War II was going on, and the Eagles didn't want to go too far south to train, so we stayed at Virginia Union University in Richmond. We had a great spring training and an outstanding ball club.

We had Lennie Pearson and Bus Clarkson on the corners. Pearson was a super first baseman and Clarkson could hit, had a great arm, and a lot of power. Dick Seay had been traded to the New York Black Yankees, and since Clarkson couldn't play second, they moved Bus to third and put Dandridge on second. That gave us Dandridge and Wells in the middle. Leon Ruffin was catching. He couldn't hit, but his throwing and defensive skills were just as good as Campanella's. What an infield that was.

Our pitching staff had Leon Day, Jimmy Hill, Max Manning, Len Hooker, and a kid by the name of James Brown, who also played left field. Ed Stone was in right field, and I played center field. Biz

Mackey was our manager and he was also still catching some. In his prime he had been a great receiver and was still a terrific player.

I think this team was even better than the championship club we had in 1946, but the Manleys didn't keep us together. Abe and Effa Manley were pretty good owners, but it's just too bad that they didn't know about promotion. They must have been worth at least two million dollars from the numbers and real estate business.

They could have made so much more money if they had just purchased the Grand Hotel, remodeled it, then given the players a job during the off season. Because a lot of them didn't really want to go to the Islands to play in the winter. For guys like Dandridge and Wells, the Manleys could have given them jobs as bartenders, waiters, or something else like that. Then they could stay at home, get some rest, and make some decent money.

Our team could have stayed together for years. I'm talking about guys like Mule Suttles, Jimmy Crutchfield, Ray Dandridge, Willie Wells, Terris McDuffie, Leon Day, Max Manning and Jimmy Hill. We had a hell of a club. But the Manleys didn't have that kind of entrepreneurship. They didn't have that kind of sense. They were penny wise and pound foolish.

In 1942, I was considered one of the best players in the league. I'd had a terrific spring and was hitting well over .500. One day I called home and my mother said that I had received a telegram from Jorge Pasquel. He wanted me to come to Mexico, and was willing to give me five hundred dollars a month with two months in advance. I was only making one hundred fifty dollars a month with the Eagles and I thought a thousand dollars was all the money in the world. So my fiancée Dee and I decided to get married.

I went to Mrs. Manley and told her about this great offer and that I was going to be married. She asked, "Well, how much are they going to give you?" I told her and she said, "I can't afford that." "Just give me a twenty-five dollar raise," I said, "and make it one hundred seventy-five dollars a month." She said, "Well, I can't pay you that much because I'm paying these other guys." "Mrs. Manley, they're not getting married - I am," I said. "You can find twenty-five dollars more a month anywhere." She said, "Well, it's just not in the books, and I just can't do it."

"Well, if you don't do it, then I'll have to accept the offer from Jorge Pasquel to go to Mexico. He's giving me two months in advance and he's paying me five hundred dollars a month plus two hundred dollars for an apartment. I'll have to accept that." I told her. "I really don't want to leave this team. This team is too good to leave, and we should keep it together." It was a perfect blend. We had youth and experience, speed and defense, pitching and hitting. We had everything. But Effa said, "Well, I just can't do it. You'll just have to go, Monte, because I can't afford it."

So I went on home to Orange. The next morning, I looked up, and Effa was standing in my living room. She said, "You mean to tell me, you're really going to leave our team?" "Yes, Mrs. Manley," I answered. "I told you what they're offering. I told you what I wanted from you and you can't see fit to do that. There's only one thing to do and that's to go ahead and leave." "Well, I just don't think it's right," she responded. And then she stormed out. But she never said a word about raising me twenty-five dollars a month. Never said a word.

Mrs. Manley was tough to deal with. She always wanted to give you something other than money. A few years later, in 1946, I went over to her house to talk contract with her and Abe. When I got there, she came to the door in her negligee. I asked her where Abe was, and she said he had to go out of town and would not be back until tomorrow. She invited me in so we could sit and talk. I sat right across from her and, as we talked, the negligee got higher and higher until, all of a sudden, I noticed it was up around her navel.

This made me uncomfortable because I had a lot of respect for Abe and I had a lot of respect for her. I just thought that her acting that way wasn't the right thing to do. "Mrs. Manley," I said, "I don't really think you have contract talk on your mind today. Maybe I had better come back at another time when Abe is here." She assured me that it was okay to continue the discussion and not to be uncomfortable because she was just a little warm and only wanted to air things out a little bit. But I got up and went to the door. "Well, I'll come back sometime," I said and closed the door as I left.

After leaving, I stopped by Ray Dandridge's house on my way home and told him the story. "Monte," he said, "you're about the dumbest guy I know. You could have probably gotten your raise and anything else you wanted." Then he laughed, and we didn't talk about it anymore. But that shows the difficulty in negotiating with Mrs. Manley.

In 1942, after my first attempt to negotiate with Effa had failed, Dee and I did get married and went on down to Mexico City for our honeymoon. We took the train from Newark to San Antonio to Laredo, and flew from there to Mexico City. It was a small airplane, and as we were flying over the mountains going into Mexico City, the plane suddenly fell two or three hundred feet before righting itself. We found out later it was caused by an air pocket but, needless to say, we were really concerned at the time. That was my first plane flight and I thought it was going to be my last.

I joined the Vera Cruz ballclub and was playing good ball. About two weeks later here comes Ray Dandridge from the Eagles for the same reason. Effa wouldn't raise his salary either. In another two weeks, here comes Roy Campanella, who had the same problem with his owner.

It's easy to see how miserly the owners were. It would have been easy to keep these real good players at home, just give them a little bit more money. If they had to raise salaries a little bit, they could have always played more games to generate the necessary capital. We had the nucleus to have a good club for at least ten years. But Mrs. Manley saw fit to break that great team up and subsequently suffered for it.

Dandridge and I were playing on the same team, the Vera Cruz Blues, but it was so hot in Vera Cruz that they moved the team to Mexico City. Campy played for Monterrey, and they had a great team, managed and led by the great Cuban Lazaro Salazar. He was an excellent left-handed pitcher, a good hitter and a fine all-around ball player.

By the last game of the season, Monterrey had already won the championship, but they were playing us a key game in Mexico City on a Saturday afternoon. Salazar had shut us out and was leading 1-0 with two outs in the last inning. Then Dandridge hit a high fastball over second base for a single. I was hitting in the third spot and came up next. I never will forget it.

Jorge Pasquel, our owner, was sitting in the box seats behind home plate. As I approached the plate, he was waving for me to come over to his box. He hollered, "Monte, ven-aca. Come here." I said, "Jorge, I'm getting ready to hit." "No, never mind," he said. "Come here just for a minute," and motioned again for me to come over. So, I went over to his box. He leaned over, put his arm around me and said, "You hit a home run for me and win the ball game, huh?" Just like that. That was the first time I had ever been commanded to hit a home run.

The whole damn ball park knew what was happening and what he was saying. "Jorge, don't you see how hard Salazar is throwing the ball?" I said. "I'll try to keep the rally going. That's the best I can promise you." "No, no," he said. "Never mind. You hit a home run for me." "Well, I'll do the best I can," I finally told him. And I got a little mad because that was the first time I'd ever been *ordered* to hit a home run.

They had held the game up while Jorge and I got this thing going. I went back to the batter's box, and Campy said, "Hey, dude, what did Jorge want?" I looked at him, sort of half smiled, and said, "He wants me to hit a home run." Campy looked up at me and said, "Are you crazy? No way today, dude. No way." "Well, that's what he wants me to do," I told him. I stepped out of the box, got some rosin, and stepped back in. At that time, I used to always take the first pitch. I figured you only needed one to hit it anyway. The first pitch was a fastball, a called strike. The second pitch was a curveball and I fouled it back over the grandstand. Then something told me, "Be ready now. Campy wants to strike you out on three pitches." So I guessed fastball and I got it. Salazar threw me a low fastball and I hit it on a line over the center field fence for a game-winning home run.

The crowd was going crazy as I was rounding the bases. By the time I reached home plate, Jorge was there to greet me. When we shook hands, he had five hundred pesos in his hand. Campy still hadn't left the field yet, and he was waiting a little way off. We were supposed to go out together after the game. He had a few hours to kill before he went back to Monterrey, so we were going to have a few beers. "Man, you've got to be the luckiest son of a gun in town," he told me. "You'll never do that again." "Well, I did it this time," I answered. "Furthermore, just calm down and stop jumping up and down. And take it easy. Jorge just gave me five hundred and told me to give you half for calling the right pitch." Campy said, "My man. My main man."

We went in the clubhouse, got dressed, and then went out and had a few beers. That was as good as I ever had. Always after that, when I reminded Campy about it, a smile would come to his face.

Even when he was down, when I told that story, he couldn't help but just laugh.

Campy and I were friends all our lives, right up until the day he died. We started in baseball the same year, 1937. He thought he was the hottest rookie and I thought I was, too. When he first came to Newark, I went over to him and introduced myself. "You may be king in Baltimore," I told him, "but when you come to Newark, you've got to come by me." We laughed together and immediately became friends. We would kid each other, have a beer together, and just fool around. We were just good friends and always had the highest respect for each other. We only played *together* on all star teams. Most of the time we played opposite each other like we did in Mexico.

The quality of play in the Mexican league was good that year, mainly because so many good black players were down there. Martin Dihigo was pitching and playing outfield, and Silvio Garcia, the great Cuban shortstop, was also there. Dihigo was simply an outstanding hurler and won pitching's triple crown with a 22-7 record, 2.53 ERA, and 211 strikeouts. Ramon Bragana, our ace, was close behind Dihigo with a 22-10 mark. Silvio Garcia was a good hitter, had good power, could run, could field and was happy-go-lucky. So it was real good baseball, and the crowds were better that year than they had been in a long time.

Dihigo was a big, tall, regal guy and had a lot of confidence. One night we were playing Torreon, the team that Dihigo pitched for and managed, and the lights were not very good there. Three straight times he got me three and two and then broke a curveball right on the outside corner and struck me out. After the third time, I said to him, "Martin, you son of a gun, I'll get even with you if it's the last thing I do. I'll get you when you come down to Mexico City." "Well, you might get me in Mexico City," he replied, "but I got you tonight three times." That's the way he was. He was the greatest Latin American player I had ever seen and a pleasure to be around.

It was just a terrific year for me in every way. On Sundays, the game would start at ten o'clock in the morning, so we could play the game, get dressed, and then go to a bullfight in the afternoon. They started at two o'clock, so you could see a baseball game and still have time to see a great bullfighter in one day.

I saw Manoleté, one of the greatest Spanish bullfighters ever, and I had never seen anything like that. Women would throw their hats, scarves, coats, and flowers, because of the action in the center of the ring. Manoleté had this big handsome bull and he just embarrassed the bull. He tired it out until the bull's tongue was hanging out. He got real close to the bull, and then got down on his knees as if to say, *Toro, charge me you big dumb so-and-so. Ah-hah!*

Then Manoleté got up and did that dance matadors do, turning around with his cape. They have a certain way they do it. And then he did that little step they do when they walk away. When Manoleté finished that little dance, he turned his back on the damn bull. And the bull was too tired to charge. As I watched that, it was like something hit me right in the top of my head. I had never felt that kind of sensation before.

Ray Dandridge used to perform that same ritual on the ball field at second base after making a great play. It was something to see Dandridge do his version of the matador's dance. From going to the bullfights, he had learned how to do it precisely the same as those professional bullfighters, and the fans would scream with delight. The game would be held up for about ten or fifteen seconds while he did this dance and the crowd would go crazy. The fans would yell and chant, "Olé, Ramon! Olé!" Of course, after the applause was over, it was "Let's play ball." Ray became very popular in Mexico because he was able to do this dance. He was in a class by himself and the fans really loved it. They ate it up.

Dandridge was not a hot dog. He never did that little dance in the States because nobody would have known what he was doing. But they knew precisely what he was doing when he did it in Mexico. He just had that flair and charisma about him that made him a big favorite with the fans. There will never be another Satchel. There will never be another Josh. And there will never be another Ray Dandridge.

When we went to a nightclub together, we'd be sitting around and the more beers Ray had, the noisier he'd get. We'd tell him "Hey, don't be so noisy. Take it easy." He'd say, "Take it easy? What do you mean take it easy? When I'm good, I get loud and, when I'm not good, I keep quiet." So he was noisy quite a bit because he was some kind of a third baseman.

Some of the other American players down there that year were

Quincy Trouppe, Theolic Smith, Leroy Matlock, and Bert Hunter, who used to pitch for the Crawfords. Of course Dandridge and Andy "Pullman" Porter played on my team.

Dee and I shared an apartment with Trouppe and his wife. Mexico City was a great city. At that time they had just recovered from an earthquake and practically all the buildings were brand new. There were only about two million people in the city and it was just a wonderful place to be. I got a chance to buy some gold, some jewelry and some great Mexican luggage. We had just one hell of a good time there. I was on my honeymoon, and I had the greatest year I ever spent in baseball. I hit .398 and led the league in both battting average and home runs, and I was the toast of Mexico City.

And I played for Jorge Pasquel, who was the George Steinbrenner of Mexico. He was rich, young, good-looking, and he loved baseball. Jorge liked me so much that we became close friends. He said, "I want you to come back down next year." "Well, Jorge," I told him, "sure I'll come back, but we'll have to talk about money. He said, "Don't worry about money, just come on back. I'll take care of you." So money was never a problem. I went home in October and Jorge sent me fifty dollars a month from November until March. Fifty dollars a month was a lot of money then and, along with the job I had, I was doing pretty good. I made a little over a hundred dollars a week, when the average salary at that time was about twenty-five dollars a week.

I was planning to return to Mexico for the 1943 season. In February, I went to the draft board and asked permission to go down to spring training. "Sure you can go if you don't pass your physical," they said, "but you have to take your physical exam first." Because of my football knee, I didn't think I would pass the examination. Along with the fact that I was married with a child and I had a job, I thought that I would have no problem. I didn't have any idea that I was going into the armed service. But I took the physical, they passed me, and off to the Army I went.

The date I got the news was March 9, 1943, and I will never forget it. The draft board was in Newark and Sarah Vaughan was appearing with Billy Eckstine down at the Brandford Theatre in Newark. John Knox, a high school classmate, was with me that day. We were feeling so low about being inducted that we said, "Well, we might as well go see the show to cheer ourselves up because it will probably be the last one we see for a while." So we saw Sarah Vaughan in her debut in Newark. She was terrific, just wonderful. I knew that she would be a star for a very long time.

13 World War II

Being in the service and not playing ball for three years does something to you. It has an effect on you. After getting home again, spring training was almost like therapy. There was a feeling of comfort and it let you kind of get back on track.

—Max Manning, Newark Eagles

I HAD STARTED out to turn things around in 1941, and in 1942 I was even more improved. I felt that I was really coming into my own. But then I had to go in the Army and that wiped out everything that I had accomplished. There's no question that World War II made some radical changes in my life, but I had foreseen that possibility right from the beginning.

Almost everyone remembers where they were when they heard the news about Pearl Harbor. I was standing on second base in Puerto Rico. I had just doubled when the announcement came over the loudspeaker that the Japanese had attacked Pearl Harbor and that the United States had declared war on them. When the announcement was over, the people really began to cheer. And I said to myself, *Don't they realize what this means? Don't they realize what a hardship it's going to create on this island? And don't they know that many of the soldiers stationed at the bases here in the Caribbean will go to war?* But, anyway, they cheered like crazy for a little while. And in three weeks the price of rice had tripled because the Germans had their submarine warfare going and some ships had been sunk out in the Caribbean.

After the winter season was over, everybody wanted to get back to the United States, so I had to get on the waiting list. There was not much air service between Puerto Rico and the United States at that time. They didn't have fleets of planes like now. They only had a few planes and if I had to wait my turn, it would have been almost a month delay. So around the first week in February, I decided to talk it over with Roy Campanella, Lennie Pearson, Bill Wright, and Johnny Hayes, who were also playing down there. We decided we would take a chance and go back on a ship, rather than wait three or four weeks. They had a ship that left once a week. So, we boarded a ship hopeful that we would reach the United States safely.

That was a terrific break but if I had it to do over again, I wouldn't have taken it. The second day out at sea we got into a terrific storm with twenty-foot waves. It was raining, the wind was blowing, and the ship just crept along. Usually it would only take four days but we were running a zigzag course and the waters off Cape Hatteras was very choppy, so we didn't reach the coast of North Carolina until the sixth day. And it was still storming.

When we left Puerto Rico, the owner of Campanella's team had given him a case of *Don Q* rum that Campy had won. When the storm started, he went below, broke out a gallon of that rum, and said, "Well, if we're going down, we may as well go down happy." So he and I met every day at the bar and had a few rum and Cokes.

As we were sailing along, we knew that sooner or later the ship would right itself. But I remember one time we were laying in our bunks when one of those waves hit. The ship headed down and the rudder came out of the water because we were on such a steep angle, and the whole ship shook. "Come up out of there," we said. "Come on. Come up out of there." And we said another silent prayer. To look outside at those twenty-foot waves would just scare you to death.

When we reached the North Carolina coast, we hugged the shore and finally got to New York on the seventh day. After we docked, the people ran off the ship and kissed the ground and thanked the Lord for delivering them. It was a sight that I will never forget.

There must have been between a thousand and fifteen hundred people aboard the ship. Roy Campanella and I were two of just a very few people who escaped seasickness. I think it was because we drank so much rum and were so happy we didn't think about it. In fact I have never been seasick. But after that experience, I vowed never to get back on another ship. Not ever. But three years later, after I had been drafted, I was back aboard ship when my outfit was sent to England in 1944.

I was assigned to an all-black engineering outfit and served in England, France, and Germany. But before I was shipped overseas, an unfortunate thing happened. I guess you could call it a quirk of fate. One day we were in an army chow line, and I saw Tommy Dukes, the catcher for the Homestead Grays, dishing out chow in the mess line. We had been in Mexico together in 1942, and he said, "Monte what are you doing here?" "Can't you see?" I answered. "I'm getting ready to go overseas." "No you're not going overseas," he said. "The colonel needs good ball players and we're not going to let a guy like you go overseas. We're going to keep you here. Just wait until I go and see the colonel." "You'd better hurry up," I said, "because we're going to leave on Sunday." So Dukes went to see the colonel, but he was away on a two-day pass and wouldn't get back until Monday. I left for England on Sunday, so I missed out by one day.

I was very disappointed because I wanted to stay up there, and I didn't want to go overseas. I didn't want to leave the States for various reasons. Mainly I didn't want to leave my wife and my daughter, who was only five months old. But all that went out the window.

We sailed nineteen days in the North Atlantic. On the second day out, we connected with a convoy of about five hundred other ships. The ship I was on was called the *Brittania*. It was a huge English luxury liner but, naturally, all the luxuries had been taken away. I think at that time the capacity was about three thousand people, but there must have been ten thousand troops aboard ship.

Since it was an English ship, they served a lot of mutton and just to smell that mutton would make you sick. So I spent a lot of time up on deck in the fresh air, trying to keep from getting sick. It was a difficult task to remain healthy under the conditions. Seeing soldiers throwing up all over the ship, along with the smell of that mutton coming from the kitchen really tested one's mettle. You'd have to have a cast-iron stomach not to be affected by it.

Everybody had to take turns sleeping, so there were eight hours on and eight hours off. I spent most of my time up on the decks watching the dice and card games. You couldn't move without bumping into somebody. I felt fairly safe because as far as I could see there were aircraft carriers, destroyers and cruisers. I figured that we couldn't be that unlucky to be hit since there were so many ships. We arrived safely in Liverpool, England, without losing a single ship or a single man from our convoy, which was a terrific feat.

We didn't lose anybody because we had terrific air coverage from the airplanes on the aircraft carriers. The only time that we were really in trouble was when our ship went beyond the areas that the land-based airplanes could cover and where the aircraft carriers didn't patrol. Those liberty ships would be on their own, because the military could not provide aircraft carriers to escort individual ships or small groups of ships, and they would rely on their speed and ability to outrun the enemy submarines. There was a blind spot near the Azores, where the planes couldn't cover completely and that's where the German wolfpacks would lie in wait. That situation existed until they were able to remedy it so that the air coverage extended over the entire north Atlantic.

When we got to Liverpool and were ready to get off, I couldn't stand up because we had been swaying back and forth for nineteen days. After I got my legs back under me, they put us on a train. We rode for a day down into southern England to a little town called Redruth. A lot of the English people had never seen any black people before. They tried to be as friendly and as accommodating as possible. When you talked to someone, they would ask, innocently and simply, "Do you have any little pickaninnies." So we would say "No, I don't have any pickaninnies," or "Yes, I have a little pickaninny." After we were there for a while, they started to invite us to their houses to have a home-cooked meal, a cup of tea, or something.

Lieutenant Black, from Texas, was our company commander. Usually a company commander was at least a captain, but this man was only a first lieutenant. When he got wind of the fact that we were being invited out, he called a formation and said, "You married men, you'll just have to wait until you get back to the States. You single men, I hope like hell, that you don't get lucky." We thought it was so strange for a company commander to say a thing like that.

As soon as Lieutenant Black sat down, a black chaplain, who was a captain and outranked Lieutenant Black, got up and spoke. I'll never forget these words as long as I ever live. He said, "Men you're members of the United States Armed Forces and if anybody invites you to their homes or invites you anywhere, by all means, you go. You have the right to go any place you're invited. And secondly, I can assure you that Lieutenent Black will not be with this outfit very much longer." When he finished the chaplain looked right at Lieutenant Black and he was red as a beet. Sure enough, in about ten days he was gone and we got a new black company commander who was a captain.

Before we shipped out to France, we were guarding a supply depot in an area near Plymouth, also in the south of England. We moved out of the area on a Saturday morning and that evening the area was plastered by the German air force. If we hadn't moved, all of us might have been killed. We went back later and saw where they had bombed, and they had really blasted the place. We said, "Thank God we moved because we could not have survived that bombing."

It was lonely for me over there and it was a very tough time, being so far from home and not having anybody to care for. D-Day was June 6, 1944, and we didn't get to France until August. By that time, when we landed at Omaha Beach, the beach had been cleared and a path had been made so that we could land safely.

My outfit was the 1313 General Service Engineers. We built bridges, built roads and did guard duty. We headed toward Paris and camped about thirty miles outside the city. We had a chance to go to Epernay, a great champagne center. There were a few big châteaus around there and we were quartered in one of them. We discovered a wine cellar there with just lots of bottles of great champagne. For several weeks many of us never drank any water. We would fill our canteens with champagne. When the officers learned what we were doing, they issued an order against it saying that anybody that got caught would be dealt with severely.

By this time, hundreds and hundreds of German prisoners were coming through, and we would guard them before they were processed and sent someplace else. There were so many of them that we almost got to the point where we didn't care where they went or what they did. The prisoners were just happy to be safe behind our lines because for them the war was over. They were tired, disgusted, disheveled, and were glad to be safe and to have someone feed and house them. They were a sorry sight to behold. Some were very young and some were very old, but they were all completely defeated and glad to be out of the war.

During the Battle of the Bulge, we were in Reims. If the Germans had broken through at Bastogne, where the American colonel said "Nuts" to the German general's surrender demands, Reims would be the first French city they would hit. So we were put out on the lines. Mainly, we were guarding a big French gasoline depot. It was cold as could be and must have gotten down to four below zero.

We were told to look out for Germans who were dressed in American uniforms. We were told to ask them, "Who was Joe DiMaggio?" or "Who was Ted Williams?" and any baseball questions or other technical questions that only a true American would know. But it never got to that. Our troops stopped them at Bastogne, so we never did actually start any fighting.

But we *did* have to fight the cold. It was so cold that we were kept busy trying to keep warm. I just tried to keep inside someplace because if we went outside, we could hardly stand it. Finally, after about a week, the weather broke a little bit.

Out of all this, I was dismayed with army routine. They didn't know what to do with us and they didn't use us properly. Actually, we wanted to fight and we didn't feel like we were really making any contributions. Then some of the 101st airborne paratroopers came back and said, "Fellows, you don't know how lucky you are. You don't want to be up there at the front. Those German eighty-eights are really mean, and you've got the cold and hardships up there, too. Know when you're well off. Just go ahead and do your thing right here because you're very lucky to be here." After that, I didn't hear too much complaining anymore.

I developed a little nerve condition, an inner-ear imbalance, so I went to the hospital to try to correct it. And I was sent back to the States. From Normandy, I boarded a hospital ship and came back to Charleston, South Carolina. That was in August of 1945, and September 1, I was discharged from the Army. Right away my thoughts turned to baseball. The doctor told me that my condition would probably improve when I got back home around friends and family and got busy. That was what I tried to do.

When I got back, I rejoined the Eagles and played a couple of weeks before the season ended. Then I headed for Puerto Rico to regain my form, since I hadn't had a chance to play any ball in the service. After I came out of service, I was never the same guy that I was when I went in. I had lost my timing, and I was three years older. Right away, I realized that I had lost something and I worked hard trying to come back.

In the meantime, before I went to Puerto Rico, the Brooklyn Dodgers contacted me. Clyde Sukeforth, one of their top scouts, came over to my house and said the Dodgers were interested in signing me to play for them. "Well, I'll sign with you," I told him, "but I'm not up to par yet. I'll let you know when I'm ready." "Well, that's okay," he said. We went over to Brooklyn, where I talked to Branch Rickey and told him the same thing that I had told Sukeforth. "Fine," Rickey said. "When you get ready just let us know."

So I went on down to Puerto Rico and started to play with the San Juan Senadores in the winter of 1945. I had a pretty good year and started to hit the ball again. I was also fielding and throwing the way I had before the war, but I still was not quite ready yet.

When the season began in 1946, I was still with the Eagles, and we trained in Daytona Beach, Florida. Leon Day had also returned from the Army and was our ace again that year. He had been able to play ball part of the time in Europe. I understand he was able to beat Ewell Blackwell in a key game in Nuremberg in the G. I. World Series. They had a big stadium and there were about one hundred thousand soldiers there. I think Willard Brown hit two home runs for the only two runs in the game to give Leon the win. Day more or less had stayed in shape, but I had to almost start all over again.

14 1946 Negro World Series

Going into the seventh game of the Negro World Series that year, we were tied with Monte's Newark Eagles, but Satchel didn't show up for the last game. That could have made the difference.

—Buck O'Neil, Kansas City Monarchs

Monte was the key to our winning the 1946 Negro World Series. His presence made the difference. He was a clutch performer and you felt good that Monte was on your side. He was the key to the whole thing.

—Max Manning, Newark Eagles

IN ADDITION TO Leon Day, the Eagles had Max Manning and Len Hooker back, and Rufus Lewis came into his own to give us a good pitching staff in 1946. Jimmy Wilkes, Bob Harvey, and Johnny Davis were the outfielders. Mrs. Manley had acquired Pat Patterson to play third base, and Larry Doby was back from the Navy. He played second base, I filled a hole at shortstop, and Lenny Pearson was at first base to complete the infield. Leon Ruffin and Charlie Parks were our catchers. Biz Mackey, one of the greatest catchers ever, was our manager. We had a lot of speed, a lot of power and good pitching.

Doby, Davis, Pearson, and myself were considered the big four sluggers in the Eagles' lineup. I batted cleanup and had a good season, finishing with a .394 average to win the batting title. After Leon Day's opening-day no-hitter, we continued our winning ways and ended the Homestead Grays' string of nine straight pennants. Our league had a split season, and we won each half easily, finishing with a combined 47-16 record.

We met Kansas City for the Negro Leagues Championship. Their best known player, of course, was Satchel Paige. I was later to play in two World Series with the New York Giants, but this was my only Negro World Series and it went a full seven games.

The first game of the Series was played at night on September 17, in the Polo Grounds. Of course, Mackey selected Leon Day to start for us and Hilton Smith started for Kansas City. They locked in a tight pitcher's duel that ended with us on the short end of a 2-1 score, but neither of the starters figured in the decision. Rufus Lewis relieved Leon and was tagged with the loss and Satchel Paige got the win in relief for the Monarchs.

In that game our right fielder, Bob Harvey, took out their shortstop to break up a double play and, as it turned out, put him out for the Series with a broken ankle. It was not intentional on Harvey's part but Jim Hamilton, the shortstop, was a rookie and just didn't know how to make the pivot and protect himself. He was a good-looking prospect and if he had not been injured he might have developed into a star and probably played for a long time.

The action moved to Newark for the second game. Joe Louis, the heavyweight champion, was present and saw us even the Series. Max Manning, my old college buddy, pitched a complete game for a 7-4 victory. Ford Smith started for Kansas City but Satchel came in to relieve him with the game on the line, just as he had done in the first game. But this time we pinned the loss on him when Larry Doby hit a two-run homer. Willard Brown homered in the game for the Monarchs and, as it turned out, both of them would be in the major leagues the next year.

The next game was originally scheduled for Kansas City on the following Sunday, but it was rained out, and we had to play on Monday. Not only did we lose a good payday from a big Sunday crowd, but we also lost the game. Lefty LaMarque pitched the complete game for them and Len Hooker started for us but was knocked out. We lost by a big score, 15-5.

We played again in Kansas City the next night, and I hit a home run to help stake Rufus Lewis to an 8-1 win. Ted Alexander started for the Monarchs, but Satchel made his third relief appearance and suffered his second defeat in the Series.

We traveled to Chicago for the next game, which was played in Comiskey Park, but we lost 5-1 to go down by one game in the Series. Both Hilton Smith and Max Manning pitched complete games.

In the sixth game we had our backs to the wall. One more loss would end the Series. We knew we had to win, so we started Leon Day again. The Monarchs started LaMarque, who had defeated us in the third game. To top it off, scouts from both the Dodgers and Giants were in the stands. Maybe that brought out the best in everybody. Willard Brown hit a three-run homer and Buck O'Neil had a grandslam for the Monarchs, while Lennie Pearson homered for us. I had my best game of the Series, going three-for-three with a pair of homers.

Despite all the hitting, the game turned on an outstanding defensive play. The man who made the game-saving play was Leon Day, who had moved to center field earlier in the game after Len Hooker relieved him on the mound. Buck O'Neil hit a deep line drive to right center field and Leon made a great over-the-shoulder catch to save the game. That catch preserved a 9-7 victory, and sent the Series back to Newark for the seventh game.

After a day off, we played the final game on a Sunday afternoon, and it proved to be a thriller. Rufus Lewis and Ford Smith were the starting pitchers in the deciding contest. I knocked in a run in the first inning to give us a 1-0 lead that stood up until the top of the sixth inning when Buck O'Neil homered to tie the game. In the bottom half of the inning, Doby and I both walked and Johnny Davis doubled to left-center field to bring us in and give us a 3-1 lead. As it turned out my run was the one that made us the Champions because the Monarchs scored again in the next inning to narrow the score to 3-2. Rufus held them the last two innings and that was the final score.

Satchel Paige was supposed to pitch that seventh game against us, but we got an unheard-of break. Satchel and Ted Strong, two of their main men, didn't show for the game. I understand that they were over in New York City negotiating with owners from a team in the Islands to play winter ball.

The bottom line was that, after seven tough games, we were the Champions. I had a pretty good Series. I had at least one hit in every game and led all batters with a .462 average. Lennie Pearson also had a good Series and finished with a .393 mark. He was tied with me going into the last game, but he went hitless for the only time in the Series. Doby, who had been one of our top hitters during the season, was a bit off his normal production and hit only .182. But numbers are not as important as winning, and that's all we really cared about.

I've never seen a woman so happy as Mrs. Manley. She gave a big party for the team. You *know* all Newark celebrated. I think for winning the Series, we each received six hundred bucks. It was great for us because it was the first time that Newark had ever won a championship. Mrs. Manley strutted around Newark all winter and the press published pictures of her accepting the Championship trophy. One of the local politicians even gave us a big party because her picture had appeared in the newspapers.

15 Jackie Robinson

Under the circumstances that he played big league baseball and what he had to go through, Jackie Robinson was the greatest competitor that I've ever seen.

—Alvin Dark, New York Giants

WHILE I WAS playing in the 1946 Negro World Series, Jackie Robinson was playing with Montreal, the Dodgers Triple-A farm club in the International League. When Branch Rickey first signed him, we didn't think that much of him as a player. At the time, we thought there were better players in our league. But when Jackie reported to Montreal in 1946, he tore up the International League. He hit, ran, and played good all around baseball. And he just constantly improved.

I knew that if he succeeded there would be new opportunities for the young Negro ball players coming along after Jackie. But I also knew that it would mean the demise of the old Negro leagues. The younger guys like Sam Jethroe, Don Newcombe, Dan Bankhead, and Larry Doby were happy because it meant they had a chance to play in the big leagues. But the older guys figured they wouldn't get the chance because of their age, and soon they wouldn't have a league of their own anymore. We all knew, once Jackie signed, that was the end of the Negro leagues. It was just a matter of time.

I had already gone to Puerto Rico when I heard that Jackie had signed with the Dodgers. I had gone down there to get back into shape shortly after I was discharged from the Army on September 1, 1945. Branch Rickey announced that he had signed Jackie on October 23rd of the same year. I was very happy for him. I wasn't jealous of Jackie's success, but I was envious. I thought, *Gee whiz, why couldn't that have been me?*

Most people don't know that Oscar Charleston was involved in the process of finding a player for Rickey to sign. Oscar was very smart and an astute baseball person. When they had their meetings, he was telling them who was out there, who was signable, and who would probably be able to make it. Oscar was probably working directly under Clyde Sukeforth. Clyde couldn't have picked a better man to help him than Oscar, and Rickey couldn't have picked a better man than Jackie Robinson.

I didn't really know Jackie at that time. I was in the Army when he played with the Kansas City Monarchs, and when I was with the Eagles, he was playing football at UCLA. I knew Kenny Washington and Woody Strode many years before I was introduced to Jackie. They all played on the same team out in Los Angeles, and there were good times and bad times between the three of them. They might have been close friends in the beginning but later on in life, they were not that close.

Someone told me once that Kenny and Jackie had a disagreement about something and they went under the stands to settle it. When they came out, Jackie was declared the winner. Kenny was about six feet three and two hundred and ten pounds, and Jackie was a little under six feet and weighed about one hundred and eighty-five pounds. But Jackie was no patsy when it came to defending himself.

Sometime later, I asked Kenny about Jackie. "I don't really know Jackie," I said. "Tell me about him. What kind of guy is he? Is he easy to get along with?" "Let me just put it this way," Kenny answered. "Jackie always wants to be first." I said, "Well, that's not the worst thing in the world." And he said, "I'm just telling you, that's the way it is." Now, you can't knock a guy for wanting to be number one, and I think you need a certain amount of that to succeed. But at other times, a person like that will automatically rub some people the wrong way.

There were certain players on the Dodgers who didn't get along with Jackie very well. They preferred to just play with him on the field and then go their separate ways. Campy and Don Newcombe had some disagreements with Jackie because he wanted to be the spokesman and tell them what to do. Robinson was aggressive and standupish, and he wanted them to be the way he was. It was like, *If you see me doing something, you be like me.*

One day Campy had to tell Jackie, "Now listen, my name is almost as big as yours, and I have no problem with race or color. My father was Italian and I've been through all of that. So, I have no hang-up on race. And, so far as you telling me what to do, you just do what Jackie wants to do, and Campanella will do what he wants to do." For a long time, there was an alienation between Campy and Jackie. And also between Newcombe and Jackie.

I didn't play with Jackie like Campy and Newk did. Jackie was an upcoming, rising star, and he was feeling his oats. He always wanted to be in command of the situation. He was a tremendous, well-rounded athlete. He starred in baseball, basketball, football, and track. And he was a good tennis player, golfer, and card player. He didn't think that anybody else could do all these things as good as he could. He was also a good speaker, smart, and naturally aggressive. Being able to excel at all the things that he did, he just figured that he was number one. He acted that way at all times, and it seemed like he thought he was just a little bit better than other players.

One year around 1949, the Jackie Robinson All-Stars went barnstorming. On that team was Jackie, Campy, Newk and Larry Doby. They had all agreed that they would split their part of the revenue into four equal shares. After the first game, Jackie and his promoter saw that the park was filled and, consequently, there was a lot of money to be made. So they got together and said, "We'll give these guys their five thousand dollars now, and then we'll split everything else." I understand that both of them made over one hundred thousand dollars apiece before the trip was over. This caused a lot of hard feelings between Jackie and the other three, and a further deterioration in their relationships.

I heard that near the end of his career in Brooklyn, almost to a man, Jackie's teammates really didn't like him. Simply because he had said and done things that had alienated them. That's not a good situation when you alienate everybody. You've got to have at least one friend. Sometimes you need more than one.

I'll always remember when Campy and Jackie finally got back together and buried the hatchet. Campanella's daughter was getting married and Ralph and Ann Branca were at the wedding. Ralph came over to them and said, "Listen, you guys, you know, you've been mad at each other for many, many years. Don't you think it's about time for you to shake hands and be friends again?" So they shook hands and, as far as I know, they were much closer when Jackie passed away than they had been for about ten years. I saw that happen and I was glad to see it.

In his later years, Jackie and Dodger owner Walter O'Malley didn't see eye-to-eye about many things. It came to a head one year when the team went to Japan. Jackie got on Mr. O'Malley about some of the traveling accommodations and how some of the players were being treated. The two of them really had words and it was an unpleasant situation. Jackie's wife Rachel, being the wonderful woman she is, told Jackie that he was wrong. He went to Mr. O'Malley and apologized, and that made everything okay, at least for the moment. From that time on, everything between them was not peaches and cream the way the press would have you to believe. They had their moments.

These differences may have contributed to Jackie being traded to the Giants and, consequently, to his retirement. He could have played a couple more years, but there were several factors that entered into his decision to retire. Number one, Jackie's health was not the best in the world. Number two, he had always been a Dodger but had been traded over to the hated Giants. Number three, *Look* magazine had promised him that if he ever wanted to retire, they would give him a lot of money for the exclusive story. Number four, he had also been promised a job as a vice-president in charge of personnel at the Chock Full o' Nuts coffee company. Number five, and I think this has to be considered, Jackie had always been the star player for the Dodgers and Willie Mays was the recognized star with the Giants. Jackie's personality being what it was, he probably would not have wanted to play second fiddle to Willie.

Considering all these points, Jackie probably decided this was the perfect time for him to retire. Maybe he was right. He had a job where his income would be even more than it was with the Dodgers, and he could spend more time with his family. He could help the NAACP and the other organizations with their programs through speaking engagements across the country. And he wouldn't have to be second best to anybody on the baseball field.

In making his decision to retire, Jackie probably discussed it with his wife. Rachel Robinson is a highly intelligent, handsome woman who has the ability to get along with people. She had the kind of foresight to make anything all right when Jackie was hell bent on screwing it up. When he had problems with O'Malley, Buzzie Bavasi, or some other Dodger executive, Rachel would tell him that he had been a little hasty in his remarks and persuade him to apologize for some of the things he had said. Then Jackie would go to the person he had offended and apologize, and things would be all right until the next time it happened.

Jackie was fortunate to have a wife like Rachel in his corner. This was especially true when Jackie trained in Daytona Beach that first spring. Jackie had Rachel to go to after practice was over, and the two of them could go out, have dinner, and enjoy themselves. Johnny Wright, the other black player who was in camp that year, was about the same age as Jackie. He didn't have much formal education, and he had no one to talk with like Jackie did. I think that was why he didn't stick with the team.

I had known Johnny long before then, because he was with the Eagles even before I got there. When I was with the Eagles, he pitched for the Grays and was a good pitcher. All he needed was just a little more control, because he could throw hard and had a good curve. But he just wasn't tough enough. I think being around white people would sometimes scare him, and he never did overcome it. Johnny was not like Jackie. He was kind of timid, and you could hurt Johnny's feelings. He would just go into his shell and not pitch as well as he could. Jackie was aggressive and outgoing, so things like that didn't bother him at all. He would just take it out on the ball or an opposing player.

Jackie had a mental toughness that seemed to bring out the best in him when he encountered adversity. Some people think that he had a chip on his shoulder and carried grudges. When Jackie, Sam Jethroe, and Marvin Williams had a tryout with the Boston Red Sox in April 1945, they were not really given a chance. And I think that soured him on the Red Sox and Joe Cronin. I guess he never forgot the fact that he was treated so shabbily and he said something about it in the papers. There was no love lost between the two of them during the time that Jackie was playing or after he retired.

I remember something that happened between Jackie and Joe Cronin while I was working in the commissioner's office. During the 1972 World Series, everyone knew that Jackie was pretty sick and maybe wouldn't last too much longer. Jackie was going to throw out the first ball before a game at Cincinnati, and there would be a ceremony on the field to honor him.

Bowie Kuhn said, "Monte, in about five minutes we're all going to assemble on the pitcher's mound. Reds' owner Bob Howsum is here and Chub Feeney, the president of the National League, is here. But I don't see the president of the American League, Joe Cronin. Would you seek him out and ask him if he would join us in a few minutes on the mound?"

I immediately went to find Joe and when I found him, he and a friend were on their way to the stadium club. I told him what was happening and he said, "You just tell the commissioner that I won't be there, and he'll have to proceed without me." When I told Bowie Kuhn what Joe Cronin had said, the commissioner just shrugged his shoulders and they had the ceremony on the field without Joe. Apparently that feeling was still there, and they didn't even want to be on the same mound together. As far as I know, they never did make up. Now, whether Jackie held grudges or not, who knows?

16 The Color Line

I think Monte could have been the one to break the color line. Jackie Robinson did it and he was hot-headed. Monte was easygoing.

—Leon Day, Newark Eagles

Monte was the type, who played his ball game, took care of himself, did a good job, had no controversy, and was a great ball player. In my mind, if he had been the first black player in the major leagues, he would have been very successful in that role.

—Preacher Roe, Brooklyn Dodgers

SOME PEOPLE SAY that Branch Rickey's choice of Jackie Robinson was a bad decision that worked out right. Simply because it went against Jackie's true nature to take all that he did without being able to retaliate. In that regard, Rickey *did* give him an almost impossible assignment. Fortunately, Jackie succeeded, and the rest is history.

The great honor, of course, was being the first black to play in the major leagues. The question has been asked and debated many times, "Suppose Jackie had failed. What would have happened?" I think that if he had not suceeded, it would have only set the program back just a little. Because guys like Willie Mays, Hank Aaron, Don Newcombe, Roy Campanella and Larry Doby were coming along. One of those fellows would have eventually broken the barrier. But it's a moot question because Jackie did a perfect job of pioneering. What Jackie did was make it easier for them when they did come along, and I'm sure that they realize this.

Jackie was a great spokesman and an electrifying baseball player who helped change history. He made baseball better because his success opened up a new source of talent for both the American and National leagues, and it gave these young black players a chance for a great opportunity. Jackie made it better for us athletically, socially, professionally, and every other way.

Soon after Jackie proved himself, the other baseball teams started to add black players to their rosters, and the door was opened in all sports. Some young people today, including black major leaguers, have no understanding about how things were fifty years ago before Branch Rickey signed Jackie Robinson.

Between 1884 and 1947, there was no black player in the major leagues. Racism affected black Americans in critical ways. First of all, it never let you reach your potential because there was always a doubt in your mind about how good you were. If the major leagues represented the best and you could never reach the major leagues, how could you ever say, "Well, I know I'm good because I'm a major leaguer?"

As far as I can see, one of the most significant things that ever happened in the long history of baseball was the decision in 1947 to allow black players to enter the major leagues at long last. In my opinion, black players have been the absolute salvation of the game since that decision was made.

The real losers in the years prior to Jackie Robinson breaking the color line are the many millions of fans who were deprived of the opportunity of seeing the great black players from the first half of the twentieth century. I'm talking about Josh Gibson, Buck Leonard, Oscar Charleston, Satchel Paige, and countless others. Just think about how many thrills the fans of this nation missed because they never saw these marvelous athletes in action during their prime.

Before World War II, there was some talk about taking blacks into the major leagues. But no one said, "Damn it, if you can play baseball you can play anywhere." It wasn't until late in 1945, after the war and after Happy Chandler replaced Judge Landis as commissioner, that Branch Rickey finally made the decision to challenge the gentleman's agreement that excluded black players from the major leagues.

When Rickey was scouting the Negro leagues for the right man to become the first black player to go into the majors, I was one of the leading candidates. But Jackie did such a great job, how could anyone criticize the job that he did? The only thing he lacked as a ball player was power, and he didn't hit a lot of home runs.

As far as the other aspects of what he did, I don't know if anybody could have taken what Jackie did. Don Newcombe once paid me a compliment when he said that Campy and I were the only two others who could have broken the color line.

Campy's father was Italian, and he was a popular player. He would be back there by himself with all that catcher's gear on, and he wouldn't be as conspicuous. By comparison, Jackie was out there in the middle of the field and, because he was black, he stood out like a sore thumb. And he was so aggressive and proud, that he was not going to back down. It's well known that Jackie had a rough time with some of his teammates and players throughout the league. He said, "To hell with it." He just had that type of attitude.

Campy, on the other hand, had an easy manner about him and would have handled the problems differently. Campy was the kind of fellow who was not hung up on race. He got along with everybody, teammates and opponents alike. Even though you might not have liked the Baltimore Elite Giants, because of Campy's great talent and charisma, you had to like him. And almost everybody did.

Mrs. Manley once told me in Ashland, Kentucky, at a Negro leagues reunion in 1981, that I was supposed to be the guy to break the barrier. She said that I had been selected by her and the rest of the owners for that role. If it had not been for World War II, I might have been the one to break the color line. Before the war, I had a good arm and was doing great fielding but, more than anything else, I could hit and I had an easy time. I was playing my best baseball. But, like they say, timing is everything, and fate intervened.

If I *had* been the first one chosen, I think I could have done the job because all you had to do was *play*. I grew up in an integrated situation, where I played sports in grade school and high school with white teammates. I never had any problem. I didn't care about skin color, and I think I had the type of personality to handle any situation. I also had a fair amount of education and some talent. If given the opportunity, I *think* I could have done the job. But, again, so could those other fellows that I mentioned.

There is more than one way to handle a situation. If a guy does something to you, it can be handled in such a way as to let him know not to do that anymore. You don't have to get into a fight or say nasty things. I think there are other ways that it can be done. You could ask the person, "Where is your sense of fair play?" or "Don't you believe in the golden rule?" Try that technique rather than be confrontational. I find sometimes that really works. You don't have to square off. If you're just naturally pleasant and go a step farther, you can get the message across.

When Dixie Walker and some of those guys didn't want to play with Jackie, he could have told them, "Well, I'm sorry you don't want to play with me, I want to play with you. I think that all of you are fine baseball players. Maybe if we all play together, we can win the pennant." It's possible to use that kind of approach and succeed. His teammates would probably have applauded him, and maybe it would have made things a little easier. Maybe those guys would not have wanted to be traded away from the Dodgers.

Even after World War II, I could have gone with the Dodgers because Rickey contacted me in 1945 after I got out of the Army. At that time they said they were going to start another league, and I didn't know what he intended to do. I had only recently returned from the service with three years of athletic rust and a bad case of war nerves, and I needed to work back into my pre-war playing condition. So I told them I wasn't ready and I'd let them know when I could play.

I knew that, in time, my inner ear problem would get better and I didn't let that stop me. I was still fairly young. So I said, "I'll start to climb back slowly." And, in order to regain my old form, I went down to San Juan, Puerto Rico, and played ball that winter. That familiar surrounding helped me. Neither my arm nor my eyesight was as good as it was before and I wasn't as fast as I had been. I had probably lost a step while I was in the Army, but I couldn't let that stop me.

I was smarter and more experienced, so I said, "I'll let that help me." That's the way I started to come back. After the 1947 season, I went to Cuba and played down there. I hit a few home runs and my power started to come back a little bit. I played good enough for the Almendares team to invite me back the next year. In the Cuban League, they played the best brand of baseball outside of the United States. That was before Castro took over down there. I understand that in his earlier years he had been a baseball player and, if we had known he wanted to be a dictator, we'd have made him an umpire.

But I worked hard in the winter leagues, and I was doing all the right things on the field and off. I was not staying out late or drinking too much. I was a beer drinker, and I'd drink a few beers and then say, "That's enough." I would go out with the guys but I wouldn't stay too late. I tried to do all the things that would keep me in there for the long haul. And it worked out just that way. By 1948 or 1949, I was almost back to where I was when I left for the Army.

I probably *could* have gone up to the majors sooner than I did. But in 1947, when Jackie broke in with the Dodgers, I went back to the Eagles. The Dodgers didn't contact me anymore, and I didn't contact them. I can't remember what kind of season I had, but I didn't think it was good for me although I was selected to the All Star squad again. I was waiting to get a call from the major leagues but I was turning twenty-eight. At that time, they didn't want to sign players older than that, so I felt like I had to be ready.

That year, Larry Doby started to really come on with the Eagles, and Bill Veeck signed him for the Cleveland Indians, making him the first black player in the American League. I thought that Larry would be a sensation with the Indians, simply because he hit the ball to all fields with a lot of power, and he could run, field, and throw. He didn't spend a day in the minors, so he had to sit around until he felt comfortable with the Indians.

After Bill Veeck signed Doby, I understand that Mrs. Manley asked him, "Why don't you give me another thousand dollars and take Monte, too?" Veeck told me later that not signing me was one of the dumbest moves that he *didn't* make.

I wasn't jealous of Larry but I was a little bit envious of the opportunity, just as I had been when Jackie signed. I said, "Well, damn. I sure wish it had been me. He got a good break. I wish I could get a break like that, too." I just kept going and waited for my chance.

Now, Jackie Robinson had played just a short time in the Negro leagues and it only took him a year to become a star in the major leagues. It was the same thing with Doby. He progressed real fast, too. He came up in mid-season with Cleveland as a second baseman, but they found a spot in the outfield for him later on that year. In one year he became an All-Star performer in center field, which shows what kind of talent there was in the Negro leagues.

For some reason major-league owners were slow to tap this great reservoir of raw talent. Mrs. Manley was very outspoken about what she considered the major league owners' oversight in not signing me. She said that I was the best all-around player they had in the Negro leagues and called me "Our Superman." The Manleys had been losing money for a couple of years and when the Negro National League folded following the 1948 season, they sold the Eagles franchise and all of their club holdings, which included players' contracts, to a Memphis dentist, Dr. W. H. Young.

When the news about the Newark Eagles ball club disbanding got out, Branch Rickey acted quickly and sent a scout, Clyde Sukeforth, to sign me to a Dodger contract to play with the St. Paul farm club. I was playing winter ball in Cuba and staying at the Hotel San Luis, in Havana. When Effa Manley read about Rickey's actions in the *Newark Evening News,* she immediately sent a letter to me at the hotel. Her letter included a clipping of the *Evening News* story about me signing with the Dodgers and asked me if I actually had signed with Mr. Rickey. I wrote her a prompt response, dated January 7, 1949, saying:

> "The article that appeared in the *Newark Evening News* is true. I have been approached by one of the Brooklyn Dodger scouts and I signed to play in St. Paul this summer.
>
> I read in the paper that you had sold the team so there was not any hesitancy on my part, since I didn't have too many years left to play. I sincerely hope that I did the right thing and that I can play good enough to make the team."

I felt it was entirely proper for me to sign a contract with the Dodgers, since the Newark Eagles baseball club had disbanded. Effa understood my position and my reasoning, but under the original agreement with Dr. Young, monies received from any major-league club for a player's contract were to be divided equally between Young and the Manleys. So, from a purely business standpoint, Mrs. Manley felt that Branch Rickey was obligated to compensate her for my contract.

That position probably delayed my entry into the major leagues and many members of the black press, and black fans in general, disagreed with Effa's action. They thought that it was spiteful and felt the black owners should help players get into the major leagues. I felt precisely as the fans did, and that she was acting selfishly with only her own monetary interests at heart.

The Dodgers released me because Mrs. Manley wanted some money and Branch Rickey said he wasn't going to give her any compensation. I found out later that he asked why he should spend five or ten thousand dollars when he could get me for free. Mrs. Manley told Rickey that he had taken Don Newcombe for no money but she wasn't going to let him take me without some compensation. Furthermore, if he tried to do it, she would sue and fight him in court She hired a young Jewish attorney, Jerry Kessler, to represent them in a test case. Rather than get into a hassle with Effa and get involved in an unnecessary lawsuit, or get any kind of unfavorable publicity, Rickey contacted her to say he was no longer interested and released me.

I understand that Kessler then contacted the New York Yankees to try to sell my contract to them, but they were not interested at that time. So the New York Giants picked up my contract. That was the best thing that ever happened to me.

III

The Major Leagues

17 Black Giants in New York

When Monte joined the team, he was obviously such a gentleman and a high class person, that there was no way you couldn't like him.

—Whitey Lockman, New York Giants

Class distinction, race distinction and religious points had nothing to do with our ballclub. Everybody was pulling together. The only thing Durocher thought about was winning, and we never had a thought about anything else.

—Alvin Dark, New York Giants

HORACE STONEHAM, owner of the New York Giants, paid five thousand dollars for my contract and Mrs. Manley accepted although she had hoped to get more. She wanted to set a precedent to stop the major-league franchises from raiding the black teams. Of the five thousand dollars that the Giants paid for my contract, the attorney Jerry Kessler got two thousand and five hundred, Dr. Young got one thousand, two hundred and fifty dollars, the Manleys got one thousand, two hundred and fifty dollars and I got nothing. Mrs. Manley used her share to buy herself a beautiful mink stole. Thirty years later, she still had that mink at the Negro leagues reunion in Ashland, Kentucky. I told her, "You made a good buy, Mrs. Manley." She said, "Not as good as the Giants did."

That's why Alex Pompez was in Cuba on behalf of the Giants to sign me and Hank Thompson in 1949. I had a fine year with Almendares that winter, and we won the championship over

Havana. Pompez informed Hank and me that the Giants were interested in us, and asked if we were interested in playing for them. I informed him that I still belonged to the Brooklyn Dodgers, but he said that Mrs. Manley had contacted Branch Rickey and they had released me. "That being the case," I said, "I'd be happy to sign." If the Giants wanted to give me a chance, that was fine with me.

Hank and I reported to the Giants' Jersey City farm club of the International League for the 1949 season. I had been waiting for this opportunity for a long time. When I finally got a chance, I went to spring training and tried to do the best I could. We trained in Sanford, Florida, and Hank and I had to stay apart from the club, but we didn't care. I wasn't getting any younger and wanted to find out what I was going to do with my baseball career. So I worked hard and got in real good shape.

We played with Jersey City until July 1st, and I was playing good ball. It was much easier there because I was living at home, so I didn't have a lot of expenses. That's one of the reasons I wanted to sign with the Giants. I was just delighted to be able to see my wife and daughters every day and to go home every night.

My family and friends would come out to see me play. People from Orange and East Orange used to flock to the games, particularly when we played the Bears in Newark. So I helped attendance. We also had a natural rivalry with Buffalo and Rochester. I enjoyed playing near home, but I wasn't there very long because the Giants wanted me in New York. When I was called up, I was hitting about .500 with a lot of home runs and was driving in a lot of runs. I was also fielding real well and throwing out everybody that ran.

When Hank and I reported to the Polo Grounds, our uniforms were laid out for us. I went over to the locker to get dressed, and when I put on the New York Giants uniform for the first time, that had to be one of the greatest thrills of my life. It was like a dream coming true, and something that I never expected to ever happen. I thought about the long road that I had traveled to get there, and the fact that it was finally happening was a feeling that is indescribable.

When Leo Durocher finally came in, he came over and said hello to us. Then, after everybody got dressed, he called a meeting. Leo said, "About race, I'm going to say this. If you're green or purple or whatever color, you can play for me if I think you can help this ballclub. That's all I'm going to say about race." After that we felt great. Each player came over and wished us good luck.

I know that Jackie had some trouble with the Dodgers, but we never had any problem on the Giants. I was happy about that and I think Leo Durocher was responsible because of the way he handled it.

We got along okay in those early days, and most of our teammates treated us cordially enough, but one could feel an underlying uneasiness through it all. There were some players that made us feel particularly welcome. My favorites on the Giants were Bobby Thomson and Whitey Lockman. Whitey was perhaps the friendliest of all. The character of each of the Giant players was one of the reasons that we had an easier time than Jackie. The club hadn't won a pennant in quite a while, so I guess they figured if Hank and I could help the team, then they would help us.

Our talented trainer, Doc Bowman, and coaches Herman Franks, Freddie Fitzsimmons, and Frank Shellenback were four of my favorite people. They were all very encouraging. All of this made our task much easier. But most of all, the reason why things went so smoothly in the beginning was the fact that Durocher laid out the ground rules so explicitly.

After joining the Giants, I didn't start to play regularly right away and sat around for a while. Then one day Leo said, "Well, we'll put you in and see where you fit in." He tried me at third base but I didn't do that well there. Before the war, I was a natural third baseman but my reflexes had suffered some. Neither myself nor Hank Thompson got much of a chance to play the balance of the season. I didn't get a real chance until the next year, and then I started to come on.

I went to my first full spring training camp with the Giants in 1950, and we trained in Phoenix, Arizona. Phoenix was a nice western city but, except for the hotel where we stayed, we ran into that same old southern situation. Black players could stay in the hotel but we couldn't linger in the lobby and had to go right to our rooms. We also couldn't eat in the dining rooms, so we would get room service and have all our meals in our room.

I went to Eddie Brannick, the traveling secretary, and said, "Eddie, we're members of the Giants and we hope to make the team. Why is it that we are the only two guys that can't eat in the dining room?" "Well, for some reason, that's the law out here," he answered, "and until they get the law changed, we'll just have to suffer with it. I empathize with you and I wish that wasn't the situation." *But it was.* We didn't raise a lot of hell because we were trying to make the team. And we didn't want to make that a big issue, without having made the team. So, we just accepted it and went along with the program.

After spring training, I returned to Jersey City at the start of the regular season. However, I was recalled to the Giants a month later, and this time I stuck. I played some at first base, and started to play right field more. I felt much better out in the outfield.

I was more confident and had begun to learn the pitchers and their patterns. And I got to know Stan Musial, Enos Slaughter, Robin Roberts, Del Ennis, and all the rest of those guys. I saw how they played and I thought, *They're no better than I am. I can do the same thing.*

But where everything before came naturally, I now had to work a little harder to get the job done. And the hardest thing was getting used to not being the top player. I want to emphasize this as much as I can because in everything I had done, particularly in baseball, I had always been the best. I could do more things than anybody. I could hit like crazy, had a lot of power, had the best arm, could run like a deer, and I was a real good fielder. And I never got hurt. So, as far as baseball skills were concerned, I never had a problem.

There were, however, three adjustments that I had to make in the transition to the major leagues. Getting rid of the athletic rust, getting used to not being the top player, and learning organized baseball's way of doing things. This last adjustment was important because of the comfortability factor. I think that contributed to the reasons why Hank Thompson and Willard Brown, who had played briefly with the St. Louis Browns in 1947, didn't stick at that time.

Hank told me, in effect, that they were given a fair chance. I know now that he probably would have made it then, if they had just given him just a few weeks in the minor leagues to get comfortable in organized baseball. I think every player, no matter how great he is, should spend some time in the minors. When you leave the minor leagues and go to the major leagues, you automatically work harder, because you don't want to go back to the minors. You want to play in the majors where you make the money and are treated so royally.

That was especially true for those of us making the transition from the Negro leagues. The gap was just too wide. We had some good ball players, but they played individual baseball. If they had first learned the organized way of playing, the adjustment would have been easier. It was just a matter of playing in the minors until you start to feel at ease. Then, after a while, it's a brand-new game. There was need for a transition period, and the minor leagues was a good time to do it. Jackie Robinson would have never made it if he hadn't had the year at Montreal, and the best thing that could have happened to Willie Mays was to start in the minors.

They didn't know what to expect, because they had always been told the major leagues were so tough. So they were bound to wonder, *Can I make it?* The first thing they had to be taught was discipline. They had to learn to show up every day on time, and to play team ball, rather than individual baseball.

For instance, when Willard Brown and Hank Thompson were with the St. Louis Browns in 1947, they were in a game with runners on first and second. Willard Brown was sent up to bunt the ball down the third base line to advance the runners. The first time, he failed to advance the runners, and the second time, the pitcher threw him a high fast ball. Brown was a high fastball hitter, so he swung at the ball and hit it over the center field fence for a three-run homer. But when he got to the dugout, Luke Sewell, the manager, jumped on him for not following instructions. Willard said he knew then that he couldn't play for the Browns because anytime you get chewed out for hitting a home run, you know you're in the wrong place.

The best approach would have been to take them to spring training, keep them in the minors where they could play, and bring them up slowly. Then they would have been all right. But the Browns didn't do that with Thompson and Brown. So both of them got disgusted and wanted to leave St. Louis. Hank, of course, later got another chance with me on the Giants and proved to be a good major-league ball player. Once you see what it's like, it's a piece of cake.

When Larry Doby became the first black player in the American League, he went directly to the major leagues, but he would have benefited from an adjustment period in the minors. I don't think Doby had as tough a time as Jackie, but he wasn't nearly as outgoing and competitive at the beginning as Robinson. Still, he became a star in a very short time.

Both the Giants and Indians trained in Arizona, so after breaking camp both teams would go to Los Angeles to play a series. Next we would go to San Francisco and then head back East by playing in Salt Lake City, Denver, Oklahoma City, Dallas, and other southern cities.

Jackie hadn't played in all those places, so we would receive the brunt of a lot of bad remarks because it was the first time those fans had ever seen a black player in an integrated situation. We received some harsh treatment from the fans, but never from our teammates, simply because Durocher had laid down the law. I think it was the same way with the Indians. Al Lopez was their manager, and at that time they had Doby, Minnie Minoso, Luke Easter, Harry Simpson, and one or two other black players. Neither team had any problems with teammates. All the problems came from the fans. They would call you everything, but we had heard all those words before. We tried to respond by playing well.

I remember we were playing a game in Dallas, and home plate was right near the stands. There was a big loud-mouthed guy sitting right there near home plate, and his voice carried all over the stands. A ball was hit to Minoso, he threw it to Luke Easter at first base but Luke missed the ball. This guy hollered out, "Hey, Lopez! No wonder you can't win, you've got too many of them niggers out there." Easter, in reaching for the ball, had pulled a hamstring and wasn't able to get up. So this same guy yelled, "Get up, nigger! Get up!"

Durocher looked at me and laughed, and I had to laugh, too. It was a funny situation. Here's this big son of a gun laying there on the ground unable to get up. And this guy in the stands was hollering "Get up!" It was really comical, and wasn't nearly as bad as it sounded. The guy was trying to be funny because he had four or five beers too many.

But again, we were used to that kind of stuff, so it didn't make any difference. We made a lot of money for the Indians and Giants by

I earned 16 letters as an all-around athlete at Orange High School. Here I am as a triple threat back in 1934.

This is me as a 17-year old in 1936 with a watch and trophies awarded to me by the Oakwood YMCA for my performance at Orange High School.

Here I am with the Orange Triangles, a semi-pro basketball team, in 1938. I'm seated second from the left and my future teammate on the Newark Eagles, Lennie Pearson, is standing second from the right.

World War II interrupted my baseball career while I was in my prime. This photo was taken in France in 1944 when I was in the U.S. Army.

I began my professional baseball career with the Newark Eagles in the old Negro Leagues.

This is me with Larry Doby. In 1946 we were the keystone combination for the Champion Newark Eagles.

This is Ford Smith, manager Joe Becker, Hank Thompson and myself at Roosevelt Stadium with the Jersey City Giants of the International League in 1949. Hank and I went up to the Giants later in the season.

This is the first all-black outfield to ever play in a World Series. Me, Willie Mays and Hank Thompson in 1951.

I was the first Giant to sign a 1952 contract. This is me with owner Horace Stoneham at the New York Giants' office.

(COURTESY OF *THE NEW YORK TIMES*)

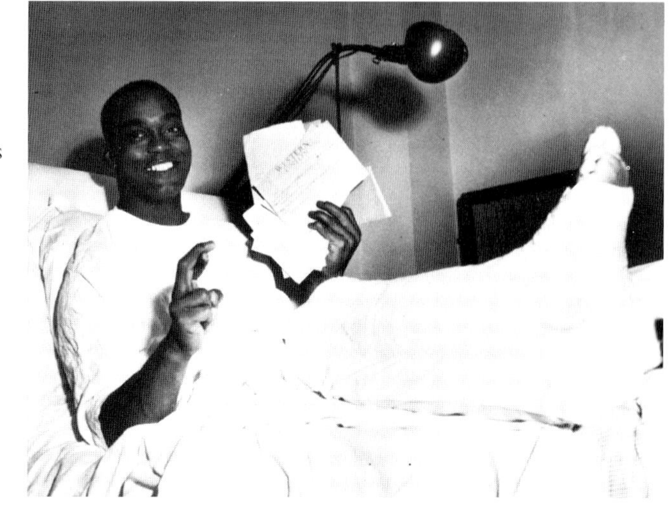

Here I am at New York's Columbia Presbyterian Medical Center holding up a handful of get-well messages while recuperating from my broken ankle in 1952.

In Puerto Rico I played with the San Juan Senadores. Here I am being presented the MVP trophy.

This picture of Leo and me was taken in the dugout at the Polo Grounds in 1954.

Willie and I attending a function in the late '50s.

This photo of me with my mother, Mary Eliza was taken in 1960.

This is me with Rev. Martin Luther King and Rev. Abernathy, as he spoke at the Westchester Civic Center in White Plains, NY in early 1964.

This photo of my father, Cupid Alexander, was taken in 1962, a year before he passed away.

Here I am with the Jackson Five. I arranged for them to sing the National Anthem at the World Series in 1973. Michael is the youngest one standing in front.

Commissioner Bowie Kuhn presented me with my Hall of Fame plaque when I was inducted in 1973.

Satchel and I are at a black tie affair in his honor at the New York Hilton in the 1970s after his election to the Hall of Fame.

This is me with Leon Day and Ray Dandridge, who were on hand for the ceremonies when the Grove Street Oval in East Orange, New Jersey was renamed Monte Irvin Field.

This picture of me with Muhammed Ali was taken at a memorabilia show.

The picture of me with my daughter Patti and my first granddaughter, Stacie, was taken in 1980.

This is me with my daughter Pam and my wife Dee. Dee and I have been happily married since 1942.

(Photo by Ross Forman)

traveling together. This was before television and, wherever we went, people flocked to see us. And they saw good games. The Indians had many stars, including a great pitching staff, and we weren't short on talent either. So, it was a good match-up.

The year 1951 was the big one. By that time, most of us had been together for a year and had developed into a cohesive team without any racial tensions. I've already mentioned Bobby Thomson and Whitey Lockman, and how they helped in this regard. Alvin Dark, the team captain, was an okay guy and so were Eddie Stanky, Larry Jansen, Dave Koslo, Bill Rigney, Don Mueller, Wes Westrum, and Sal Maglie. They were all high-class fellows and easy to get along with. And they really made us feel welcome without any reservation.

We got along like a big happy family. There was a lot of respect between the white players and the black players on the team. And we had a lot of fun. We'd kid each other and I think that prevented anything serious from flaring up in a game.

Ray Noble, a black Cuban, was our backup catcher. That year a very popular circus came to town with a big ape. The ape was called Bushman and they advertised this big ape as a star attraction. Eddie Stanky thought that Noble kind of resembled Bushman. Each day when Stanky came into the locker room, he would say to Noble, "What do you say, Bushman?" One day Stanky came in and said that, and Noble went over to Hank Thompson and asked, "What is this Bushman? Who the hell is Bushman?" "You mean you don't know who Bushman is?" Hank answered. "He's that big ape that's appearing with the circus. And that's what Stanky means. He's calling you an ape."

So Noble went over to Stanky's locker and grabbed him by the collar. Stanky started to laugh and Noble picked him up and kind of hung him on a hook there. And he said, "You don't call me Bushman, no more, huh?" "Oh no, no, no." Stanky replied, "Don't kill me. Don't kill me. I was only playing." After that there was no more Bushman story. When Stanky came in he'd say, "Hello Noble." That ended the Bushman thing.

Of course, when Willie Mays arrived, everybody saw right away what a sensational young budding star he was, and that really helped the racial situation all around. We'd get in the clubhouse before a game and kid around, and we'd carry that same confident attitude to the playing field. It got to the point where it was a real pleasure to come to the ball park to see what great catch or throw Willie would make from day to day.

18 Willie and Leo

They always gave Leo credit for putting his arm around Willie and bringing him along. From what I saw, it seemed to me that Willie had an awful lot of respect for Monte. Monte was like a father to him.

—Bobby Thomson, New York Giants

Monte roomed with Willie and had a lot of influence on him. Monte was like an old professor. When he talked, you listened. He helped Willie get straightened out.

—Dusty Rhodes, New York Giants

WHEN I FIRST SAW Willie Mays, I saw all the things in him that I had before I went into the Army. So, when Leo assigned him to me as a roommate, it was wonderful because I knew I could help him. I had been through it, and I knew what it felt like to have all that talent. That's why we got along so well, and why our friendship has lasted. He and I have never had an unkind word to say to each other in all these years. I understand that I was his last roommate because, after I left, he started to room alone.

I remember during the 1951 season, the Giants were playing pretty good baseball. We went into Pittsburgh for a series and we were staying at the Crosley Hotel, right across from the ball park, Willie and I went down to the hotel dining room about eleven-thirty in the morning. We got about halfway through eating, and the waiter said, "Aren't you guys going to play today?" We said, "Yeah, why do you ask?" He said, "Well, I think they're playing now. In fact, I know they are because I've got it on the radio." And here we were, the two of us, sitting at the table eating. So, we finished our meal, paid the bill, and hurried on over to Forbes Field.

We thought it was a one-thirty ball game, but, because of some holiday, the game had been moved up an hour and we were supposed to be there about twelve-thirty. When we came into the clubhouse, somebody told Leo that we were there. He came in and his first words were, "It'd better be good." Just like that. I said, "Yes, Skipper. Nobody told us about the game time being changed, and we hadn't found out about it." He said, "All right, get dressed and come on out."

He didn't put us in the game right away but an inning or two later he sent us in. I think I went zero for nine in the doubleheader, and Willie dropped one of the few balls in a key situation that I ever saw him miss. And we got beat the doubleheader.

After the games, Leo told us he was going to have a meeting in his room at the hotel. So he started the meeting and the first thing he said was, "I don't know why you guys were late and why you didn't know the game had been moved up an hour. Monte, you ought to know not to be late. You're old enough to know better." And he told Willie, "And you, you little son of a gun, you haven't been here that long, and you ought to have more respect for Monte than to keep him up late." Willie didn't say anything because we hadn't been breaking any rules or anything. Leo said, "I'm going to say this and then I'm finished with it. The next time it happens, it'll cost you five hundred dollars." From that day until I left in 1955, he never did collect that five hundred bucks because we were always on time.

The only thing we were guilty of was the fact that we failed to notice that the time had been changed on the bulletin board and nobody told us. We hadn't been doing anything wrong. That's not bad compared to some of the things the guys do today. But it shows how something can happen, and sometimes kind of wake you up. In fact we went to St. Louis and, one game later, started on a sixteen-game winning streak.

The Cardinals had a stable of left-handers and every time we'd go to St. Louis, they'd pitch those left-handers against us. They had Al Brazle, Harry Brecheen, Howie Pollet, and Max Lanier. And during the season in 1951, they traded Pollet for Cliff Chambers, another left-hander, and they were all tough to hit for a left-handed batter.

When we got to St. Louis, Hank Thompson didn't expect to play against them because he batted left-handed. He thought Leo would play Bill Rigney or somebody else at third base like he usually did against the Cardinals. So Hank was out all night carousing. But somebody got hurt and he had to play the next day, and he must have struck out about four times in key situations.

In the clubhouse after the game, Durocher called a meeting and said, "We've got too good of a ballclub to be playing the way we're playing. You guys are trying too hard. You're not relaxed enough. I want you to go out tonight, and if anybody is in the hotel before six o'clock in the morning, it'll cost you five hundred dollars." Then he looked at Hank and said, "All except you, Hank Thompson, you little sonofabitch." Leo had heard that Hank had been out carousing the night before and he said, "It's twelve o'clock now and one hour from now, at one o'clock, I want you in the hotel, in bed, by yourself, alone."

We were staying at the Chase, and I don't know what everybody did, but we all went someplace, and we sure as hell didn't get to the hotel until early that morning. We played night games there anyhow, and if we had a few highballs and a few cocktails, we could sleep it off the next day and be ready for the game that night. But that remedied the situation at that time and it was a smart move on Leo's part.

Durocher had the foresight to see what the problem was. It relaxed us, and then we went on our streak and won sixteen in a row. It was just a change and that was what did it, I think. We were just trying too hard and were too tight.

Hank was known as a carouser, and I remember another time when Durocher got on him. Our lockers were right next to each other, and Leo came over and said, "Monte, I'm going to put you in charge of Hank while we're in St. Louis. Watch him and make sure he doesn't go astray. Make sure he gets to the hotel on time. Make sure he catches the bus. You're in charge of him." And Hank said, "Hell, who's going to be in charge of that sonofabitch?" Everybody got a big laugh out of it, and we let it go at that.

Durocher had a knack for knowing how to handle certain players. He handled Mays just right and that had a lot to do with our success. Willie needed instruction off the field in little things, and I helped him in that way. But Leo was like a second father to Willie.

Leo was not the most popular man off the field, but he was a hell of a manager. Durocher was dictatorial. If he said that we were going to pitch a batter a certain way, and a pitcher was going to vary from that pattern, he'd better let Leo know so he could move the players around accordingly. If a pitcher didn't do what Leo said, he'd chew him out. And he *could* chew somebody out. It would happen quite a few times during a season.

I remember once when Bill Voiselle got two strikes on a hitter and then didn't waste a pitch. When he threw that next pitch, the guy hit it for a home run, and Leo fined him five hundred dollars. Most managers want you to waste a pitch in that situation unless you've got overpowering stuff.

To avoid incidents like this, we would have a quick meeting before every game where Leo and the starting pitcher would discuss the other team's batting order. Sal Maglie's nickname was "The Barber" and when he pitched, regardless of who we were playing, his rundown of the opposing lineup was about the same.

They'd call the lead-off batter's name and Sal would say, "Well, the first pitch I'll come in high and tight and knock him down. Then I'll start to work on him." And he would describe how he was going to pitch to him. Then they'd go to the second batter and Sal would say, "Well, the first pitch I'll come in high and tight and knock him down." Then he would tell how he was going to pitch to that batter. And they would go right on down the lineup and every time it was the same thing on the first pitch. When he got to the end of the batting order, he had knocked the entire lineup down. Everyone got the same treatment and the Barber was known to shave all the batters real close - not just a once-over job.

After we decided how we were going to pitch to each batter, every fielder knew how they were going to play him. When a pitcher was going to vary from the established pattern, we had signals so we would know precisely what each pitch was going to be. That's a big help because sometimes you miss a ball just by a half step. Even if you're not moving on the pitch, if you've got an idea where the ball is going to be hit, sometimes you can catch up with it. You will find that well-coached teams know what's going on between the pitcher and the catcher and how they're going to pitch a batter. Sometimes that can mean the difference between winning and losing. That's why Durocher made sure we always had our heads in the game.

By contrast Leo had a very relaxed clubhouse. We played cards, but no poker. We played mainly hearts but sometimes gin rummy or something like that. We usually had about forty minutes to kill before a game. So guys would get out a deck and we played cards to relax and take our minds off the game. Then we'd go on out and try to win. If we got on a long losing streak or were playing lousy baseball, Leo might cut out all card playing. There would be no card playing at all until we started to win, and then we could start to play cards again. Durocher, himself, was a terrific card player, one of the best, and played cards all the time. A lot of times, it was Leo and Herman Franks playing partners against Dusty Rhodes and Bobby Hofman, after they joined the club.

Rhodes was also a carouser and a big drinker, and he got along with everybody and helped keep things loose. Don Mueller was a practical joker, and he liked to give players a hotfoot. The first year I was with the Giants, we had a guy by the name of Bert Haas, who played some at first base. He was one of the best bench jockeys I've ever heard. He could say some of the funniest damn things, but he kept it clean. He had the ability to really get on anybody on the opposing club and kind of upset them. He became the best bench jockey in the entire league and Durocher kept him there just for that reason. Bert had been a pretty good ball player, but he was in the twilight of his career, so he made a career out of bench jockeying. The things he would say were absolutely comical, and sometimes the guys he was ragging would have to laugh themselves.

Freddie Fitzsimmons, one of our coaches, was also a natural comic. The kind of things that Freddie would do and say to keep us loose was amazing. Herman Franks was like a diplomat. If something got serious, we would tell him and he would take care of it. Frank Shellenback was tall, elderly, reserved but knew pitching. He knew how to improve a pitcher, and was an outstanding pitching coach. He, Fitzsimmons, and Franks worked perfectly together. We had a super coaching staff.

Eddie Logan, the clubhouse man, and Doc Bowman, our trainer, were two others who were with the Giants during my years with the team. Doc Bowman gave the rubdowns and he didn't like anything electrical. He wanted to do everything by hand, and he had strong hands. He'd give you a rubdown every day if you needed it, but a player had to get to the park early for the rubdown. Doc had a lot of regulars and one of them was Johnny Mize. Before he went over to the Yankees, he was on the table every day. Some of the guys thought it was bad luck to get on the table all the time, so they would only get a rubdown every once in a while. Doc spent a lot of time with pitchers, stretching and rubbing their arms, because they've always got something wrong.

If you had an injury, you reported to Doc Bowman and he would advise Leo how serious it was and whether or not he thought you could play. If Doc Bowman thought you could go and you didn't think you could, you'd have to tell Leo, "I just can't go today. Give me a couple of days and I'll be ready." Now and then, there would be some goldbricks, but that was rare because Leo had little patience in that regard.

Durocher was a smart manager and really knew the little things that can make a difference, and he made sure that we were well versed on it, too. He always wanted to be in command of the situation on the field. He was very resourceful and, whatever it took for him to have the advantage, he would do it. That's the reason you had to admire him for being a strategist and an exceptional manager. He knew what moves to make and what it would take to get the team going. Sometimes he would get in a fight purposely to shake up the club and to get more spirit into them. He was very experienced and had managed a lot of clubs. So he knew all the tricks, and that's why he's in the Hall of Fame.

We won in 1951 because Durocher knew how to turn a bad situation into a good situation. We always learned something from it. If it wasn't too serious, he'd make us laugh about it. If it was serious, then he would say, "Well, it could have been worse," or something like that. Durocher had the ability to do whatever was needed.

I think he was probably the only manager who could have brought us back from thirteen and a half games behind in August to catch the Dodgers on the last day of the season, and win it on the road. He was so precise in the things that he did and the things that he said. He managed with style and he had charisma. That year, after we got behind the Dodgers, he never said, "Let's catch 'em." He always said, "Let's see how close we can come." That's a big difference. If he had said, "Let's catch 'em," that would have put a lot of pressure on us. But "seeing how close we can come" meant if we caught them, fine. And if not, there was always next year. That was a very important distinction. His phraseology was very important. That was one of the reasons why we were able to do it

19 The Giants–Dodgers Rivalry

When we played the Dodgers, it was nothing to get knocked down the first time you walked up to the plate. Usually, if a guy hits a home run, the next guy gets thrown at but, in this case, you walk up there to lead off the game and the first pitch is behind your ear. That's the way we played.

—Davy Williams, New York Giants

The rivalry between the Giants and Dodgers was so great that it was kind of a year highlight. Whether you liked it or not, or even knew what caused it, it was there in front of you all the time. I can look back now and see how enjoyable it was just to get in there and battle.

—Preacher Roe, Brooklyn Dodgers

THE GIANTS-DODGERS RIVALRY started way back in the days of John McGraw, when he was managing for the Giants and Wilbert Robinson was managing the Dodgers. It continued over the years and even intensified as time passed. It was an inter-city rivalry and whenever these two teams got together, the game took on a special significance. The Giants and the Dodgers were really the working man's teams. The Yankees, being in the American league, were in another class.

Brooklyn, as I later learned after visiting over there, was a wonderful place. But we in New York considered it to be too far away. We thought of Brooklyn in terms of Coney Island and hot dogs. Way back, the Dodgers had some good ball clubs for a few years and they had a good club when I came up to the Giants. But no matter where they were in the race, the records went out the window when these rivals played. Whenever the two teams met, it was a special game and there was a special feeling because each team was trying to knock the other's block off.

After Bill Terry took over from McGraw, the Giants won a pennant in 1933, his first full season as manager. The next year a reporter asked him about the Dodgers and he said, "Is Brooklyn still in the league?" At the end of the season, the Giants were tied with Dizzy Dean and the Gashouse Gang, with only two games left. The Dodgers were a losing ballclub mired in sixth place under Casey Stengel. But Casey used Terry's comment to inspire the Dodgers and they beat the Giants those last two games of the season to knock them out of the pennant. That's the kind of feeling that had built up between the two clubs. And these kind of emotions were even stronger when I joined the Giants.

I guess the whole thing was fueled by the fans. The Giants' supporters were not quite as vocal as the Dodger fans. They were a little more reserved. Dodger fans were really vocal and, as they say, had no couth at all until they got that real good club in the early forties. After Branch Rickey and Walter O'Malley took over, they had the real good clubs and the franchise is still fielding quality teams right up until today.

When you look back, you have to say that the greatest fan in baseball was the Dodger fan who lived in New York and rooted for the Dodgers, or the Giant fan who lived in Brooklyn but rooted for the Giants. They took their lives in their own hands. Their lives were at stake because that was something that you just didn't do. They had to be careful about what they said. If they rooted for the Giants in Brooklyn, they did it silently. The rivalry got so hot and heavy there that a lot of fights broke out. They used to argue about who was the greatest pitcher, Hugh Casey or Carl Hubbell. Later, it was Don Newcombe or Larry Jansen, and Preacher Roe or Dave Koslo. And, of course, who was the greatest centerfielder, Duke Snider or Willie Mays.

The two teams eventually moved on to California and the rivalry still exists today. But not to the degree that it was, because in New York we were in the same city and in California, they're about four hundred miles apart. But it's still one of the greatest rivalries of all time.

Now the fans ate this big rivalry up, and the newspapers flamed it. Whenever we'd meet it was like a World Series game. Leo Durocher and Charlie Dressen, as managers, fit right into this scenario and had their own private feud. Dressen had coached under Leo in Brooklyn and when Leo left, Dressen took over. He was a real smart baseball man but he wasn't flamboyant like Leo. In certain ways, Durocher tried to embarrass Dressen and downplay him. It was apparent that Charlie and Leo didn't like each other, and they definitely liked to show each other up.

Certain players on the Dodgers also didn't like Leo because he left them and went to the Giants. The main culprits were Jackie Robinson and Carl Furillo. When the two teams met, there was a lot of jockeying on the bench. They'd call over and say, "The same team that won last night is gonna win again tonight." It was that kind of thing. And then, too, sometimes it got personal.

And, of course, the Brooklyn fans didn't forgive Leo for leaving the Dodgers and joining the hated Giants. When Leo first returned to Ebbetts Field, the fans booed like crazy. They hollered, "Hey Leo, what are you doing in that uniform?" and "Hey Leo, you're going to get beat again tonight." It was that kind of thing when he went back. They'd get on him. They even had the band on their side. That little orchestra they had, the Brooklyn Symphony Five, would get on him, too. Every time Leo would do something they would hit the drums or do something to antagonize him.

Every time he sat down, they went "Brrrrtttttt" with the drums, trombone, and all the instruments. One time Leo bent over like he was going to sit down, but he didn't sit. And while they were in between, he sat down and got them out of their rhythm. But that didn't stop them, they still did it the next time. They always make a big deal out of that, like they were kind of razzing him musicwise. All the fans got into it and it was effective. It was a very funny thing, too.

Ebbetts Field was such an intimate ball park that you could hear what these loudmouths were saying. It was an experience, just going in there and getting out alive. We hated to go to Brooklyn. Since we lived at home, we would all drive to the game in our cars, whether it was a night game or day game. There was never enough parking and we had to go through all that traffic to get there. We would just park and walk from the parking lot into Ebbetts Field. Then when we came out of the ball park, we feared for our lives. It was simply terrible. I wish that we had met at one central spot and taken a bus over there. I would have felt more secure. We never knew what was going to happen when we went over to Brooklyn.

I think our fans were a little better behaved. The Polo Grounds was a bigger stadium, the parking lot was larger and more secluded, and the security was tighter. The Dodgers may have had a hard time, too, but not as hard as we had when we went over to Brooklyn.

There was some animosity between the players. We didn't like them *off* the field and we hated them *on* the field. So, it was a natural thing. We wouldn't speak to them, except to say something bad about them or to try to embarrass them. And the newspapers would fan the flames. At that time, there were several papers in New York. We had the *News*, the *World*, the *Journal*, the *Telegram*, the *Times*, the *Post*, and two or three other papers. All these writers would get their shots in and really fan the flames.

Leo used to get on some of those writers, who were a pain in the neck. He and Dick Young had a running feud. There was another writer from the *New York Journal*, and he and Leo went at each other one night and I thought that they would never speak to each other again. But the next day, that had all been forgotten and they were acting civilly. Leo could turn it on and off like that.

It wasn't until much later, as we all got a little older, that we realized this wasn't the way to be. The bitterness of the rivalry also affected Campy and me to a certain degree. We had became good friends way back when we played in the Negro leagues and in Mexico. But after we got to the majors and became a part of that rivalry, we wouldn't act too friendly on the field. But, off the field, we would forget about it. Campy was the kind of guy who would want to beat your brains out on the field, but after the game was over - the game was over. I was the same way. We'd do a little kidding and things like that, but some of these other fellows really took it to heart.

On the other hand, Jackie and I were never close. I didn't know him from the Negro leagues, because I was in the Army when he was playing there. I did see him play with the Montreal Royals and knew he had the potential to be a real star before he ever went up to the Dodgers. I also admired the fact that he had taken so much abuse without cracking those first couple of years. But nevertheless, when he was with the Dodgers and I was with the Giants, I stayed away from him. We got along all right but whenever I saw him, I just said, "How are you doing?" and kept going on my way.

When the Giants and Dodgers met on the ball field, the worst would aways come out, or the best of baseball would be played. Durocher told us, "Stay in right after them. We can beat these S.O.B.'s. We're going to beat them because we've got *me* on our side. You've got me here and I'm going to see that you win. All you've got to do is do what I tell you to do." And I guess Dressen probably felt the same. He was smart but with him, it was always "*I* did this" or "*I* did that." He liked to take credit for things and wouldn't give his players much credit. He took credit for everything except losing.

One day Dressen outdid himself with his grandstanding. When Artie Wilson, our utility infielder, came to bat in a game, Dressen came out of the dugout and called time. Then he motioned Furillo to come in from right field to second base. Then he moved Robinson from second base to shortstop, and moved Pee Wee from shortstop into the hole, and Cox over on the foul line at third. Then he brought the left fielder in and over towards the foul line, and had Snider over in left-center. He left right field and almost all of the right side of the infield open. He made a show of moving the players one at a time while the game was held up until he finished. That kind of posturing really upset Durocher.

Dressen liked to show how smart he was. He was mainly trying to show Durocher up, but he was also trying to show Artie up. Artie was a left-handed batter but he always hit to the left side. We felt sorry for him and were rooting for him to pull the ball this time. But Artie just couldn't pull it. He hit a one-hop comebacker to Newcombe on the mound.

Shortly after that, they sent Artie down to the Pacific Coast League. Although nobody wants to admit it, there was an unwritten quota system at the time that limited the number of black players on a ballclub. But Durocher was going to send Artie down anyway because Leo thought it was simply outrageous that he couldn't pull the ball. If he had been getting basehits, it might have been different. Artie had hit the ball with the Birmingham Black Barons in the Negro leagues and hit over .300 after he went to the Pacific Coast League. But that's the difference between major-league pitching and minor-league pitching. Dressen knew that Artie had never pulled the ball before and couldn't in the majors. That was all in the plot. Dressen thought that he was a genius manager, and he was trying to show that he was a better manager than Durocher.

So, that's the way it was. Those two managers were ideally suited for this rivalry. It didn't matter whether they were in first place and we were in second or whether we were in first place and they were in third. That's the way it went for a long, long time. And it made for real interesting baseball. Because some of the best plays that I've ever seen, and some of the best baseball that I've ever seen, was the result of the Giants and the Dodgers getting together. It was fantastic. It was like war. And it was like a World Series game each time we met.

By Durocher and Dressen always trying to outdo each other, we often got into a throwing contest. When the Giants and Dodgers played the saying always was, "If you knock one of our guys down, then two of your guys are going to get it." One time in 1952, after I had recuperated from my broken ankle and was back in the lineup, we were trying to close in on the Dodgers during the pennant stretch and we got into that kind of game. We had a doubleheader at the Polo Grounds, and Gil Hodges was hit by a pitch in the fifth inning. Then he spiked Bill Rigney on a play at second base and put him out of the game. Just the day before, Hodges had put Davy Williams out of commission when he almost cut him in half with a hard slide at second. So that made two second basemen in two days that he had put out of action.

Then Joe Black, the Dodgers pitcher, started knocking batters down. We had an outfielder that year named George Wilson, and Joe threw a high hard one inside that went between Wilson's head and his cap, as he ducked out of the way. When we went in the field, our pitcher Monte Kennedy returned the favor and dusted off both Hodges and Black the next time they came to bat. By the eighth inning, Larry Jansen had relieved Kennedy and he hit Andy Pafko. The umpires knew what was happening and warned both teams. But Jansen still hit Billy Cox in the ninth, to get Durocher's "two-for-one," and was ejected from the game. We would yell, "Let 'er rip!" to our pitchers. That's the kind of games that we had when we played the Dodgers, and shows the kind of rivalry that existed between the two teams.

Leo's favorite cry was "Stick it in his ear!" He was particularly tough on the Dodgers pitchers and other people that he really didn't like. Jackie Robinson and Carl Furillo were two of those. There was no love lost on either side. Furillo was having a pretty good season against us in 1953 and Durocher told Ruben Gomez, "Any time he comes up, I want you to knock him down." Ruben did as Leo instructed and the second or third time, he finally hit Furillo. First base was over near the Giants dugout, and after Furillo went to first, he looked in and said to Durocher, "I know that was you, Leo. You told him to do that." And Durocher hollered out, "That's right, you Dago prick, and the next time you come up I'm going to have him to do the same thing."

When Leo called him what he did, Carl saw red and charged the Giants dugout. When he got almost to our dugout, I stepped out and tried to stop him. You don't let anybody come right in the dugout like that. So I tried to grab him and to restrain him. But he pushed me aside and tried to get at Leo. As Furillo wrestled around me, Durocher was coming toward him. So they finally got to each other, but they couldn't swing because there were too many people around by that time. The Dodger players had come over, and they said, "Let them fight. Let him kill him." They were wanting Furillo to do harm to Leo. The bullpen people had come in and everybody on the bench had come over, and we had one heck of a melee right there in front of the Giants dugout.

That's when I found out how strong Gil Hodges was. I looked up and saw Hodges picking guys up like they were babies and sifting them out. Just weeding them out of the crowd. He was pulling them off, and taking them out of the middle, and throwing them out. Somebody had already rescued Durocher, but Furillo was on the ground and his finger was stepped on and broken. They never did find out who did it, because it happened in the melee and it was impossible to tell who it was.

Always before, there had been a question of who was the strongest, Gil Hodges or Cincinnati's Ted Kluszewski. Big Klu had those huge arms, and he weighed much more than Hodges. But after that incident, I laughed and said, "Well, I thought Ted Kluszewski was the strongest man in baseball, but now I think we've got a new champion in Gil Hodges. Because I've never seen such strength." Hodges was a peacemaker that day and I'm just glad that he tried to break up the fight because if he had wanted to get involved, there would have been four or five knockouts right there on the field. They were really going at it there for a while before order was restored. But finally, after a few minutes, it was broken up.

That was in early September and Furillo couldn't play anymore for the remainder of the season. Furillo, Stan Musial, Red Schoendienst, and Don Mueller were all going for the batting title. Furillo won the batting championship when he had to sit out the rest of the season because of the broken finger.

The next season, I noticed that Furillo was acting funny around me when I was on the field. One day, I asked Campanella if something was wrong. Campy said, "He hates your guts." "Why?" I said. "I never did anything to him." He said, "You kept him from killing Durocher." So I went up to Furillo and asked him about it. "Carl, I never had any stake in that fight," I told him. "I was trying to break it up. I hope this doesn't affect our friendship, but you can do whatever you want to do." And then I just forgot it. He finally got over it, but it took him two or three years. But Furillo and Durocher, never made friends with each other again.

There was another time when I thought we were going to have another fight similar to that one. That was the incident between Alvin Dark and Jackie Robinson in a game at Ebbetts Field. The inning before, Jackie had bowled Davy Williams over at first base when Davy covered on a bunt. Jackie was really out to get Sal Maglie because Sal always pitched him inside and had knocked him down earlier in the game. But Maglie didn't field the bunt, and when first baseman Whitey Lockman fielded it and tossed to Davy, Jackie went into him hard and bowled him over. Leo wanted to take Davy out of the game, but he refused to leave, although he was out of action for about two weeks beginning the next day.

The visitor's dugout at Ebbetts Field was level with the playing field and leading up to the dugout was a tunnel. Immediately after the inning was over, Durocher took us all off the bench and we went down into this tunnel. He said, "Are we going to let this son of a gun run us out of the ball park? The first man up that gets on, I want you to just keep running and I want you to give him what he gave to Davy." Then Leo turned to me and said, "Monte, how do you and Hank feel about it?" I said, "Leo, we've got *Giants* written across our shirts."

I could have been the one to send the message, but as luck would have it, Alvin Dark was the first man up and he doubled to left-center field. Jackie was playing third, and Dark just kept running and he jumped at Jackie like he was going to jump right in his lap and ride him up into the stands there at third base. Jackie was very hard to get a clear shot at and he kind of sidestepped, and Alvin missed him. But Jackie got the message. He knew that what he had done was wrong and that we were trying to retaliate. That was all that happened and all that was said about it. Jackie knew what Dark was doing and he accepted it as, *Okay, I roughed up one of your players and, if you want to rough me up, that's fine.*

This was at Brooklyn, so we expected to go on the field and we were ready to go. But Jackie just laughed, rather than try to come back at Alvin, and that kind of eased the tension a little bit. There was no need for us to go out for another melee.

There were other situations though, where we would have those free-for-alls. In fact, each time we met, there was a good chance that there was going to be another one. Durocher knew that Maglie and Jansen and all the rest of our pitchers would retaliate if the Dodgers tried to intimidate our players. And Leo would always look over at the Dodgers dugout and say, "It'll be two-for-one every time you try to pull a stunt like that." And he kept his word.

Even before that incident, Durocher didn't like Robinson. He used to tell Jackie he was swell-headed and he would get a towel and wrap it around his head. Sometimes we would be playing the Dodgers and when something came up on the field, Jackie would be out there really giving it to the umpire. Maybe an umpire missed a strike or there was a disputed call. That was a situation when either Pee Wee Reese, the captain, or Walter Alston, the manager, should be arguing the point, and I think it was a little embarrassing to Pee Wee.

Durocher used to get on them about it. He would holler over there at Jackie, "You! You swell head! Pee Wee's the captain of the team. When something happens, why the hell do you go out there every time? Who's the captain here? Who's the manager? Every time we look up, you're out there before the manager or the captain. Don't you think you're going a little beyond your authority. Why in the hell don't you sit down and not embarrass anybody? And furthermore, I've never really liked you anyhow." Leo would only do that to make players mad and try to upset them. So that was a tough rivalry.

When we played at Ebbetts Field, only a wooden door separated the clubhouses. And after the games, if the Dodgers won, they would yell and bang on the door with their bats and laugh at us to rub it in. Early in the 1951 season we were off to a bad start, mired in last place, and we had just lost a doubleheader to the Dodgers to extend our losing streak to eleven games. The Dodgers were celebrating and banging on the door with their bats and yelling at us through the door. Furillo and Robinson yelled, "Eat your heart out, Leo, you sonofabitch. You'll never win this year."

A few months later, after we'd lost another doubleheader to give them a sweep of another series, they were yelling and ragging us. They were ahead by eleven and a half games and had beaten us eleven out of the fourteen games that we had played. And they were really banging on that wooden door and yelling, "The Giants are dead! The Giants are dead! How do you like it now, Leo?" They were laughing and taunting us and then they started singing, "Roll out the barrell, we got the Giants on the run!"

Robinson was usually the leader of these taunts and one day Eddie Stanky got so riled up that he began cursing Jackie, and added some racial epithets. When Eddie realized that I was standing there, and what he was saying, he looked at me. I just smiled and said, "That's just fine with me, Eddie." I understood that he didn't really mean anything by it and I took it in the spirit in which it was given.

Another time, Leo said something that could have been misinterpreted. We were playing the Dodgers and Jackie Robinson was sitting in their dugout between some white players. We were about thirty yards away and you couldn't see Robinson in the dugout. Durocher looked over there and he turned to me and said, "You know, Monte, this is the first time I realized that Jackie is so black." I just looked at him and smiled and said, "Yeah, Leo, he's black. No one will ever mistake him for white." Leo didn't mean anything by the comment and I knew how he intended it.

Leo and Jackie never did get along, even when Leo was managing Brooklyn. Durocher used to kid around with the players there and they put up with him, but there was no real fondness. The friendship was superficial. They used to kid him after he left the Dodgers. They would holler at him, "You traitor. You were in the best place. Why in hell did you want to come to this second-rate club?" The two main ones were Furillo and Robinson. Both of them were very vocal, and Durocher had rabbit ears. He wouldn't take anything. He would always retaliate, and say or do something.

With Leo and Jackie, there were always words exchanged between them and sometimes the language would get pretty bad. Once, not long before the Dark-Robinson incident, Pee Wee Reese had to restrain Leo from charging on the field after Jackie because of the words being hurled between the two. Durocher was in the third-base coaching box and was using some pretty rough language, with some racial remarks interspersed throughout. Hank Thompson and I were on second and third base at the time and, although his tirade was directed toward Jackie, he was shamed when he realized that Hank and I had heard everything he said. Afterwards, he apologized and we understood what had happened and why.

What really teed off Durocher was one time when Jackie got personal. They were yelling back and forth, and Jackie said, "Well, I may be this and I may be that, but at least I don't wear my wife's perfume." When he said that, Leo charged and here we go out on the field again. He was going after Jackie, and we had to restrain him. "Why don't you keep it non-personal?" Leo said. "Keep your remarks about baseball, and don't get the wives involved." He made some more remarks like that and called Robinson a no-good S.O.B. That kind of verbal exchanges continued between the two for the rest of their baseball careers. Many years later, when Jackie was just about ready to leave this earth, they finally made peace with each other.

The rivalry between our two ballclubs could also generate other hard feelings at times. Roy Campanella used to give Willie Mays a tough time. Willie was a rookie and Campy would try to rile him. Willie would come to the plate, and Campy would start talking to him. "What do you say, pup? What do you say? What do you say Willie? When you going to get married? You getting much?" That kind of banter would kind of upset Willie. So he told Durocher about it. Leo said, "Well, the next time you go up there and he starts to talking, just take the bat and tap him lightly." It never did get to that but Willie was tempted to do it. Because that first year, Willie caught everything and threw out everybody that ran, but he didn't hit that much. He got some home runs and had some key hits, but his average wasn't that high because he hadn't got his confidence and didn't know what to look for.

And then there was old big Don Newcombe. Mays had hit two or three home runs in a row, and the reporters asked him how he was going to do against Newcombe in that particular game. "Well I don't know," Willie answered. "I don't think I'll have any trouble with him. I'll hit him like I've been able to hit everybody else." That was like waving a red flag in front of a bull. So three straight times, old big Newk threw at Mays and knocked him down. Willie was hard to hit, but Newk threw at him until he finally hit him with a pitch.

I hollered out and told Newk, "If you want to pick on somebody, why don't you pick on a veteran like me? Somebody who can defend himself, for Christ's sake." And Newk and I would get into it and curse each other out. But after the game, we would forget it for the moment. But the next time we played, we'd think about it. And it would be business as usual, with both teams trying to knock the other's brains out. That was the general feeling with the players, black and white. We hated the Dodgers on *and* off the field. And they hated us.

20 The Giants of Summer

Monte Irvin hit me so good you can't believe it. He could hit me at midnight with the lights out. He'd just get up there and you'd throw your best and he'd hit at your best. And I admired him very much.

—Preacher Roe, Brooklyn Dodgers

I can't believe that anybody else in the league was hitting the ball as hard as Monte was through that sixteen-game period and through the rest of the year. If he didn't get basehits, they were just shots at everybody. He really was hitting the ball super.

—Davy Williams, New York Giants

THE DODGERS, man for man, from 1947 on, really had a great club. From the time that I joined the Giants their lineup had been the same. They had Billy Cox at third, Pee Wee Reese at short, Jackie Robinson at second, Gil Hodges on first, and the great Roy Campanella behind the plate. In the outfield, they had Carl Furillo in right, Gene Hermanski in left, and the great Duke Snider in center. On the pitching staff, they had Don Newcombe, Ralph Branca, Preacher Roe, Carl Erskine, and Clyde King.

The only thing that was lacking was depth on their pitching staff and a real good left fielder. When they traded for Andy Pafko during the 1951 season, the Dodgers thought all their problems were solved and they now had the perfect club. And they did - at least on paper. But you don't win pennants on paper. They have to be won on the ballfield. And that was not so easy because the Giants also had a good ballclub.

After having been long identified as the manager of the hated Brooklyn Dodgers, it was a radical change for the Giants when Durocher replaced the extremely popular Mel Ott during the 1948 season. Ott had been a fixture with the Giants for twenty-three years, including the last seven as manager, when Leo came in.

That's when the Giants fortunes turned, because Durocher was the perfect manager. He might not have been the perfect father and he might not have been the perfect citizen, but he was the perfect manager. He made very few mistakes, was confident, and was a great strategist. Leo liked to take chances on the field. He would gamble that something he did in the first inning would pay off in the last inning. His favorite saying was "just stay close to them, and I'll think of something to beat them." And that's the way he managed. We were very fortunate to have him because he knew what to do and what to say in any situation. He always protected his players and would look out for their best interests. If you played hard for him, he would always get you as much money as he possibly could.

Of the players that he inherited in 1948, only two regulars were still in the starting lineup in 1951 - Bobby Thomson and Whitey Lockman. There were also two pitchers, Larry Jansen and Dave Koslo, who were holdovers from the 1948 starting rotation. So four key players were carried over from his first season. Leo continued to add his kind of players to the ballclub for the next two years to form the nucleus of the team that pulled that miraculous comeback in 1951.

Except for Willie Mays, the pieces that fit together to win the pennant in 1951 were already in place the previous year. We finished five games behind the Phillies, but I think we could have won if we'd had Ray Dandridge. He was having a super year at Minneapolis and was a proven veteran player who would make few mistakes. Several of us who had played with Ray tried to get the Giants to call him up, but they said they needed him at Minneapolis as a gate attraction.

In 1951 we had a real good club, and we were solid. When Willie Mays joined us, Leo moved Bobby Thomson to third base. When Bobby first came up to the majors, he was a third baseman and he was comfortable there. Leo also moved me from first base to the outfield, and put Lockman on first. He played the position as if he had been playing it all his life. That gave us our best combination and

I was more comfortable playing in the outfield. Whitey had good hands and was a good gloveman. And he was a solid hitter and hit in the clutch. He hit left-handers, even though he batted from the left side.

Joining me in the outfield, was Don Mueller in right. When he first came to the Giants, I was playing there. But I switched over to left and also played first base until they made the switch with me and Lockman. Of course, the sensational young rookie, Willie Mays, was patrolling center field at the Polo Grounds like no one had ever done. He was simply outstanding.

One day we had a meeting and Durocher said, "Monte you and Don just give Willie plenty of room. If there's anything that he can get to and wants to catch, let him have it. You two just play your own position and help Willie whenever you can." Don and I always remembered that and we never had a problem. We never did run into each other. Willie was great at coming in on a ball, was great going back, and had a rifle for an arm. He was just outstanding in every way as an outfielder, and he always seemed to rise to the occasion when we needed a great play.

One of the greatest throws that I've ever seen was one that Willie made on Billy Cox. A ball was hit to right field and Willie went over into Don Mueller's territory in deep right field to make the play. He wheeled and threw a strike to Wes Westrum to get Billy Cox at home plate. The ball was hit so far that Billy didn't really run, and Westrum gave him the big decoy. Then all of a sudden he caught the ball and put the tag on Cox, who was the most surprised person in the world. That one play won the ball game for us.

Westrum had been behind the plate ever since Durocher took over the team. He didn't have the notoriety that Roy Campanella and Yogi Berra did, but Wes was smart, had a good arm and was a fine defensive player. He was a pull hitter with power and could hurt you in close ball games.

We got our middle infielders, Alvin Dark and Eddie Stanky, in a trade with the Boston Braves in 1950. Leo sent Sid Gordan, Willard Marshall, Buddy Kerr, and a pitcher named Red Webb to the Braves. Dark and Stanky were the heart of our infield. Both of them had good years and were great guys to have on the team. They added a lot to the team through intangibles, as well as talent. They were smart and would always try to do something to rile the other club.

They had played on the Braves pennant winner in 1948, so they brought a winning attitude to the team. Since the Giants hadn't won a pennant since 1937, that was something that was needed.

Eddie Stanky played second base and was a great fielder. He didn't have that much range, but he had good hands. He was a streetwise veteran and a pepperpot. He couldn't hit, he couldn't field, and he couldn't throw. The only thing he could do was beat you. Eddie was a pull hitter and one of the best leadoff men I've ever seen. He would foul off fifteen pitches until they would finally walk him.

Stanky had played with the Dodgers for quite a while and he and Durocher got along fine. Stanky was a little teed off at Leo, because he got rid of Eddie after Jackie Robinson came to the Dodgers. But once they got back together on the Giants, there was no problem between them. Leo had traded Eddie to the Boston Braves and that's when he and Dark first teamed up.

Alvin Dark was a rugged individual and our team captain. He was a solid shortstop, a good team man, and a great guy. And he came to the park to play every day. He could run, he could throw, and he was a good hitter. He was particularly adept at hitting behind the runner. He wasn't flashy as some shortstops are, but he was steady and, in a clutch situation, would come through most of the time. He had a dry wit about him, and was just a good fellow to lead our team to the championship in 1951. Almost to a man, all the other players liked him.

When Dark was managing the Giants during the sixties, a situation came up where some writers and some players said that he was a racist. But I never knew him as that. Alvin and I have only had the highest of regard for each other. When that trouble started in San Francisco, where Dark supposedly made derogatory references about black and Spanish players, writers tried to find someone to provide validation. So they asked Jackie about the situation and what he believed about the allegations. He had only complimentary remarks to make about Dark. I'll never forget that. He said that Dark was a hard competitor and a guy who wanted to win.

Then they also asked Willie Mays about it, and Willie had complimentary things to say about Alvin. Finally somebody got to me and I told them, "I don't know about the situation out there. I don't know whether its true or not. I only know Alvin Dark as a gentleman. We were teammates for six years and we were friends then and we're friends now. And that's all I know about it."

It wasn't until later on, when the papers inflamed the issue a little bit more, that some other things were said about it. But remember, the immediate reaction was that Dark is an okay person. He was supposed to have said these things off the record but the reporter said, "Maybe *you* said they were off the record, but *I* didn't say they were off the record." It was unfortunate that something like that ever came up, because a team has to have cohesion and unity. The type of togetherness that I'm talking about is what we had in 1951 that enabled us to make up all that ground in the pennant race.

Our pitching staff that year wasn't bad, either. It was led by our meal ticket, Larry Jansen. I used to compare him to Tom Seaver. He threw hard and had two kinds of curves. Larry had a slider that he would throw left-handers and he had one that broke a little bit deeper. He had a stout heart and was a money pitcher.

Backing him up of course was "El Senor" Sal Maglie, who had learned how to pitch under Adolph Luque in Mexico. Sal had three kinds of curves and all of them were just awful to hit. When he'd catch a batter looking for one kind, he'd throw the other kind. Then when he'd catch them looking for the curve, he'd bust a fastball in that inside part of the plate for a called strike three. Maglie knew how to pitch, and was our number-two man.

Our number-three man was Dave Koslo, a left-hander. He'd win because he knew how to pitch. He didn't throw that hard, but he knew how to change speeds, and was a very effective pitcher.

For our other starter, we were able to pick up big Jim Hearn from the St. Louis Cardinals. Jim came over and fit right in. He saw how these other guys were doing it, and he started to develop the winning habit. And he became real tough for us.

In the bullpen, we had a big stout fellow named George Spencer, who turned out to be a great reliever. He threw the ball hard, improved his control, and was real tough in key ball games. And we called up Al Corwin from Minneapolis, and he was a big help. He was a lean, thin right-hander, who came up and won four key games in a row to keep us going in that streak when we were trying to catch the Dodgers. I don't think we could have won that year without the contributions that he made.

Once we got our pitching staff squared away, we started to roll.

We had a well-rounded ball club, and we just tried to outsmart the Dodgers. Even though our personnel was not supposed to be as good as theirs, somehow we always got the job done. I'm just grateful that I came along in time to be a part of it, and to witness all the great baseball being played.

The Giants were a perfect club, personnelwise. We all complemented each other in a positive way. A lot of the guys were southerners but we all got along fine. Somebody would crack a joke and nobody took anything too seriously, and nobody ever said anything that was too bad. As the first blacks on the team, Hank Thompson and I carried ourselves pretty well and commanded respect. We gave respect and we got respect from the other players. They saw that we were trying to help them and we *did* help them. So it carried throughout all my years with the club.

Willie Mays, of course, was Leo's favorite. He was the only one who received special handling from Durocher. Leo's relationship with other players, even those he liked, was different from the one he enjoyed with Willie. Others that were among Leo's favorite players were Whitey Lockman, Alvin Dark, Wes Westrum, and Sal Maglie. Leo liked old Wes because he would get out there and catch the whole game with a broken finger and never complain. Leo would kid a lot with Maglie, but he knew if he had one game to win, Maglie was the man who would do it for him. Durocher and Bobby Thomson were not that close but they respected each other.

And for me, Leo knew he didn't have to do anything with me. I was going to do my best at all times. I was in the twilight of my career because I was almost thirty-two when I came up. So he never really had to get on me. I never had to go into the office. If he had something to tell me he would always come over to my locker or tell me to come over to his locker, which was across the room. And he would say something to reassure me.

Consequently, I had an excellent season in 1951. I had always liked to hit in a clutch situation and I was especially dangerous with men on base. It seemed like all my hits turned out to be key hits and came at just the right time. I led the National league that year in RBIs with 121, and finished the regular season with 24 home runs and a .312 average.

Many things contributed to the remarkable record we achieved that summer and fall. However, the single greatest factor of all, beyond the shadow of a doubt, was the presence of Willie Mays. From the time that he was brought up from Minneapolis, Willie kept the entire ball club very loose with his clubhouse antics and infectious humor. I remember one thing that he would do when he wanted to really annoy you. Willie had big hands and he let his nails grow. So, he'd take that big index finger and put it in your ear and turn it, and then laugh like hell. So when anybody saw him coming, they covered up their ear. It was all done in good fun and helped to keep the team loose.

His sensational play, day after day had a terrific impact on our morale. He was always making an impossible catch, or an out-of-this-world throw from the outfield to cut down some thoroughly shocked base runner. Willie Mays was truly our greatest inspiration.

When we got our team squared away and started to win, it was a sight to behold. I remember the famous stretch run we put on that year just as if it were yesterday. We won sixteen games in a row and thirty-nine out of the last forty-seven to catch the Dodgers on the last day of the season. Then we beat them two out of three in the playoffs for the pennant. That year was a dream year because it's the most fun I think I ever had playing baseball because we did the impossible. Without *knowing* it, we were *doing* it. We played one day at a time, got some breaks here and there, and took took advantage of almost all of our opportunities.

Coming from thirteen and a half games back in mid-August to wind up the regular season in a tie with the Brooklyn Dodgers, then beating them in a dramatic playoff, is a special feeling that is almost impossible to explain. And that was the kind of experience that every baseball player should have. Every athlete should experience the kind of feeling that we had in chasing the Dodgers and finally catching them on the last day. Of course all that was culminated by Bobby Thomson's game-winning home run that was called "the shot heard 'round the world."

21 The Shot Heard 'Round the World

Monte was the ultimate of the guy that you want on your team. He was my kind of guy, a real team player all the way. He was strong and tough, but a gentleman at the ball park and in the locker room. He was just a presence that I respected. And I've always said this about the playoffs - Monte is the one who got us there.

—Bobby Thomson, New York Giants

ABOUT THE ONLY thing that anyone remembers about the playoffs that year was Bobby Thomson's "shot heard 'round the world." To set the stage for Bob's famous climactic homer, we took the opener from the Dodgers at Ebbetts Field, 3-1, behind Jim Hearn's five-hit pitching. I had a homer and scored two of our three runs. Thomson homered for our other run and Andy Pafko hit one for the Dodgers' only run. Ralph Branca was the losing pitcher and, ironically, yielded the home run to Bobby Thomson.

The second game was played at the Polo Grounds, but the Dodgers came right back and grabbed the second game, 10-0. Clem Labine, who was a rookie that year, shut us out and the Dodgers pounded three of our pitchers for thirteen hits.

The third and deciding tilt is the one that produced great drama and some mild controversy. Brooklyn led 4-1, going into the ninth inning. Don Newcombe was pitching some great ball for the Dodgers and had struck out the side in the eighth inning. Things didn't look especially encouraging for us, but we had become accustomed to this kind of situation all year long.

Dark opened the ninth for us with a single to give us a baserunner and some hope. Then, something happened that was somewhat controversial and caused some questions in some people's minds. With Dark on first and Don Mueller, a left-handed hitter, at the plate, and with the score being what it was, Gil Hodges held Al Dark on first base. Don Mueller followed with a single to right field.

Actually, Hodges shouldn't have held Dark on first. He should have been playing halfway, a couple of steps off the bag. If he had, then the ball that Mueller hit would have been a perfect double-play. In fact Hodges just missed it by inches anyway and Mueller got the hit to keep us alive. But that was just the breaks of the game. Nobody told him to play halfway and that cost them. In a game you get the breaks, and we got the breaks.

I was the next hitter. Nine out of ten times, I would come through in the clutch with a basehit or a home run or something. I felt confident that we were going to pull it out. But I fouled out to Hodges, trying to pull one of Newcombe's sliders into the left field stands. Maybe I was trying too hard to tie the score. I was very disgusted with myself at the time but today I say, "At least I didn't hit into a double-play." I could have killed the rally. As it worked out, I was very happy that I fouled out, because I set the stage for what ultimately happened.

Whitey Lockman followed me with a very important hit that has often been overlooked. He doubled into the left-field corner, scoring Dark to make the score 4-2. But Mueller was hurt sliding into third base. He broke his ankle and had to be carried off the field. Clint Hartung came in to run for him. Some people question why Leo picked Hartung to pinch run for Mueller. I think he picked Hartung because he didn't want to waste any players. Leo didn't think that he would be used and that's the reason he used Clint. Besides, Clint wasn't the fastest guy in the world, but all he had to do on a basehit was just run ninety feet and score. And on a home run, of course, just trot on home. So all he had to do, as it turned out, was to trot on home. I think it was a wise choice to pick him because it was the ninth inning and, ordinarily, we wouldn't have needed him in the game.

There was about a fifteen-minute delay when Mueller was injured. Some people speculate about whether that wait might have affected Newcombe. Maybe Newk got cold during the delay and that was a contributing factor in the decision to take him out of the game. But I actually think he probably would have been taken out anyway. Charlie Dressen wanted a fresh pitcher, and he knew from past history that Newk would get weak in the late innings and then give up a key hit. I think he wanted to get somebody in there, who would get the next couple of outs and get the job done for them.

When Dressen called down to the bullpen after Lockman's double and asked who looked good, he told Ralph Branca and Carl Erskine to get up. Erskine was wild during his warm-ups and that little, quick curve of his got loose once or twice. And they had to hold up the ball game to retrieve the ball and throw it back to the bullpen. I guess that's why Dressen went with Branca. So Branca came in and warmed up. Then Bobby Thomson strode up to the plate. The rest is baseball history.

Allen Roth, one of the statisticians who had been traveling with the Dodgers, said he could have fallen off the bench when Dressen selected Branca. Because Bobby Thomson had hit four or five home runs off him during the season and had also also hit one in the first playoff game in Brooklyn. Roth thought it was an awful bad choice and he said he was fit to be tied. He thought it should have been either Erskine or Labine, who had shut us out in the second game. Labine could have come in and thrown his sinker.

But again it was the luck of the Irish. Bobby just happened to be the right man in the right place at the right time. Everyone who knows anything about baseball knows what happened. Branca threw two pitches, both fastballs. Bobby took the first one, then jumped on the second one, and hit a low line drive into the lower deck in left field. And the Giants won the pennant.

I don't know, with first base open and only one out, if the Dodgers ever considered walking Bobby to set up a possible double play. That would have been going against the book by putting the winning run on base, but Dressen sometimes went against the book. Willie Mays, who was only a rookie then, was the next batter and was kneeling in the on-deck circle when Thomson hit his game-winning shot. Later, after all the dust had settled, I asked Willie if he was ready in case Bobby had failed to get the job done. Willie laughed nervously, in that little characteristic way of his, and said he was glad he hadn't been forced to face that situation. Because his knees had been knocking so badly that he wasn't at all sure whether he could have made it up to the plate.

Another strange thing, that might add another bit of controversy, was that Roy Campanella didn't catch that game. Campy said he could have caught. I didn't know that until much later. I said, "You know, Campy, another break we got was that you didn't catch. Because I knew when Branca threw that first pitch - that high strike inside to Bobby Thomson - that you would have gone out and said, 'Now wait a minute, keep the ball down. Let's keep the ball away from him. If he hits a home run on a pitch down and away, then we just deserve to lose.' " But Rube Walker was the catcher, and Ralph figured that by throwing Bobby the same pitch, he would cross him up. And, of course, Branca guessed wrong. Because Bobby hit a pitch that never should have been thrown. He should have probably been thrown a curve, or something low and away.

I thought Campy had a real bad sprained ankle and couldn't catch, but he said he could have caught the game. They were just resting him so he could start the Series against the Yankees. But, again, things just broke right for us that year. I guess it was just Leo's year, and it was the Giants' year. It was an indescribable feeling and when I talk about it, even now, I get a warm feeling. Particularly for Bobby and the great thing that he did.

Many years later I talked to Bobby about that homer. I thought the subject had been covered as much as possible. But then, at a fantasy camp in Arizona, we had been talking about this situation. So I went over to Bob and asked, "After we got runners on second and third, with one run already in and the score 4-2, what do you remember about the inning?"

"You know," he said, "the only thing I really remember is, on the way up to the plate, I said to myself, *Hit a good pitch. Don't be a donkey. Don't go at something bad. Make sure it's a strike.* And then, after the first called strike, I remember hearing Leo saying and gesturing, *If you've ever hit one, hit it now.* When I hit it, I didn't know if it was going to be in the stands or not. But when it did disappear into the stands I really don't remember rounding second and third and finally jumping on home plate. It's all really very vague in my mind."

"That's understandable because it was like a dream," I said. I remember I watched Jackie Robinson as Bobby rounded the bases and Jackie watched him touch each base. And when he finally jumped on home plate, Jackie took his glove, wrapped it up, put it in his pocket and headed for the clubhouse. I said to myself, *Jackie is playing it right to the hilt. He's hoping that Bobby will make a mistake and he'll be able to take advantage of it.* But I also thought, *What umpire would have had the nerve to call him out, if he missed one of the bases?* Probably none of them. And I remember watching Ralph Branca when the ball went into the stands and heading for the clubhouse, too.

After the ball went into the stands, we all looked at each other and my immediate reaction was, *We finally did it! We finally did it! We're the champions! We've come so far. How did we do it? I can't believe it. We don't have to wait 'til next year.* All those things went through my mind. By then, Bobby was almost at second base, and all of us rushed to home plate to greet him. As he rounded third, we were already there waiting for him. Of course, you didn't have to worry about Durocher and Stanky, because they had wrestled each other to the ground along the third-base line. Every time one would try to get up, the other would pull him down.

As Bobby was almost at home plate, we all kind of got back and cleared a path for him so that, when he jumped, we made sure that he jumped on home plate. So that Jackie Robinson, the umpires or nobody else could say that he didn't touch home plate. That's when we had the greatest feeling of all. Because we had finally done it. And we started to the clubhouse.

We calmly walked from home plate to deep center field to the clubhouse. And the fans were so kind. Nobody tried to steal our hats, or our gloves, or to tear our uniforms off. They just patted us on the back and said, "Nice going. Nice going, guys. Get the Yankees tomorrow. Beat the Yankees."

When we got to the clubhouse - to show how much confidence the clubhouse man had in us winning - he had put the champagne away. He had to hurry to get some champagne out, put it in some ice, and try to chill it. Actually it never really got cold, and we had to drink warm champagne. Willie Mays drank a couple of sips - he had never drunk anything before - and he got excited and fell out. So most of us, instead of drinking warm champagne, went back to our cold beer. We must have stayed in the clubhouse a couple of hours. We just wanted to savor that victory.

Big Newcombe told me that he was in the showers when he got the news. He never saw the home run. Somebody came in and Newk said, "Well, what was the score?" And they said, "The Giants won." "The hell they did!" he said. And he really didn't know that the Giants *did* win until the cameraman broke his camera down and took it right over the way to the Giants' clubhouse.

I remember Pee Wee Reese coming over and saying, "You know, I don't believe what's happened. I'm going to go on to Yankee Stadium just as if we won." Somebody told him, "Pee Wee, don't go because you'll be the only Dodger there if you do." He said, "I still just don't believe it." And I remember the Dodger players coming in and congratulating us. We were on cloud nine because we just couldn't believe what happened.

We were going on to the World Series against the New York Yankees. The main thing we were concerned with was hurriedly getting our World Series tickets so that we could distribute them. That was a real chore and we had a lot to do. But we reported to the Bronx about eleven o'clock the next day, still on a high and still half loaded, but beat the New York Yankees 5-1 at Yankee Stadium in the first game.

22 The 1951 World Series

We both hit over .400 in the '51 World Series, but the great thing about Monte in that Series was stealing home in the first game. I thought that ignited the ball club. That World Series typified Monte and the year that he had. That kind of capped off the season.

—Alvin Dark, New York Giants

AFTER THAT DRAMATIC playoff, the World Series was anticlimactic. We had done the one thing we wanted to do. And that was to beat the Dodgers. Everything else was a plus.

We got a bad break before the World Series ever began because we lost Don Mueller for the entire Series, and he was our hottest hitter the last month of the season. We had to go away from our set lineup when Mueller got hurt, and it kind of upset the balance a little bit. Our continuity had been broken.

We had to put Hank Thompson in right field. He did a creditable job, except he didn't hit that much. Hank was a pretty good hitter, but he had been sitting around on the bench for a quite a long time and needed a few more days to get acclimated to playing every day.

Another factor to be considered is that our pitchers were tired, particularly Maglie and Jansen. If Maglie and Jansen had performed for us in the Series and if Mueller had been in the lineup, I think we would have won it easily. We didn't get those good breaks in the Series, but we didn't care.

As I look back, my greatest thrill in baseball was stealing home in the first game of the 1951 World Series. It was the first time in thirty years that anyone had done that, and I guess it might have embarrassed the Yankees a little. There were two outs and I was on third base. I noticed that Allie Reynolds, the great Yankee right-hander, was taking a long time to deliver the ball. He was ducking his head and going into that long pumping motion before he let go of the ball. And I was really confident that I had a chance to make it because I had stolen home five times that year. So it was nothing new to me.

Actually, I had stolen home six times, but on one steal the umpire ruled that there had been a foul ball on the play. We were playing the Phillies in that game and Wes Westrum was at bat for us. I broke for home and the pitcher, Bubba Church, threw the ball. I got in safely, and the ball hit the string on top of catcher Andy Seminick's mitt and went on back to the backstop. The umpire ruled that the ball tipped Westrum's bat while he was trying to get out of the way. But the ball did *not* tip Westrum's bat. Wes argued vociferously that I had made it but the umpire held to his ruling. So I was not credited with a sixth steal, which would have tied the record at that time.

Anyway, in the World Series, I saw that I could steal home on Allie Reynolds. Durocher was the third-base coach and I went over to Leo and whispered so that Gil McDougald, the Yankees third baseman, couldn't hear, "Leo, I think I could make it." Leo said, "Get a big lead, get a good jump on the next pitch and go ahead." Bobby Thomson was at the plate, and there were two outs and no strikes on Bobby. So, I took a big lead, but I eased off. I just kind of walked off and, just when Allie Reynolds went into his pumping motion, I took off and ran as fast as I could.

Allie tried to hurry his windup and he threw the ball high. By him throwing the ball high, I was able to slide under Yogi Berra's tag. He missed me maybe four or five inches. If the throw had been lower, Yogi would have clearly had me. So when I slid past Yogi and the umpire called me safe, Yogi says, "No. No." And I said, "Yes, Yog." "Why?" he asked. "How do you know?" I said, "You'll see it tomorrow in the *Daily News* and the *Daily Mirror*. It's just that simple." We were laughing and I just walked away. But sure enough, the next day on the front page of the *News* and the *Mirror* was a picture showing me sliding in and just evading Yogi's tag.

We won the ball game 5-1, and the fact that I was able to pull off something like that in the first inning of the first game of the World Series was a great thrill for me. In fact, of all my thrills, that was my biggest one.

I was batting cleanup and I was four-for-five in that first game, and one of the basehits was a triple over DiMaggio's head. I had gotten four hits in a row and in the eighth inning, when I came to the plate for the fifth time, Yogi said, "We don't know how to get you out. We throw you high balls and you hit it, and we throw you low balls and you hit it. Can you handle one right down the middle?" I never said anything to him but, sure enough, Reynolds reared back and threw a fastball right down the middle. And I hit a line drive to Joe Collins, who was playing back, at first base. I was surprised to get the pitch, because I didn't believe Yogi. All I had to do was believe him and I probably could have gotten another basehit.

Yogi was very talkative behind the plate, but Campy used to talk like that, too. I didn't really believe anything Campy said, and I wanted to check Yogi out, too. I knew that he was noted for talking and not telling the truth. The next day, he said, "I told you." Just as if to say, *I told you what was coming, you dummy, you should have believed me.* I said, "Yogi, I've never believed anything you said." Yogi *was* a talker.

Dave Koslo was a surprise starter in that first game, and he pitched a great game for us. After winning the opening game in their home park and still having our two top pitchers to use, things looked pretty good for us. The fact that we were hitting the ball pretty well was also encouraging.

In the second game, Eddie Lopat beat us 3-1 on a five hitter. I went three for four, stole second base in the first inning, and scored our only run in the seventh inning, when Bill Rigney pinch hit and lofted a sacrifice fly to right field. That cut their lead to one run, and Willie was on third base. Ray Noble then pinch hit for Larry Jansen, but fouled out to Yogi to end our threat. Jansen had pitched good ball for us up to that point and had only allowed four hits when he left the game. The Yankees added another run in the eighth inning for the final margin of victory.

That win evened the Series at one game apiece, but the victory was costly for them. That's the game where Mickey Mantle injured his knee. A ball was hit into right centerfield and Mickey, who was playing right field, slipped on a drain cover and wrenched his knee. When they had to take him out, I thought that the Yankee luck was over. But they put Hank Bauer in and he had a good Series from there on out. So again the old Yankee luck held out.

A lot of people say that Mantle could have been greater if he had not hurt his knee. I don't think his knees actually affected him that much. Although Mickey played in great pain, he could still run like a deer and became a superstar. But if he'd had two healthy legs, he might have played twenty-some years instead of only eighteen, and hit a whole lot more home runs. Because he was awesome when he was right.

The next three games were at the Polo Grounds, and we took the Series lead again the next day with a 6-2 win, thanks to good pitching from Jim Hearn and a five-run fifth inning, in which Whitey Lockman's three-run homer chased Vic Raschi. The rally was ignited by an incident between Eddie Stanky and Phil Rizzuto at second base. Stanky had walked and was trying to steal second, and Yogi's throw had him. Rizzuto had the ball waiting for him, so Stanky figured the only chance he had was to put his foot right in Rizzuto's glove and maybe the ball would be dislodged from it. And he did just that. The ball went one way and the glove went the other, and Stanky was safe.

Since that time I don't think they have spoken a word and they've had this feud all these years. Simply because Rizzuto thought it was an illegal act and Stanky should have been called out. The press kept this thing in the limelight for a lot of years, and even now it's still talked about. I believe Stanky was justified in what he did, and Rizzuto should not have been that critical of Eddie. Scooter was just outmaneuvered and he should have accepted it as that.

Sometimes things follow a pattern. The Yankees were good *and* extraordinarily lucky. We had them on the run, but that Sunday it rained and gave Allie Reynolds an extra day's rest that he needed to come back and beat us, 6-2. Without the rain, they would have had to pitch Johnny Sain, or Reynolds without enough rest. That was a real bad break for us. Sal Maglie was a tough competitor, but he was not effective for us in that game.

It was a one-run game until the fifth inning, when Joe DiMaggio hit a two-run homer into the upper deck of the left-field stands to give them a cushion. Nineteen fifty-one was Joe's last season and that was the last home run he ever hit.

But I wasn't thinking about that then. I was on a roll, and had two more hits in the game. Reynolds was known as a clutch pitcher but hitting is contagious. When you're on a roll, sometimes you're swinging good and you're in a groove. You just go up there and look for the ball. He just threw the ball where I was swinging and I was able to get a few hits. Nobody was able to consistently hit Allie Reynolds, because he was a tough pitcher with a lot of speed and a good curve. I was just lucky to get a few hits off him.

I knocked in Alvin Dark in the first inning to give us an early lead, but then I got caught stealing. It was a pitchout and I should never have run. I went on the green light and I blame myself for running. I was too aggressive. I should have stayed on first and waited to see what would happen, but I was feeling rambunctious. When I went down, I slid into second base hard and hurt my leg when I hit the ground.

We got blown away in the fifth game, 13-1, with Gil McDougald's grand slam in the third inning being the big blow. That gave the Yankees the lead for the first time in the Series. Lopat five-hit us again, but I managed to get two of them. Both hits were on changeups. I waited on them and I was able to hit the ball back up the middle. With Lopat you had to try to guess right. If you did, you were fine but if you didn't, he was tough, because he changed speeds so well and had good control. He had a lot of heart and beat us twice in the Series.

When I singled to center field in the sixth inning, that gave me eleven basehits in five games to tie the World Series record for hits at that time. I was hoping to set a new mark. I remember in the ninth inning, I hit a a low line drive to left center. I looked at DiMaggio and knew he couldn't get it. So I thought, *Well there it is.* But Gene Woodling came from nowhere and must have dived five feet on his belly and caught the ball. If he had not made the catch, it would have been at least a triple and maybe an inside the park home run. I was very disappointed that I didn't get that hit.

We went back to Yankee Stadium for the next game, and I still had four more chances at the record. I blooped one into left field in the eighth inning and, again, Woodling came in and slid on his belly and caught the ball. And in the ninth inning, with the bases loaded, I hit one way back in left field that would have been a home run in the Polo Grounds, and he caught that one, too. After the Series was over I told Gene jokingly, that I would've given him five thousand dollars if he had let just one of those balls fall in there.

Breaking the record was secondary to winning the ball game.

Koslo and Raschi were locked in a pitcher's duel at one apiece. Raschi was one of the best pitchers I've ever seen. I was just glad that I didn't play in the American League and have to try to hit him on a regular basis because he had that great delivery and was tough in the clutch. Raschi had control to go with his good speed and curve.

Hank Bauer's two-out, bases-loaded triple in the bottom of the sixth inning gave them the 4-1 lead. In the ninth, we staged a rally and almost pulled it out. With the bases loaded and nobody out, we were very surprised when Casey Stengel brought in Bob Kuzava, a left-hander, to pitch to power hitting right-handed batters. But Casey knew that Kuzava got right-handers out better than he did lefties, and he got us out.

But again, the Yankees were just lucky. Kuzava gave up two long flyballs that would have been home runs in the Polo Grounds. I hit the first one, and Bobby Thomson followed with one that was even farther than mine. Both of our drives scored a run, so we were only one run down with the tying run in scoring position. But Yankee luck continued through the ninth inning. Sal Yvars came up to hit for Hank Thompson and hit a screaming line drive to right field, but Hank Bauer fell down and caught the ball for the final out.

That gave the Yankees the championship. Raschi, Reynolds, and Lopat each started two games against us. I can see why the Yankees were the best in the American League because it was quite a feat to get by those three. But I was on a roll in the Series and finished with a .458 batting average. Considering how tough those three guys were, I was very fortunate to have had the success that I did. I just wish that we could have had the same lineup that we had down the stretch and that our pitchers had not been tired. Then, I think we could have probably beat the Yankees.

23 Between Pennants

We went down at homeplate - getting knocked down by the opposing pitchers - more than any club in the game of baseball. I think Durocher felt like that if they knocked us down at homeplate, we'd get up and be a better hitter. And I really think that happened in most cases and we were a better ballclub when those kind of things started on the field. And Durocher was a master at that.

—Alvin Dark, New York Giants

We would never start a knockdown affair but we would end it. And we always figured two-for-one. If they got one of us, we'd get two of them. That usually ended it.

—Larry Jansen, New York Giants

In 1951, I was voted the team's MVP and had a good World Series. Horace Stoneham, the owner of the Giants, called after the Series and asked me to come over to his office to talk salary. We sat down and he asked me what I wanted. So I said, "Mr. Stoneham, you know, we've never had any problem about money. Whatever you think is fair." I took the onus off me and threw the ball right back in his lap. He said, "Well, you're making twelve thousand five hundred dollars, suppose I double it?" All I could think of was, how fortunate I would be to make twenty-five thousand dollars. That was more money than I thought I would ever make.

At that time, a top player in the league - guys like Ralph Kiner, Duke Snider and Jackie Robinson - were making about thirty-five thousand dollars or forty thousand dollars. So, when he said twenty-five thousand dollars, I jumped at it right away and signed a contract.

We had pictures taken, and a photograph was on the front page of the newspapers the next day. The story said, "Monte Irvin signs his new contract" and had the salary and everything else in the article.

As I was driving home that day, I was thinking about it and felt that I might have been too hasty. Instead of jumping at the twenty-five thousand dollars so fast, I should have said, "Mr. Stoneham, I came up late, and instead of twenty-five thousand dollars, could you make it thirty-five thousand dollars?" And I'm sure he would have gone for the extra ten grand.

But as fate would have it, I broke my ankle in 1952 during spring training and stayed out most of the year. I only played about a month and even then I couldn't play regularly. When 1953 came along, I received the same salary and I made the same amount in 1954 and again in 1955. If I had signed for thirty-five thousand dollars, Stoneham might have said, "Well, I'm paying this guy too much, let me trade him. Let me get rid of him because I can't pay anybody thirty-five thousand dollars to sit on the bench." I think the whole thing evened itself out. Sometimes it's better to take a little less and make it up in the long run.

After having my salary doubled, I started off very well in the spring of 1952. Mays was now in his second year, and I was hitting in the third spot with Willie hitting number four. We had a good spring and we expected to win the pennant again. We were touring with the Cleveland Indians during the preseason and, when we got to Denver, there was a snowstorm. So the groundskeepers cleared the snow off the ground and piled it over on each foul line. Then we started the game because the park was filled.

In the first inning, I singled and then Mays singled up the middle and I was going from first to third. The air is kind of rare in Denver so I got tired and didn't pick my foot up when I got ready to slide. That's when I broke my ankle, and that put me out for most of the season. When my ankle popped you could hear it all over the stands. Everybody said it made a terrible noise. I can't remember it popping, but I know it sure hurt. It took the ambulance a long time to get in because there was still a lot of people trying to get into the stadium.

So, while I was laying there, Doc Bowman made a tourniquet. He took a sock and then a bat and bound it tightly around the calf of my leg so the blood wouldn't run down into my ankle. I never did lose consciousness but it sure did hurt like the dickens. I think he gave me some kind of little shot to try to ease the pain.

While I was waiting on the ambulance, I looked up and Willie Mays and Harry Simpson were crying like babies. "What's the matter?" I asked them. "Why are you crying like that?" Willie said, "Well, maybe if you hadn't done that we might have won the pennant again and there would have been more money in our pocket." I laughed and said, "Thanks a lot!" So, in any bad, some good comes out of it, and a little humor came out of this.

Meanwhile, the ambulance finally arrived and they put me in it and gave me another shot. When we arrived at the hospital, they operated on me right away and the next thing I knew, I woke up the next day with Leo Durocher and Herman Franks sitting there.

The team needed to get a replacement for me and they were able to pick up Bob Elliott from the Braves. Bob was near the end of his career and he didn't have the best season in the world, but he did the best job he could under the circumstances.

I worked real hard to rehabilitate my ankle. I broke my ankle on April the second and I came back the first of August and was playing again. The first time I came up, I got a hit to right field, which was my area when I really wanted a basehit. I would wait a little longer and then offer at the pitch. So, I hit a single between first and second, and the crowd gave me a fine standing ovation. I was very appreciative of them for that.

After I got back in the lineup, I batted .310 for the remainder of the season, but I had missed most of the year and we finished about four or five games back. If I had been healthy and able to play all year, I might have made the difference in a half a dozen games. Willie Mays missed most of the season, too, because of military service. If we both had been in the lineup all season, we probably would have repeated in 1952.

One thing that kept the Giants in contention that year was the addition of Hoyt Wilhelm to our pitching staff. When he got there, first of all, we had to find somebody to try to catch him. Wes Westrum was the best at trying to catch that knuckler. Wilhelm was tough to catch *and* tough to hit. When we put him in with the lead, we didn't have to worry about it. He was really tough. He gave up very few home runs and he didn't relinquish any leads. Even though Joe Black was rookie of the year with the Dodgers, Wilhelm's statistics are even more impressive. If the Giants had won the pennant, it might have happened just the other way around, with Hoyt getting the award.

The two seasons between our pennants were contrasts for me personally. In 1952 I suffered a broken ankle and broken dreams, but in 1953, I had a comeback season. I had lost some of my speed, but I still finished the year with a .329 average. Although I missed about thirty games, I finished with a team high 97 RBIs to go with 21 homers and a .541 slugging percentage.

The Dodgers' celebrated Boys of Summer won the pennant during both of these seasons but lost the World Series to the New York Yankees each time. Our sensational comeback win over the Dodgers in 1951 had merely intensified the already heated and fiercely contested rivalry, and Durocher and Dressen continued their on-going battle. But the Dodgers replaced Dressen with Walt Alston for the 1954 season.

The Dodgers still had a virtual all-star team. They had Campanella behind the plate and Hodges, Reese, and Cox in the infield. Junior Gilliam had replaced Jackie Robinson at second base, and he won the Rookie of the Year honors in 1953. He was smart, had a lot of talent, and was a solid ball player. He could run and was a good leadoff man. He could hit and field, but had a mediocre arm. Gilliam had played in the Negro leagues with the Baltimore Elite Giants, the same team that Campy had played on.

After he joined the Dodgers, he and Jackie became great friends. Junior had a wonderful personality. He was likeable and easy to get along with, so he and Jackie got along fine. He didn't have any problem because he would go along with whatever Jackie wanted to do. He just wanted to go out and play his game.

With Gilliam at second, Robinson moved to left field to fill the hole left when Andy Pafko went to the Braves. Sometimes George Shuba, a left-handed hitter, played in left field. Of course, Furillo and Snider were still firmly entrenched in the other two outfield positions.

They had a great pitching staff led by Newcombe and Erskine. And they had Labine, Loes, Meyer and Branca, all right-handers. They had Preacher Roe, the left-hander who used to get everybody out, and another good left-hander, Johnny Podres. Joe Black, before he hurt his arm, was in the bullpen. A couple of years later, they had

Don Drysdale and Sandy Koufax. When I was playing, Koufax was just a rookie and when a team signed a bonus rookie, they had to keep him for a while. But he couldn't find the plate and didn't develop until the fifth or sixth year that he was in the league. I'm glad I missed Koufax because I think he was one of the hardest throwing left-handers I've ever seen. When he got his confidence and control he was just about unbeatable.

So they had a fine staff. They had a lot of power and good reserves, so they were tough. In looking back I think the Dodgers could have won the pennant about ten years in a row. But Walt Alston, at that time, was a new manager and he was not the manager that he became later on. I think it took him a few seasons to develop his own style. But in my view they had the best team. And they hated Durocher.

But the Dodgers were not the only team that didn't like Leo. We always had a little melee with the Cardinals because they hated Durocher. Enos Slaughter and big Walker Cooper were over there. When I was coming along, I liked that Gas House gang connotation that the Cardinals had. I liked the way they ran the bases and fielded the ball. I liked Slaughter's all-around hustle and the fact that he would run to first base all the time. But when I first joined the Giants, I had an incident with Enos in a game against the Cardinals.

When I was trying to learn how to play first base, Slaughter hit a ground ball and hustled down the line to make it a close play. I had to try to take the ball out of the dirt and didn't get out of the way, and Slaughter stepped on my heel. He could have avoided it and didn't have to spike me. So I said, "Enos, you didn't have to do that. You stepped on my foot." He said, "Get your goddam foot out of the way." "Well, don't do it again," I said. "Hear? Because if you do, I'll take a bat and I'll beat your goddam brains out. So just be sure you don't ever do it anymore." And that's all there was to it, it never happened again.

When Enos was elected to the Hall of Fame, I mentioned that incident to him. He said, "Well, at that time, I was tough on everybody." He had a similar run-in with Jackie Robinson when he was at first base in his first season with the Dodgers. But that's a different story. Now, Enos is one of the guys I enjoy talking to because he's noisy and he's interesting, and he's always got a good story to tell.

Since he's been in the Hall of Fame, we've become quite good friends.

When Slaughter and Musial were with the Cardinals, we could expect a tough battle on the field when we played them. I always had a good arm and I remember one throw I made against the Cardinals that St. Louis sportswriter Bob Broeg says cost them a pennant.

This was in 1949, my first year with the Giants. At that time I wasn't hitting that much, so I knew I had to field well. Red Schoendienst was on first base and Stan Musial doubled down the right field line. The ball got in that little gully and when I finally caught up to it, I grabbed it and threw a strike from deep right field on a line to get Schoendienst at the plate. When he rounded third he kind of slowed up because I was just getting the ball, but I unleashed one of the damnedest throws you have ever seen. It was a powerful throw right on a line. Westrum gave him the decoy and then tagged him out.

That run not scoring cost them the ball game. It was a key game and that was the year that the Dodgers beat them out by one game. If they had won that game, there would have been a playoff for the pennant. But that one throw did it.

The Cardinals had a good team and were always competitive. I admired the smooth fielding of Red Schoendienst and the play of Marty Marion, who I thought was the best fielding shortstop I had ever seen. And Marion wasn't a slouch at the plate, either. Pitching, they had Harry Brecheen and Gerry Staley, who were tough. And they added two new left-handers, Wilmer "Vinegar Bend" Mizell and Harvey Haddix, who won twenty games in his first full season in 1953. Of course, Haddix is best remembered for the twelve perfect innings that he pitched for the Pittsburgh Pirates against the Milwaukee Braves in 1959, before losing in the thirteenth inning 1-0.

Needless to say, I admired Stan Musial's hitting. Stan was the premier player in the league at that time but Durocher made no distinction when it came to knocking batters down. In 1954 Musial hit five home runs in a Sunday doubleheader against us, and Willie Mays had to reach over the fence in left-center field to catch a sixth one. Two of the home runs were off Wilhelm and it was almost unheard of to hit homers off him.

The next day, Durocher went to Monte Kennedy and said, "Monte, you're pitching tomorrow night and every time that goddam Musial comes up, I want you to knock him on his ass.'' And Monte did, about three times in a row. Then the fourth time, he hit Musial.

Stan said, "You told him to do that, Leo." "Yeah, I did and tomorrow will be the same thing," Leo said. "What do you think we're going to do? Do you think we're going to let you take the bread right out of our mouth? You're no better than anybody else. You can bite the dust just like any other ball player. And if you keep hitting the way you are against us, you can expect that every time we meet."

Whether he was going to do that or not I don't know, but Leo put that doubt in his mind and showed Stan that he wasn't immune from being thrown at. I remember that as though it were yesterday. I can see Stan in that crouch, and Kennedy wild and throwing hard. It was magical that Musial didn't get hurt. I don't think Stan had much love for Durocher after that.

When Leo was managing the Dodgers, Stan would go to Brooklyn and kill them, too. In fact, that's where he got the name "Stan the Man." Leo was simply tired of Stan Musial wearing him out, and he thought he would stop him the best way he knew how. And that was to make him hit the dirt. Durocher's saying was, "If you can hit lying flat on your back, you're a pretty good hitter."

Beanball battles could happen at any time, especially when Leo was involved. I remember one time, we got into a throwing contest with the Cincinnati Reds when Ewell Blackwell was pitching. Blackwell was throwing the ball so hard, we could hardly see it. He had us shutout 1-0 and in the seventh inning Durocher went out and called him everything in the book. Leo said, "You long, tall sonofabitch! Why don't you put something on the ball? You're not throwing it hard enough." And in that particular inning, he struck out the side. So when Dark came in he said, "Damn, Leo. What are you trying to do? Don't make him mad. We can't hit him now."

Leo said, "I know what I'm doing. Never mind. You just stay right close. Stay right after them." In the eighth inning, Leo went out and called Blackwell everything again, and he got a little more personal this time. So Blackwell came over to the third-base coaching box after Leo, but the umpires broke it up. And don't you know, Blackwell got wild and walked the bases loaded. I was next up and the count went to one ball and one strike. Then he threw me a fastball inside and, with that inside-out swing of mine, I hit the ball down the right field line and it hit the foul pole at the Polo Grounds' 263-foot mark for a homer and we beat them.

From the moment I hit the ball until I got home, Blackwell was cussing me as I was rounding the bases. He said, "You lucky bastard, you're lucky to hit one like that. You'll never hit another one." When I crossed home plate, I said, "I might not hit another one, but I hit that one, you bastard." Just like that. So we won the game all because Durocher had the guts to get on this great, side-wheeling right-hander.

But Blackwell didn't forget about the home run that beat him. The next time that I faced him, he got me three balls and no strikes. Then on that fourth ball, he drilled me in my left side and it felt like the ball went in on the left side and came out on the right side. I was down on the ground squirming in pain, and Durocher came out. He said, "Monte, show the sonofabitch up and don't rub." I said, "I have to rub, Leo, it hurts." He said, "No, don't rub. Don't let the big tall bastard see you rub. Show him up." Doc Bowman came out and gave me some smelling salts and I finally got up and went to first base.

Then Leo hollered out, "Show him up again, Monte. Steal second." So I got off the base, took one step, and fell flat on my face. They came over and when they checked me, they discovered that I had two broken ribs. I was out for about two weeks until my ribs healed and I could get back in the game. It wasn't really funny at the time because when he drilled me, it *really* hurt. Some of these incidents really stick out in your mind and that one stuck with me because he stuck that ball in my ribs.

Ewell Blackwell was probably the toughest pitcher that I ever faced. He came from the side and he could throw so hard that it got on you before you knew it. And then he had that real good curve. He'd catch you looking for that fastball inside and throw you a curve and then you're really out of there. Most of the time you would take the ball. But he did you a favor when he threw you a curveball. Because that fastball would get up on you and you wouldn't see it until it was more than three-fourths of the way home. You'd see it at the last minute, so you could kind of nick at it. And he was mean. If you took a healthy cut at him, he would knock you down.

Not only was he the toughest pitcher that I ever faced, he was one of the toughest pitchers that *anybody* ever faced during that two-or three-year period. Everybody in the National League would tell you that. He almost pitched a double no-hitter during that time, and you just didn't get more than one or two runs off him. In fact, when his name was mentioned during the season, we'd all take our baseball hats off to say *Hail to the King*. If he hadn't hurt his arm, he would be in the Hall of Fame.

Another team that hated Durocher was the Philadelphia Phillies. We always had trouble with the Phillies, and the worst fans in the world at that time were in Philadelphia. They hated Durocher and Durocher hated them. They hated the Giants and we hated the Phillies. And they all wanted to get Leo. So one afternoon we got into that free-for-all when I grabbed a bat. They were trying to get to Durocher and I was fending them off with that bat. At that time, if you hit anybody with a bat, you might be thown out of baseball. Well, I didn't hit anybody, but that melee was unbelievable.

In another game against the Phillies, the year before, Andy Seminick almost wiped out our whole infield. He spiked Bill Rigney at second base and knocked him down and stepped on his glasses. Then somebody singled and as Seminick was going around third base, he gave Hank Thompson an elbow and knocked him senseless. Just knocked him out. Then he slid hard into Westrum at home plate. So he got three of us.

After the inning, Hank Thompson came to the Giant dugout, and he was groggy. And what made it worse was when you go in the dugout, you have to duck to keep from hitting your head on the concrete overhang. But instead of ducking, his head hit that concrete and he knocked himself out again. So he got two blows, one from Seminick and one from the concrete overhang.

When the Phillies came into the Polo Grounds the next time, we vowed to get him back. We said, "Somebody ought to get Seminick for what he has done to us." So we kept it in mind. Somehow I got on second base and Alvin Dark singled sharply to right field. I took off and Seminick stepped across the plate, blocking it without the ball. So I slid in and hit him and his glove went one way, a shinguard went the other way, and I was safe. It wasn't anything dirty, I just put one of my homeplate slides on him, and getting hit the way he did was perfectly legal. When I scored that winning run, the game was over. After the game, it was discovered that Andy's ankle was fractured.

That was the third game of a series and when we came out on the field for that fourth game, I didn't know how Seminick was going to react. So when I came to the plate, I said, "How're you doing, Andy?" He said, "Fine. How're you doing?" I said, "Fine." Nothing happened, but I was ready to fight if he wanted to.

We won that game to make it four in a row and we shut them out three times. That was in 1950 and if we had another week to go in the season, I think we could have won the pennant that year. As it was, the Phillies had to go to Brooklyn and play the Dodgers with the pennant riding on the outcome. Dick Sisler hit that key home run off Newcombe and they were the champions. Then they played the Yankees in the World Series and Andy caught that whole series with his ankle injected with novocaine to kill the pain. That shows how tough he was. He never complained and that's what I admired about him.

The Phillies always fielded a good team and they would always battle us. In fact during the years that I was in the National League, the 1950 Philadelphia Phillies was the only team that broke the New York ball clubs' domination of the league. All the other pennants were won by either the Giants or Dodgers. The Dodgers won a majority of those flags, including 1952 and 1953, but I think that we would have won at least one of those, if I had not broken my ankle and Willie Mays had not been drafted. Willie was still in the service and that was a big blow to us in 1953, and kind of put us out of the race that year. But the good news was that Willie would be back in 1954 and I was confident that I could have another quality season.

24 World Champions

In the first game of the World Series, Leo said, "Grab a bat and go hit for Monte." I looked around three or four times. I thought he was kidding. But I went up there. My intention was taking the first pitch but Lemon threw me a curve and it hung about eye high and I just hit it and the wind took it into the seats.

In the fourth game, Monte was hitting and Newhouser was pitching. Leo looked at me and he said, "Go up there and hit for Monte." I looked at him and he said, "Nah, sit down. Hell, let Monte hit." So he singled in two runs and we won the game and the World Series.

—Dusty Rhodes, New York Giants

WHEN WILLIE MAYS came back, it was like heaven. I remember the first time he reported to our training camp in Phoenix after his discharge. We had all gotten dressed and Durocher was waiting for him. When Willie came out, you would have thought that Leo had just found a long-lost son. They hugged and then they started kidding around just like they used to before Willie went into the Army.

While he was in the Army, Willie had really developed that basket catch of his. After he rejoined the Giants, he kept going from where he had left off and had a terrific year. He led the league in batting average, caught everything that was hit in the outfield, and threw out everybody that ran. He just had a wonderful year, and won the Most Valuable Player award.

In 1954 we added a pitcher, Johnny Antonelli, who helped strengthen our pitching staff. Antonelli was almost unhittable in the clutch at that time. He threw the ball real hard and had a good changeup. And he was a winner. The same thing was true of Ruben

Gomez, who had joined us the year before. When Gomez really wanted to pitch, he was very tough. He had that wonderful screwball he could throw to left-handers, and he had good speed and a quick curve. Antonelli and Gomez were two real plusses, and we also got another good left-hander, Don Liddle, in the Antonelli deal.

We had two other acquisitions that made a difference for us in 1954. Dusty Rhodes and Marv Grissom. Rhodes became a premier pinch-hitter and used to go up and get the job done. Grissom was our right-handed reliever. He would come in there with that screwball, and he had great speed. Along with Wilhelm, you just couldn't score any runs off us. So we were exceptionally tough that year.

Davy Williams had replaced Stanky at second base the year before, and Hank Thompson was now playing third base and he became a good third baseman. The rest of the starting lineup was the same as it had been in 1951. Whitey Lockman was still at first, Alvin Dark at shortstop, Wes Westrum catching, and the outfield was the same with Mays, Mueller, and me. We didn't have any weakness.

I think that 1954 club was a little better than the 1951 club, talent wise. Because Mays was a veteran now. And with the acquisitions of Antonelli and Gomez, two real good starting pitchers, we had an excellent rotation. Maglie and Liddle pitched good ball, and with Wilhelm and Grissom in the bullpen, we were tough to beat. And we were more confident because we had been through it before.

We lost Bobby Thomson, who was traded to the Braves in the Antonelli deal. Unfortunately, he broke his ankle in spring training just like I did two years earlier. That enabled Hank Aaron to play regularly and the rest is history, he became the all-time home run hitter. But Hank wouldn't have gotten that chance if Bobby hadn't broken his ankle. Bobby was disappointed because he wanted to have a real good year in Milwaukee. So the trade turned out fine for the Giants and not that good for the Braves.

Dusty Rhodes had the Midas touch that year. Everything he touched turned to gold. His swing was tailored to the Polo Grounds and he hit a lot of Chinese home runs, but you can't knock him for that. That foul line was short down the right field line and he was a dead pull hitter, but it was there for any other hitter, too. They had the opportunity to take advantage of it, but not many of them could.

Dusty *could*, and he got credit for it. He turned out to be a fine player for us that year.

In the World Series, the Cleveland Indians had won a record 111 games and were favored over us. They might have swept us in the Series, if Willie Mays hadn't made that great catch off Vic Wertz, and if Dusty Rhodes hadn't hit the home run to beat Bob Lemon. It was the breaks of the game and we got the breaks and they didn't. That's why we beat them four in a row, instead of them beating us four in a row.

The one thing that people remember about that Series now is what has come to be known as *the catch*. That was when Willie Mays made that never-to-be-forgotten catch over his shoulder four hundred and sixty feet from home plate in deep center field in the Polo Grounds off the bat of Vic Wertz, Cleveland's first baseman. That unbelievable play broke Cleveland's back. All the fire seemed to go out of the entire team for the rest of the Series.

When Willie made that play, the score was tied at 2-2 in the eighth inning, with Bob Lemon and Sal Maglie locked in a pitcher's duel. The Indians opened the inning with Larry Doby walking, and Al Rosen getting a basehit to bring Wertz to the plate with nobody out. Playing the percentages, Leo brought in left-hander Don Liddle to face Wertz, who batted left.

Mays was playing over in left center because Don was pretty quick and was pitching away from Wertz, and we figured that Vic couldn't pull the ball. So Willie had to get on his horse and really get over to right center in order to catch the ball. The ball was hit pretty high but on a line, and Willie left at the crack of the bat and went over and caught the ball with not that much difficulty.

I came in to possibly get the carom off the wall, and maybe hold him to a triple. But Willie caught the ball and then had the presence of mind to turn around and throw a strike to second on the dead run. Doby was already at third base and he was able to get back to second and tag, but Rosen couldn't advance to second. Willie's throw kept him at first base. That was a key play in the game and Willie made it. Not only did he make the great catch but he made the great throw, too. So that was very vital to us.

On the way in after the side was retired, I said, "Roomie, I didn't think you were going to get to that." And he said, "Are you kidding? I had it all the way." I said, "You did, huh?" He had no idea that he was going to catch that ball. It was one of the greatest catches of all time, and fortunately it was seen on television and captured on film. That's why today they show it over and over.

Later Durocher said that he thought Willie would make the catch. But I think Leo was putting it on a little bit when he said that. I was in left field at the time, so I don't know what Leo said in the dugout. But later on, after the fact, he made the claim that when Wertz hit the ball, he was saying, "If it stays in the ball park, he'll catch it. If it stays in the ball park, he'll catch it." And sure enough it stayed in and he caught it. What made Willie a great center fielder was that he didn't play too deep, which enabled him to catch a Texas leaguer that was hit over shortstop or over second base. He could play in close because he had that great ability to go back. At the crack of a bat, he could turn and go where he thought the ball was going to fall. That put him in a class by himself.

That catch that Willie made off Wertz is the one that is most remembered, but I've seen Willie make better catches. The one that I think was his best was in 1951, in the dead summertime. We were playing in Pittsburgh in front of about five thousand people, and I remember it was a hot afternoon. We had a lead of 2-0, with Sal Maglie pitching. Then they got a walk, a hit, and another walk to load the bases with two outs.

Rocky Nelson, the first baseman for the Pirates, was at the plate. He was a left-handed batter and a dead pull hitter. Maglie was pitching him away and he had pretty good stuff that day, so Willie was playing him more or less straight away. Sal got two strikes on Rocky and figured he was looking for the curve, so he tried to throw a fastball by him.

But Rocky hit the ball directly over Willie's head in center field. At the crack of the bat, Willie turned and ran. When he turned and got ready to make the catch, the wind had taken the ball over to his right. He saw that he didn't have time to bring his glove hand over to make the catch, so at the last minute he caught the ball in his bare hand on a dead run for out number three.

Everybody would have scored and maybe it would have been an inside the park home run if he hadn't made the catch. Durocher immediately said, "Fellows, I've seen great catches in my life, but this is the first time I've ever seen anything like this."

Then Leo said, "I'll tell you what we'll do. Let's have some fun with it. Let's give him the silent treatment when he comes in." By the time Willie came in to the bench, everybody was there. Half of the guys went down one side of the dugout and half down the other side. And Leo went over to the cooler like he was getting a drink of water. Nobody said anything, and nobody looked at Willie.

That was almost too much for him to take and he said, "Leo, aren't you going to say something?" Leo said, "What do you mean?" Willie said, "Well, I thought I just made a pretty good catch out there. Aren't you going to say, 'Nice going Willie' or 'Pretty good catch,' or something?" "What are you talking about?" Leo said, "I was over at the water cooler and I missed the whole thing. What you'll have to do is go out there next inning and do it all over again."

And don't you know, he almost did it. He almost made the same kind of catch in the next inning, and we came away with a victory. To show how great that catch was, Branch Rickey was watching the game from his office upstairs by the broadcasting booth, and he sent a note down to Leo that described the catch as, "the greatest catch I've ever seen anywhere, anytime." And we all agreed with him.

There was one other outstanding catch that Willie made in Brooklyn in 1954, and *he* considers it his best. Joe Reichler, the Associated Press sportswriter at that time, did a story on Mays' nine best catches, and he rated the one in Brooklyn the greatest. And Willie agreed with that estimation.

It was an afternoon game and Ebbetts Field was filled. We were in the eighth inning, the bases were loaded and there were two outs. Larry Jansen was pitching. The Dodgers had a utility infielder by the name of Bobby Morgan, and he was a pull hitter. Jansen threw him a fast ball on the outside corner, and Morgan pulled it in the gap between me in left field and Willie.

At the crack of the bat, Willie started to run. He had a long way to go because the ball was hit on a line, and he didn't have much time to get there. Willie saw that if he kept running, he would run into the wall. Although the wall was padded, he knew even if he made the catch, it would probably jar the ball out of his glove. So he dived the last ten feet alongside the wall and backhanded the ball. When the ball went into his glove, his knee hit his head as he dived, and he kind of knocked himself out. But he still held on to the ball for the third out.

We thought he had killed himself. Actually, we didn't know what to think. Doc Bowman, our trainer, and Leo rushed out to left field. Nobody would touch him until they got there. Leo said, "What do you think, Doc?" "Well, I don't know," Doc Bowman said, "I might have to give him some smelling salts to see if we can bring him to." But, just before Doc opened his bag to get something, Leo said, "Why don't you pull back his eyelids and see how his eyes look?"

Upon Leo's saying that, a smile came on Willie's face and they saw that he was really all right. But he was just lying there. So when a smile came on his face and he looked like he was okay in every other way, Durocher kind of gave him a little slap and said, "What the hell is the matter with you, scaring everybody to death?" "I'm okay skip, I'm just resting," Willie answered. "That was a long run and I'm tired. I'm just resting." Then he got up and showed that he was okay, and the tension was off.

A lot of the Dodgers had also come out to see if he was hurt, and I walked in with Pee Wee Reese and Duke Snider. Each of them said, "I don't believe a human being could catch a ball like that. It's impossible. He's going to have to do that again because I just don't believe he caught that ball." It was a superhuman effort for somebody to dive ten feet, catch the ball, hold on to it, and save the game.

We went into the ninth inning and the score was 2-1 in our favor. Jansen walked a man and then got two outs and two strikes on Roy Campanella, but Campy hit a home run to beat Jansen. That kind of took some of the stardom away from Mays. Now Campy was the star because he hit the home run that won the game. But even though we lost the game, nothing could diminish the tremendous talent that Willie demonstrated in making the catch that he considers his greatest ever. It was an impossibility, but he did it. He made the catch.

Now, that's two catches that I saw him make that I thought were better than the one he made off Vic Wertz in the World Series. When you talk about which one was the best, it's like which comes first the chicken or the egg. He considers the one in Brooklyn off Bobby Morgan to be the best. But I thought the one he made off Rocky Nelson was the best.

It was inventive, with no glove and catching the ball in his bare hand on the dead run. And the catch off Nelson was in the stretch run, when we made up all that ground and every game was crucial. We won that game and we were tied at the end of the season so it was a very important play. If we had lost that game, it would have broken our momentum and this just kept it going by winning. That catch won the game and probably the pennant.

The game was not televised and I'm not even sure if it was even broadcast. But if somebody could have gotten a picture of it or even described how great it was, maybe it would be as well remembered as the World Series catch that he made off Vic Wertz. But anything that happens in a World Series attracts more attention and is remembered longer.

While everyone remembers Willie's great World Series catch, few people know that Vic Wertz was the only batter that Don Liddle faced in that game. After *The Catch*, Leo replaced him with Marv Grissom. When Liddle left the game, he told Grissom, "Well, I got my man. Now you do your job." Marv retired the side without giving up a run. Then he stayed in the game and got the win in extra innings, when Dusty Rhodes pinch-hit for me and delivered a three-run homer in the bottom of the tenth inning.

Dusty made Durocher look like a genius every time Leo put him in a game. And he had done it all year. I felt bad about being lifted for a pinch hitter in that situation. I wasn't having the year I had in 1951, but I felt a little embarrassed that he would take me out. I had always been a good clutch hitter but, since Dusty came through, I didn't mind. I said, "Well, I couldn't have done any better than that."

In the second game, Johnny Antonelli started for us, and on the first pitch of the game, Al Smith homered to give Cleveland a quick lead, but that's all they got. Early Wynn was pitching for the Indians, and he had us shut out going into the fifth inning. We got runners on the corners, and Leo called on Dusty to hit for me again. And again, he came through, with a basehit to center field to tie the game and advance the go-ahead run to third base. Later in the inning that run scored on a fielders choice to give us the lead. Of course, Dusty did it again later in the game, when he homered to give us a cushion run. So I told Dusty, "You can hit for me any time as long as you keep getting a basehit. But make sure you get the basehit."

And to top it off, Dusty caught Wertz' deep flyball, with the tying runs on base, for the final putout of the game. Leo may have been holding his breath on that one, but Dusty put it away to give us a 3-1 win. Dusty was not much of a fielder, but he sure could swing a bat.

That's what he wanted to do, and that's what he had confidence in doing. That's why I think he was so successful. He had a wonderful year. That was his season in the sun.

We traveled to Cleveland for the next two games. In the third game, we got the bases loaded in the third inning and Leo called on Dusty again. He delivered for the third straight time, knocking in two runs with a basehit to right field off Mike Garcia, and we went on to win 6-2.

Leo pinchhit for me in the tenth inning in the first game, and then he inserted Rhodes earlier in the next two games. I guess he wanted to break the game open earlier. And you can't complain with the results because he was successful. I guess Leo was wondering how I was going to take it. So, I never did say anything to him one way or another. I was just happy that Dusty came through. Because of that, Dusty and I have developed a closeness which exists to this day.

With us winning the first three games, Cleveland had their backs to the wall in the fourth game. This created another situation that has received a lot of attention. Al Lopez had to make a decision about his starting pitcher, and he chose not to use Bob Feller. I think Lopez didn't know what to do. Feller had never won a World Series game, and Lemon would have had to come back on two days rest. Lopez decided that he would start Lemon because he was their top pitcher that year and he had come back with two days rest to win before.

I think the newspapers created some of the controversy in this instance. Lopez was between a rock and a hard place. Because if he started Lemon and didn't win, then everybody would say, "Why didn't you start Feller?" If he started Feller and he got knocked out, they would call him a dumb S.O.B. because he started Feller. So I guess he went with what he thought was the right hunch. But it turned out to be the wrong one. I don't know if Bob Feller ever forgave Al for not starting him. In my way of thinking, Feller would have been real tough because he wanted to win a World Series game and he never had. And here was this great pitcher - for him to be denied that thrill is really something.

So Lemon got the start for the Indians and Liddle started for us. The game was pretty close. We were leading but it was still anybody's game, and we got the bases loaded. I had doubled down the left field line off Bob Lemon the first time I came up. So Al Lopez sends Hal Newhouser in the game to pitch to me. I knocked in two runs with a basehit to left field and that really broke the game open, and we won that last game pretty easy.

After the game was over I said, "Well, Leo, I thought maybe, since Dusty was hitting so well, you might start him." He said, "I knew my man was going to come through sooner or later for me." I wanted to kind of redeem myself for not hitting earlier. I could have gotten three hits in the game but Sam Dente made a great play in the seventh, and turned it into a double-play. The final score was 7-4, and we swept the Indians four straight games to reign as the World Champions of baseball.

25 Closing a Career

Monte never gave up and was always a fighter. He was one of the best men I've ever met.

—Larry Jansen, New York Giants

I RETURNED IN 1955 for my Giants farewell. I played about forty-five games with them, and then was sent down to Minneapolis for the rest of the season. I guess it was because age was catching up with me and I had that broken ankle, because I never had any problem with the front office.

Leo broke the news to me one day when we played a game in Minneapolis. He came over and said, "We want you to stay here where you can get a chance to play every day. Then if you swing the bat a little better, we'll bring you back." I felt they were not going to do it. But I went on and played for Minneapolis. I won the batting championship and led the Millers to the pennant. We beat Rochester in seven games in the championship playoffs. Along with Al Worthington's pitching and our hitting, we got the job done.

It was a surprise to be sent down by the Giants. I was shocked. I thought it was just a matter of using a little more patience. Apparently they didn't think that I was going to come back. But I did come back, because I had a fairly good year for the Cubs the next season. I don't know who was playing out in the outfield for the Giants that year but he didn't have a better season than I did.

I really didn't understand why the Giants sent me down. But I was a veteran and I knew there were no surprises in baseball. The broken ankle had slowed me down the last couple of years and maybe they figured I was going to slow down even more. And they probably had somebody playing who wasn't making as much money as I was. So, it surprised me but it didn't surprise me. I'll put it that way.

That was Leo's last year, too. He wanted to become general manager and I think owner Horace Stoneham made a big mistake by not appointing him. Leo knew the talent and he could have done a terrific job for the Giants. The decision to send me down was probably made by Horace Stoneham. Stoneham was his own general manager.

I was still making the same money at Minneapolis that I had been making with the Giants. It was disappointing to be sent down, but I didn't get down in spirit. I didn't let anything get me down. I had been through hard situations before, so I just kept on playing.

The next year I was in the draft and I understand that the Tigers were really interested in me. I was delighted because I wanted to play in Detroit with the short fences in left field and right field. And I wanted to play with Al Kaline because he was a terrific player. Instead, the Cubs picked me up. I was disappointed at first, but it turned out to be an unexpected pleasure because I got a chance to play with Ernie Banks. I didn't have that bad a year, and finished with fifteen home runs and a .271 average, while sharing left field with a kid named Jim King.

Playing with the Cubs was just wonderful. Since all our games were in the daytime, I was able to see the ball better. I wish I could have played many years with the Cubs. Wrigley Field is a good park for right-handed power hitters, and I think I would have hit a lot more home runs and probably had a higher batting average. I was thirty-seven when I finished with the Cubs. I thought I deserved a chance to play another year for the Cubs. But I guess they were on a youth program, even though they didn't have anybody better to replace me.

After the Cubs released me, I went to the Coast and played with the Los Angeles Angels in the Pacific Coast League. I started off hitting real well and I liked to play out there. We had another home-run hitter, Steve Bilko, who had been in the major leagues with the St. Louis Cardinals. He was playing first base and I was playing outfield, and we had a one-two thing going pretty good. I was looking forward to a wonderful season, when my back problems started. When I would play a game, my back would get stiff, and I would have to wait four or five days before I could play again.

Dr. Robert Kerlan, the famous orthopedic surgeon who helped Sandy Koufax, started treating me. I asked him about an operation on my back. He didn't recommend surgery at my age, and said that once I was out of baseball, it shouldn't bother me. So I took his recommendation and sometime around May, I decided to quit. After a few days, I drove back to New Jersey and officially retired. My back didn't bother me anymore for a long time. I'm glad I took the advice of Dr. Kerlan, for whom I had the highest respect.

I retired from baseball in 1957. My life as a baseball player was over, but I had to get on with the rest of my life and meet new challenges.

IV

New Challenges

26 The Commissioner's Office

Monte was superior on special assignments, especially as a pinch-hitter for the commissioner. He flawlessly handled speaking engagements and other appearances I could not make and smoothed out public relations problems.

—Bowie Kuhn, Baseball Commissioner

AFTER I RETIRED from baseball, I went to work for the Rheinagold Brewing Company, and I was glad that I had a job to go to. I had worked for the brewery in the off season since 1952, and I just went back with them full-time as an area representative. I enjoyed my association with Rheingold and stayed with them until I went to work in the commissioner's office more than ten years later.

Before I left Rheingold, there were two occasions where Jackie Robinson and I were brought together. The first time was when the vice president in charge of sales wanted Jackie to endorse Rheingold beer, and he asked me if I would set up a meeting. I called Jackie and told him what had been mentioned. "No, I'm not interested in it," he told me. "I won't endorse beer, cigarettes, liquor or anything else I don't believe in." I relayed Jackie's response to the vice president and he said, "Well, tell him he won't have to endorse it. All he will have to say is that, when guests come over, he likes to serve them Rheingold beer. Maybe we can work it out like that."

So, they negotiated on price. The price started out pretty low but, when it got up very high, Jackie agreed to do it. I sort of chuckled to myself and said, *Seemingly money will change anybody's mind.* It changed his, because it was some really decent money for just endorsing the beer. So Rheingold made a point of purchase. Jackie and

I did a promo together and they put posters in all the stores in New York, New Jersey, and throughout the area.

The other occasion occurred later on, when Earl Williams was honored as the minor-league player of the year. He was from Montclair, New Jersey, and they gave him a banquet in Orange, my hometown. There were two or three hundred people there to honor Earl for his achievement. Jackie was asked to come over from New York and, since I was from Orange and had been a baseball player, I was invited to sit on the dais with Jackie and Earl.

When Jackie got up to speak, he said that he just wanted everybody to know that baseball didn't owe him anything, and he didn't owe baseball anything. I don't know why Jackie said what he did, but I thought that it was inappropriate for the occasion. I just thought somebody should have something to say on behalf of baseball. So after Jackie finished talking, I asked the emcee if he would give me two minutes so I could say a few words.

I told Jackie, "I agree with you on a lot of things that you do but, on this particular occasion, I have to disagree with you. I think that you were great for baseball, and that baseball was good for you. If it hadn't been for baseball, maybe no one would have ever heard of Jackie Robinson. This young man is being honored simply for what he has achieved in our game. I think somebody should say something appropriate about him winning the minor-league player of the year award. And how wonderful baseball is for giving him the opportunity to excel. We wish him the best of luck as he approaches the major leagues."

In my capacity with Rheingold, I also often worked in conjunction with my good friend, Joe Reichler, who became the public relations director for baseball. So, in 1968, when I had a chance to work in the baseball commissioner's office, I seized upon the opportunity and was delighted that we would be working together again in my new position.

I was hired by Spike Eckert, who was the baseball commissioner at that time. At the beginning he wanted me to work part-time, but I told him it had to be full-time or not at all. We had a couple of luncheons before he decided to hire me, and I was able to convince him to put me on full-time. I guess he was trying to size me up and at the same time I was sizing him up.

At one of these luncheons at a local restaurant, Eckert asked what

I thought was a strange question. He said, "How would you save baseball if you were the commissioner?" I said, "Well, Commissioner, I don't think that baseball is in that much trouble. You have good years and sometimes you have lean years. But I think baseball is in good shape, and all we have to worry about is how to continue developing the stars and guys who can hit, run, field, and throw. I think baseball is going to be all right. Sometimes it takes a long time for a real star to come through, then all of a sudden you'll get four or five." I guess Eckert was impressed with what I said, because he hired me about a week later. And I was very grateful to him and happy to be in the commissioner's office.

Eckert had a very short tenure and I must say the worst hatchet job I ever saw was when they fired him. We were in San Francisco in 1968 for the winter meetings, and the General had his wife and family with him. The baseball owners called him in and fired him, and they got him to announce his own dismissal. By the things that he said, I don't think he actually realized that he was being fired. It was like he was in a fog. I never will forget what happened.

Sportswriter Dick Young got up in this meeting and asked Spike Eckert, "Do you realize that you are being fired? Do you realize that you are announcing your own dismissal?" Eckert said, "Well, I don't see it that way." Young said, "Why don't you talk straight to us. I'm not a politician. I didn't bring my political writer with me. Are you being fired or aren't you?" Well, he *was* being fired.

Joe Reichler and I had been invited by Del Webb, once a part-owner of the New York Yankees, to stop in Las Vegas for a few days before flying on back to New York. He was going to take us to dinner and to see some shows. But after the meeting where the General was fired, we had to change our plans. One of the owners came over to me and said, "Monte, kind of watch after him. We're worried about the way he looks and about what he might do. So take him back to the hotel and take care of him." Which I did.

On the ride from the Palace Hotel back to our hotel, I didn't know what to say to the General. I told him how sorry I was about what happened, and that now maybe he could do some of the things that he'd always wanted to do. It was like he was in a daze and I don't think he even heard me. I felt so sorry for the man. He didn't live too much longer after that, and I think his ouster was probably a contributing factor.

The owners found out that Eckert wasn't the man they were looking for. He didn't really know baseball. He was interested in baseball, but he just didn't *know* the game. When he got ready to make a speech, sometimes he would have to go in the bathroom and throw up. One time Joe Reichler gave him some notes to read, but the General got the cards mixed up. He was really reading the wrong notes and wasn't aware that he was saying the wrong thing. He was an embarrassment to baseball and that's the reason they fired him.

The owners admitted they wanted somebody they could control. But they didn't want anybody who was totally out of it, and he *was* totally out of it. But, his termination was not handled very well at all. It could have done more diplomatically. There were three or four owners who were leading the charge, including the leadership in Baltimore and Cincinnati who wanted to get rid of him.

Subsequently, the owners were looking around for someone who knew baseball, was a fan of the game, and also had a good legal mind. In 1969 they hired Bowie Kuhn, who was the attorney for the National League. He came in and started to do what was needed at the time. Bowie was the perfect choice and that's why they picked him. I knew we had the right man because he was a lawyer and a good baseball fan. We felt that baseball was in the hands of a competent leader. Bowie served sixteen years, and I was there with him the entire time. When he retired, I retired.

We had some wonderful moments in those years. During his reign, a lot of changes were coming about, and he made many critical decisions. He had those tough negotiations with Marvin Miller, and there were other legal problems that had to be dealt with. The players went on strike and were locked out, but he brought them back. There was also the Denny McLain case and Bowie had to make a decision on that.

And then there were problems with some owners. Charlie Finley wanted to sell his players and break up his team, but the commissioner wouldn't let him do that. Augie Busch wanted to do some things that were not baseball astute, so the commissioner fined him a couple of hundred thousand dollars. He also had to fine Ray Kroc out in San Diego. And he had to come down on Ted Turner because Turner wanted to get in uniform, sit on the bench, and manage the club. The commissioner told him he couldn't do that, so Ted Turner was mad. George Steinbrenner made his employees contribute to a political party, and Bowie had to sit him out for a year. And, for one reason or another, the commissioner had to come down on a few other people.

All these decisions alienated the new breed of owner that had come into baseball. So, in the best interests of baseball, Bowie made some enemies. Then, when it came time to rehire him, he couldn't get the necessary votes. The owners got together and said, "Commissioner, you've been in for a long time and we don't have anything against you. We just simply want a change - a new person. We want somebody who is more acquainted with the business end of the game and can make us some money, rather than just enforce the rules."

That's the way they put it, but you could read between the lines and see what they meant. Really, the owners *did* have something against him and the action they took was expected. Because the commissioner insisted on doing the right thing, and the owners didn't want to do the right thing. That's why Bowie was forced to retire and return to his law practice.

Many important decisions were made when Bowie was the commissioner, and I think he did an outstanding job. Of course, if he had it to do all over again, he might come down even harder on some of those guys.

The commissioner demanded that the integrity of baseball would always be protected for the best interests of the game. And it *was* protected under him. He will always be noted for doing it so expertly. I'm sorry that the player relations deteriorated under him, but he couldn't help it. He was trying to hold the fort against the union leader, Marvin Miller. So, it was a tough reign but he did a creditable job. One of these days, he will probably be elected to the Hall of Fame.

27 Conflicts and Controversy

Baseball must be a great game to survive the fools who run it.

—Bill Terry, New York Giants

THE YEARS THAT Bowie Kuhn and I worked together in the commissioner's office coincided with the era of free agents, arbitration, and player strikes. Of course, conflict and controversy came along with the labor disputes. The first controversy of significance that Bowie had to deal with was the Curt Flood case. The St. Louis Cardinals and the Philadelphia Phillies had made a multi-player trade, with Flood and Tim McCarver being the big-name players involved. But Curt refused to report to the Phillies and filed a suit challenging the reserve clause.

One day the commissioner said, "Monte, I wish you could arrange a meeting with Curt Flood and me at some out-of-the-way place. We could meet, just the two of us, in Palm Springs, Tahoe, or some place warm where there's nobody around. We can sit and talk and resolve the situation." I said, "Commissioner, I think that's an excellent idea. I'll be happy to try to set up a meeting."

I called Curt Flood two or three times and finally got him on the phone. I said, "Curt, the commissioner wants to meet with you with no publicity. Nobody will know about it but you two, and he wants to do it as soon as possible. If I can do this, it would really be a feather in my cap because it is a serious situation and I think that the two of you together can solve the problem before it gets out of hand."

"What will we talk about?" Curt asked. "You can talk about whatever you want to." I told him. "You can tell him about the situation that you're in, and maybe he can have some influence on whether or not you go to Philadelphia. Just open up. You give him all your views and he'll give you his views. And then you might be able to come to some kind of agreement." "Well, as far as I'm concerned, we don't have anything to talk about," he said. "And there will be no meeting." "Now, is this final?" I asked. "Don't you think that, with him being the commissioner of baseball, you should at least meet with him?" He said, "No, I have nothing to talk to him about." So we let it go at that.

After sitting out a season, Flood signed with Washington and played with them for a while. He was making over one hundred thousand dollars a year but he didn't play well. So he said that he was going to quit baseball, and was going to Europe. He wanted do some painting and make his living over there.

The commissioner then dispatched Joe Reichler to try to talk to Flood. They met at JFK Airport in New York and Joe tried to show him where he was making a mistake. He was not really the ideal player to test the reserve clause. Joe told him, "Let somebody who is making fifteen or twenty thousand do it. Not you. You're making a lot of money." Joe tried very hard to get him to reconsider, but Curt said, "No, I'm going." So he and his secretary boarded a plane and went to Europe. After they got over there, they found out that his paintings didn't sell that well. His money ran out and Curt saw some hard times before he finally came back home to the United States.

We had tried to talk him out of going in the first place. Later, he wrote a book that made reference to this meeting and to the fact that I had called him. Rather than say, "Monte Irvin had called me to try to set up a meeting," he said, "Some guy in the commissioner's office tried to talk me out of doing this and I told him 'No.' " That's the way he referred to the situation.

I didn't see Curt Flood for a long time. When we finally did meet again, he came up to me and gave me a hug. That was when he had become the commissioner of that senior league in Florida. Now, every year, I receive a Christmas card from him. I think he realized he made a mistake when he reacted toward me the way he did. Curt decided to fight the reserve clause, and Arthur J. Goldberg, a retired Supreme Court justice, represented him. The case was tried and went before the Supreme Court, but Goldberg lost it, and Curt Flood was out of baseball for good.

Whether or not he was sorry that he took that course of action, I don't know. I *do* know that many of today's baseball players don't even know who Curt Flood is, and he has received no compensation or extra applause for what he did. If he had to do it all over, it's problematic whether he would do it again. His case did open the door for free agency that came a few years later in the mid 1970s, with Catfish Hunter, Andy Messersmith and Dave McNally, and a few other arbitration cases.

Before free agency, the owners were in complete charge. They were too powerful and were not fair. Even Commissioner Kuhn wanted to change the system and make it more equitable, but he didn't want the drastic changes that are in effect now. I think what has really hurt baseball more than anything else is arbitration, where an outside guy is brought in to decide the fate of the great game of baseball. And these arbitrators work both sides. One time they will favor the player, and the next time you can bet they will favor the owner, so they will be hired again. Most of them don't know a darn thing about baseball. They aren't knowledgeable fans and don't know about the inner workings of baseball.

Of course arbitration is good for the players. They can market themselves, and since this is a free market economy, they get as much money as they possibly can. At the same time, the owners were stupid for not using good judgment when signing some of these players. Many clubs are still paying guys who are no longer in baseball. And when they permitted these player agents to come in and take their ten- or twenty-million-dollar cut right out of the game, this was money that would never return. I just thought it was wrong then, and I still think it is wrong. But that's the way it is today.

The strike that started in 1994 was really crazy. Why didn't both sides talk and settle something while they were still playing? Possibly, it's a matter of putting a salary cap on the game like is done in other sports. Basketball and football both have a cap and they are not going broke. Why can't baseball have the same thing? That is a matter that will have to be resolved.

In baseball there's also a matter of motivation. A lot of people lose sight of the fact that once players become financially independent, subconsciously, they don't try as hard. It's a psychological thing. It takes a very unusual person who can receive that much money, and not let it affect their play on the field. Those players who have done it are few and far between. The moment these high-priced free agents receive a big contract, for some reason or another, they go on the disabled list within a year or two.

I was just sorry to see the strike happen because 1994 was going to be a super year. Consider all the positive facets of the game that were unfolding. There was the Yankees situation, the Montreal situation, the Baltimore Orioles situation, and so many teams were playing good ball. And a lot of guys were going for the records. Consider the power numbers that Matt Williams, Jeff Bagwell, Barry Bonds, Ken Griffey, Jr., and Frank Thomas were putting together. And you had Tony Gwynn trying for .400, Greg Maddox winning his third straight Cy Young Award, and Cal Ripken, Jr., pursuing Lou Gehrig's record.

So, it's just a crime that baseball was interrupted. The people missed it, especially having no World Series. It was a black eye to baseball and it's going to take a lot of excellence to overcome it.

After the season was aborted, I said that if there was no agreement before spring training, the major-league clubs were going to use replacement players. I honestly believed that there would be some union players who would report, particularly guys with performance clauses in their contracts. I thought they were going to want to be playing and that there would be a lot of desertion. Some of the players had already said that they would report to camp. I knew that would pose a big problem for the strikers.

Both the owners and the union put pressure on the minor leaguers, who were caught in the middle. That's when Michael Jordan left baseball and switched back to basketball. Players had to make a decision about whether they were going to play or not. And in 1995, when some replacement players were called up after the strike was ended, there were problems in some of the ballclubs.

In this strike, the owners were right. They have a lot of money at risk and deserve to get a return on their investment and maintain some control. The owners decided they couldn't afford to lose this one. They thought if they did, they just might as well fold their tents and go home.

Even after the camps opened, I hoped both sides would get together and negotiate and play, but at the beginning of spring training they were farther apart than ever. The owners and players walked out of the meetings and went their separate ways. Fortunately they were able to get together in time to salvage the 1995 season, without having to field replacement teams. I still don't see why they couldn't have done it earlier, but each side was stubborn and that's what caused the problem.

The baseball strike did more damage than anybody could possibly have thought. When the 1994 World Series was cancelled for the first time in ninety years, the fans were mad. And they're still mad. As a result the attendance in 1995 was off twenty percent, and in some places even more.

In order to regain the confidence of the fans, the players have to change their ways. They've got to be friendlier and more cooperative. They should give free autographs at the ball parks and do a lot of little things to help bring the people back.

The owners have to figure some way to keep prices nominal. For a man, his wife, and two kids, it costs about a hundred dollars to go to one ball game. That's entirely too much money. A bag of peanuts that used to cost ten cents is now three dollars, a beer is five dollars and a hot dog is four dollars. And that's ridiculous. I just wish somehow they could get back to normal, the way it should be.

The owners also must appoint a commissioner. Somebody who will represent the best interests of the fans, the players and the owners. At present they have only an acting commissioner, who says that he does not want to be a permanent commissioner. The owners have to seek someone who's very capable to try to get back on track.

One big thing that really helped was when Cal Ripken, Jr., broke Lou Gehrig's record for consecutive games played. A lot of attention was focused on baseball that day. Ripken's accomplishment helps show that the players of today must be great because they're breaking all the old-timers' records. Cal is the kind of player that you're certainly proud of because he is very durable and very talented. He is also a nice person who is involved in community activities to help bring people out to the ball park.

Some changes will have to be made to get baseball back into the number-one spot. They're being challenged by football, basketball, hockey, golf, tennis, and other sports. However, it's still the dream of kids all over the world to play baseball in the major leagues. This is true particularly here in the United States, in Latin America, and in Japan. Baseball is also getting big in Europe, and soon they'll be playing regular schedules in China.

The things that I mentioned will have to be addressed before the sport will be healthy again. It would be great if the owners and players would settle their differences and avoid another strike.

Maybe things would be different if the first strike in 1972 had been handled differently. That season, they closed the camps and locked the players out because they couldn't reach an agreement. That's when the commissioner and I disagreed about whether to keep the camps closed. However, the disagreement was not only with me, because the rest of the staff felt the same way. The commissioner would have staff meetings every morning, where all of us were asked to give him our feelings and comments. We always gave him the very best advice that we could.

We thought the camps should stay closed, but after about five days, Bowie ordered the camps opened. If the commissioner had kept the camps closed just for another couple of days, I think that Marvin Miller and the union would have been broken. The reserve clause would have eventually been changed, but not so drastically. It would not have been as severe as it is now. There wouldn't have been any arbitration and there wouldn't have been all the other changes in baseball that have affected the game so strongly.

The commissioner decided that for the best interests of baseball, he wouldn't do what we advised. In order to have an on-going relationship with the players, he decided that he would open the camp and let them come back. That way the owners wouldn't lose a lot of money, and the players wouldn't be unhappy. Again, I think if he had kept the camps closed, then Marvin Miller would have been bested and a lot of his power in baseball would have been taken away. I would have loved to have seen the commissioner control the game of baseball, rather than Marvin Miller. But he didn't, and I think that changed the history of baseball.

Marvin Miller didn't have baseball's interest at heart. Marvin Miller wanted to make Marvin Miller a bigger person and he didn't think about the overall effect that it would have on baseball. I'm sure the fellows like Robin Roberts, Allie Reynolds, and all the rest of those guys who were instrumental in getting the players' union started, didn't have any idea that it would turn into what it did. If they had known the kind of guy that he was, they wouldn't have been so pro Marvin Miller.

What Miller did resulted in these high salaries now. They've created free agency and some people think these high salaries are going to affect baseball in every way. I guess the jury is still out on who's right. Naturally the players are going to try to get all the money they can, and it's up to the owners whether they're going to pay it or not. I don't know where the money is going to keep coming from, but it's going to have to come from someplace.

Marvin Miller has done a lot of good, but I think he could have done it in a different way. They could have changed the reserve laws, but left enough incentive in there for a player to go out and perform the way he should. And not make him an instant millionaire overnight. I think this has hurt baseball terribly. And it has also hurt the fans because, by the players making such huge sums, the cost of going to a ball game has gotten far too high.

But baseball is such a great game that nobody can kill it. People have tried. The players have tried to kill it, and the owners have tried to kill it. But it will keep going on and on. Things looked really bad during the 1994 strike, but as long as the game keeps developing stars, I don't think we have anything to worry about over the long run. After all, disputes between owners and players are nothing new. It's as old as baseball.

Another problem that has been around since the inception of baseball is gambling. As I mentioned earlier, Bowie Kuhn also had to deal with it. The Denny McLain case was like the Pete Rose situation in that it involved gambling, but was different in most other aspects. McLain was just betting that his club would win. He wasn't betting on other clubs like Pete Rose did.

McLain was convicted of gambling on the games and there were not any hidden facts in his case. He admitted that he was wrong and that he did bet. It was just a matter of how long he was going to be suspended. It could have been for a year, or he could have been thrown out permanently. As it turned out, the commissioner sat him down for a few months.

Bowie Kuhn had already retired when the Rose situation came up. Bart Giamatti was the commissioner then and he had proof that Pete was doing so many illegal things that stringent action was warranted. Not only did he bet on games, but I think it's been made clear that Pete Rose called other managers to get certain information to use in his betting, not only on his club, but on other clubs, too.

Since the commissioner's office had all the facts, they offered him a deal. If he would admit what he had done and promise to get treatment for his gambling habit, they would sit him down for a year and then probably bring him back. But Rose chose to fight them with his lawyers. He took it to court and lost. In 1990, Pete was convicted of income tax evasion and had to go to jail for about five months. There was a big difference between McLain and Rose. Pete tried to really change the rules of baseball.

That's why he's been barred from the Hall of Fame and it's doubtful that he'll ever make it. I don't think Pete Rose deserves to be in the Hall of Fame because he was offered a chance to come clean, and he didn't come clean. He has never really admitted that he did something wrong. He has never come right out and said, "Yes, I'm guilty. And I'm just sorry for the whole thing." Rose continues to stonewall and as long as he continues to do that, I think he'll be banned from the Hall of Fame. A lot of other Hall of Famers feel the same way.

I hope that Pete has learned his lesson because he was a terrific baseball player. He's doing okay now. He just should have realized what the consequences were going to be. Ever since the Black Sox scandal in 1919, rules against gambling have been strictly enforced.

Before I began playing with the Giants, Leo Durocher was suspended from baseball for a year by Commissioner Happy Chandler because he was alleged to have associated with known gamblers. Chandler had no right to do what he did because Leo was not guilty.

Leo was falsely accused and he confronted Chandler about the allegations. He told the commissioner in no uncertain words that he had done nothing wrong. It was proven that Leo was unnecessarily thrown out of baseball for a full year. Of course, Leo took it like a man. Today, it couldn't happen because a man has more rights in baseball now than back then. They have a hearing and the charges have to be proven.

Gambling and drug abuse are the two problems in baseball that should not be tolerated. They should control them and take proper actions whenever necessary. There is a drug problem in our country and it is reflected to some extent in baseball. But I think baseball has done more than other sports in this regard. When I was in the commissioner's office, we were the first to take action because the problem existed and nobody was doing anything about it. The commissioner set up a task force to determine who was involved and then he investigated the suspects.

Bowie posted signs in all the clubhouses around the leagues, and had a representative go around and warn players about the dangers of using drugs. A player could be thrown out of baseball and possibly thrown in jail. I think coming down on them pretty hard prevented a lot of guys from continuing to use illegal substances. But some players had gone so far with the substance abuse that it was impossible to stop them. Even today, some players continue to have problems.

Bob Welch developed an alcohol dependency, and Steve Howe developed an addiction to drugs. Welch sought help and apparently has his problem under control. Howe has been given numerous chances and came back and was still able to play. Of course, he's a good pitcher but he has abused the system. He's had enough chances. An addiction *is* expensive but young players today have a lot of money to spend, they have a lot of time on their hands, and they give in to drugs. They get connected with the wrong kind of people and they give in to their weakness.

Baseball has strict rules now. Dwight Gooden has been caught a number of times, and when he didn't pass the urine test, he was suspended. He was out of baseball for an entire year with no salary, but has signed with the New York Yankees and will be back in baseball in 1996. Darryl Strawberry also had a relapse and was dropped by the Giants when he failed a drug test. But then he got another chance to play with the Yankees in 1995.

That shows how vulnerable these guys are. There is always somebody who is going to take a chance and do the wrong thing. But now that they know what the penalties are, they are less prone to use drugs. I wish we could stop young people from using them completely, but there's no way to do that.

But baseball should keep coming down hard on offenders and, if need be, throw them out of baseball. For the first offense, sit them down for a year and then bring them back. If they continue to do drugs, throw them out of baseball permanently. I think that's the quickest and best way to handle the problem. It should be just like gambling. If you do it, you're out of baseball.

Those were some of the problems that the commissioner's office had with players. An entirely different set of problems came from the new group of owners, who brought in a lot of new ideas and a different attitude with them. Many of them were not true baseball owners. They were just in it for the money, and they wanted to change things and do it their way.

Charlie Finley was representative of this new ownership. He had some good ideas. He wanted to play the World Series at night and, since they adopted that idea, it has proven to be very popular. Another idea of his was to use orange baseballs in night games. It was proven that orange baseballs were easier to see at night, but they didn't adopt that idea because it came from Charlie Finley.

Bowie Kuhn and Charlie Finley just naturally didn't get along. When they got into a name-calling match, it made matters worse. Finley called Kuhn a village idiot and then apologized to all the village idiots of the world. Bowie wouldn't dignify those remarks with a response. He just sloughed it off and said, "What can you expect from a guy like that?" Finley was definitely unconventional and certainly no stranger to controversy. There were several confrontations between the two of them.

During the second game of the 1973 World Series between Finley's Oakland Athletics and the New York Mets, Mike Andrews was put into the game at second base. In a key situation, bases loaded and two outs in the twelfth inning, he made a couple of errors that caused the A's to lose the game. When that happened, Charlie Finley wanted to release him immediately, during the World Series. But the commissioner wouldn't let him do that.

Finley said Andrews was injured and so they had a hearing in the commissioner's office. I was sitting at my desk and the secretary-treasurer came in and said, "They have a hearing and Charlie Finley wants you to testify." I wondered what it was all about, but I went on over to the meeting. After I got there, Charlie Finley said, "Monte, were you in the clubhouse when Mike Andrews said he was injured?" "To tell you the truth," I said, "it was the World Series and I had many things on my mind. Maybe some of these things that you said happened *did* happen, but I cannot swear that I heard Mike Andrews say this one way or another. And that's the truth and nothing but the truth. I just didn't hear it or, if I did hear it, it just went in one ear and out the other. So, I cannot swear to it." Then they dismissed me and I went on back to the office.

The hearing lasted until about one o'clock in the afternoon. I went out to lunch, and who should I meet but Charlie Finley. Charlie said, "I wasn't trying to put you on the spot, but I needed you." "Well, the next time you want to put me on the spot," I said, "let me know. Not that the outcome would have been any different because I told you the truth."

Catfish Hunter became a free agent when he got Charlie Finley on a technicality. There was a clause in his contract that Finley ignored, and that opened the door for Catfish to sign with another club. He was declared a free agent and then signed with the Yankees. That had an impact on baseball because, although Catfish wasn't sensational, he got the Yankees back into the winning habit. That's when they started to come back and win some pennants.

And there was the time when Finley wanted to get rid of Joe Rudi, Vida Blue, and one or two other players because they were making pretty good salaries. Finley wanted to sell them because he needed the money but Bowie Kuhn wouldn't let him break up the team because it wasn't in the best interest of baseball. Finley got mad about that because he eventually lost the players to free agency and didn't get anything in return for them.

Then there was the Reggie Jackson situation, where Finley was going to send him down because Reggie had been in a month-long slump. Reggie didn't want to go, and the commissioner prevented Finley from doing that. The relationship between Kuhn and Finley was always very confrontational, and they were always at each other's throat. I think the feeling was mutual and it never did change.

Another idea brought in by the new group of owners was the designated hitter concept. As with all controversial topics that came up, the commissioner had meetings about the DH. Some people were pro and others were con. I was always against it. The reason this came about in the first place was that the pitchers were overpowering the hitters. I thought if there was to be any kind of change, they should just move the mound back, a foot or six inches. That would make a difference and would have solved the problem.

When the commissioner was considering this change, some baseball people said, "There's got to be a whole lot of situations come up and a lot of questions that will have to be answered. But they worked it out in the American League, and the Yankees' Ron Blomberg was the first DH in 1973. But in the National League, it's still the way it used to be. I think that baseball is much better off without the DH because the game is more of a challenge and the manager can maneuver better.

Pitchers can be very aggressive in the American League because they never have to come to the plate. That's a very important thing. A lot of pleasure is taken away from the game when a pitcher can't come to the plate. In order to be a complete baseball player, pitchers should be able to bat. I'm a purist. I don't like the DH, and I hope that in a few years, they change it back to the way it was before. I don't think the batting averages would be appreciably affected. Some players like Orlando Cepeda and George Crowe have prolonged their careers by being a DH. But that takes away a spot on the roster from someone else, and takes away playing time from a youngster. The DH is still a controversial issue and probably always will be, because it was something different.

Another issue that was something different was when Frank Robinson became the first black manager. The commissioner and I always talked about things that came up, and I told him I thought Frank would do a good job. I was delighted that Cleveland had selected him and he *did* do a good job. The organization realized that

Frank was a fine manager. They didn't have much material but he got the very best out of what they had. I think that Frank Robinson is partially responsible for the success the Cleveland club is having now, because he started them on the right track.

Another thing that Bowie Kuhn was responsible for was the formation of the Negro Leagues Committee for the Hall of Fame that selected deserving Negro League players for induction. That was another decision that he made that was not popular in some quarters because some people were resistant to change.

On a different note, while I was working in the commissioner's office, one of my duties was to get singers for the National Anthem during the World Series. At that time the Jackson Five was one of the hottest acts in the country. I checked with their agent in Los Angeles, and he said they were available and would like to perform. So, arrangements were made.

But some officials were worried because they had never heard of them. They had a meeting and the matter was discussed. The officials of the Cincinnati Reds club, who were the home team, thought they should get somebody else. Some people in the commissioner's office also wondered if it was the right thing to do. Neither group knew anything about the Jackson Five. I told them that they were the hottest thing going, and they would be delighted to perform. But the officials didn't want to commit to letting them sing.

After much deliberation, I decided to tell their agent about what was happening and there was a possibility that they might not perform. Their agent said, "Well, you tell them, for obvious reasons, that if they don't permit the kids to sing, we'll have pickets all around the stadium."

Then I went to Cincinnati and told the officials what the agent said. They wanted to avoid bad public relations and a possible confrontation so they agreed to let them do the National Anthem.

I was standing on the field with Joe Reichler, and just before the Jackson Five went out on the field, he said, "Are they any good? I have never heard of them." "You mean you've never even *heard* of them?" I asked. "They're great." "They'd better be," he replied, "because our jobs depend on it." The kids went out, did a sensational job and received a standing ovation. But that was an anxious moment for me because they saved our jobs. Michael Jackson was about seven or eight years old at that time and who knew then that later he would become the hottest rock star in the world and worth millions.

28 The Ghost of Babe Ruth

As a matter of protocol, I asked Monte Irvin to represent me in Atlanta and stay with the Braves until the record fell.

—Bowie Kuhn, Baseball Commissioner

FOR THE MOST PART, everything went fairly smooth during the years that I was in the commissioner's office. The one thing that I really disagreed with the commissioner about was his not attending the game in Atlanta when Hank Aaron was going for the lifetime home run record.

Hank had tied Babe Ruth's mark at Cincinnati and was going home to break the record. Bowie Kuhn had taken a speaking engagement in Cleveland and decided to go there to address The Wigwam Club, rather than go to Atlanta. I thought he should have gone to Atlanta, at least for the first series. Then, if Aaron hadn't broken the record, Bowie could have gone back home and attended to other duties instead of just hanging around waiting for the record to be broken. I thought it was important enough for him to cancel that engagement in Cleveland and attend the Braves' game. But the commissioner saw fit not to do it.

He had ordered Hank to play in Cincinnati and also ordered manager Eddie Mathews to use a set lineup for the Braves, so that there wouldn't be anything out of the ordinary. The commissioner specifically ordered them not to save Aaron so he could break the record at home. He also told Mathews that if he did not do precisely as instructed, the commissioner's office would deal with him very severely.

They wrote that up real big in the Atlanta newspapers, and the commissioner lessened his popularity in Atlanta when that happened. Bowie figured that, if he attended a game, he would not get a cordial reception. Consequently, I don't think he wanted to hear the boos of the Atlanta fans, and decided to send me. Naturally, he's the boss and he can do what he wants. So I had to go.

He was defended in the newspapers by Dick Young and some of the other writers. They said that the commissioner shouldn't follow Aaron around waiting for him to break the record. I agree with that, but I thought he left himself open for a lot of criticism. Of course, he didn't think so. By not going he kind of offended Aaron and the fans in Atlanta, too. I thought that, since this was almost like a sacred record, the commissioner of baseball should have been there. But he sent me.

The Braves' homestand was about two weeks and my wife and I packed to stay that long, just in case. We took tennis rackets, bathing suits, books to read, and everything. Naturally, the commissioner's office wasn't very popular. I called the Braves office and told the public relations director that we would be there and to leave some tickets for us.

We stayed at the International Inn, right across from the ball park. When we went on over, it took us an hour to try to get into the park. They gave us some seats way the hell up in center field, and I thought somebody might have made a mistake. So I left my wife up there and told her I would come back to get her. Then I made my way down to the Braves boxseats and I just happened to see Bill Bartholomay, one of the owners of the Braves. I told him about the seating situation and he said, "Well, you sit right down here with us, Monte, and it will be convenient."

Our office had a special diamond-encrusted gold watch made for Aaron that cost about five thousand dollars. I was going to present it to Hank when he broke the record. So Hank hit a homer off Al Downing in the fourth inning, and they had a brief little ceremony on the field. I awarded him the watch, made a speech, and wound up saying "And the commissioner of baseball would like you to have this diamond-studded watch in memory of this wonderful occasion."

After I gave it to him, Aaron said, "Where's the commissioner?" Which kind of angered me. I had just given him the watch, and I'm not the boss. The commissioner is the boss. Why should he ask me where the commissioner is? I could kind of understand it a little bit, but it still made me mad. "What's the matter Hank?" I asked. "Am I not good enough to award this watch to you? The commissioner couldn't make it and he sent me." Joe Garagiola and Tony Kubek were telecasting the game. They said over the air that the commissioner should have been there and also asked "Where's the commissioner?"

That was a very strange night because immediately, after Hank hit the home run, the temperature changed. It had been a beautiful night at first, but then the temperature must have dropped thirty degrees and the wind started to blow. It was kind of eerie.

After the ceremony was over, I made my way back to our seats in center field, got my wife, and we went back to the hotel. We planned to get a plane out the next day, but the thought came to me, *If there's a flight out tonight, why stay the night?* Sure enough TWA had a flight out sometime after midnight. We caught that flight and were back in Newark about three o'clock in the morning. We had left that morning, arrived in Atlanta a little after noon, and returned in less than twenty-four hours, after having seen Aaron hit the record-breaking home run. So it was a very unusual day. It was one of the weirdest days I ever spent. But, again, I wish the commissioner had been there because I thought it was that important. That was one of the few disagreements that we had.

Afterward, Aaron and the commissioner had this feud going. Hank continually criticized Kuhn in the press, and had a lot to say. I thought the commissioner of baseball was above that kind of criticism. Hank should have said something and then let it die. But it became an ongoing feud between the two of them. I remember Aaron came to an affair in New York when the commissioner was being given an award. Hank got up and said, "Well, Mr. Commissioner, you didn't attend my affair, but I'm attending yours."

In the meantime the Ashland Oil Company and the Tri-State Fair and Regatta honored the Negro league players in Ashland, Kentucky. Hank had promised all the guys and all the people there that he would attend and say a few words of inspiration to the Negro Leaguers, who were partly responsible for Hank being able to play in the major leagues. He promised right up until the last minute. Then, maybe a couple of hours before the affair, we got a call from him saying that he couldn't come. He said his brother had contacted cancer, but it came out later that his brother had the cancer for many years. We thought that it was just terrible that Hank didn't show. I figured that he had got wind of the fact that the commissioner had also been invited, and probably didn't want to be there and confront him again.

But the whole thing had a happy ending. When the statue of Aaron was dedicated in Atlanta, the commissioner got an invitation to the ceremony and attended. Both of them wound up helping each other and they let bygones be bygones. I think they're friends now and I hope they remain friends.

The years that Bowie Kuhn was commissioner was possibly the most tumultous period since they first had a baseball commissioner. I think that history will show that his performance in this position will compare favorably with his predecessors. Judge Kennesaw Mountain Landis, the first commissioner of baseball, was the most powerful ever. No one since has had any powers like he had back then. After the Black Sox Scandal, baseball gave him some omnipotent powers. Even though those Chicago players were charged, they were never convicted. But Landis still banned them because he was all powerful and when he made a decision, his decision was final.

Judge Landis had things his way and that included the gentleman's agreement that remained in place throughout his tenure. When asked about why there were no blacks in baseball, he said there was no ban and that anybody could play. But that was not true. There was an unwritten agreement that blacks were not going to play. Bill Veeck wanted to buy the Phillies and stock the team with blacks, but he wasn't permitted to do it. That idea was too progressive for the times. Judge Landis was a traditionalist and he wanted to retain the status quo. And he had the power to do it.

Another thing that Landis did to control the racial situation was the way he handled the exhibition games between black teams and white teams. He said they could barnstorm for one month after the World Series was over. Some of the black players used to form barnstorming teams and play teams like the Philadelphia Phillies or Philadelphia A's. And the major-leaguers would play the Baltimore Black Sox or the Hilldale club from Philadelphia. Sometimes the black teams would beat the major-league teams. So Landis came out with a ruling that only three players from any one team could participate on the same barnstorming ballclub. That way if they lost, the black teams couldn't say that they beat a major league club intact.

But Judge Landis did some good. One thing you have to say about Landis was that he was strict, and he did bring respectability back to baseball at a time when it was needed.

Landis served as the commissioner until his death in 1944, and Happy Chandler was appointed as his successor. Chandler had been the governor of Kentucky and a U.S. senator before becoming the baseball commissioner. The one thing that he is most remembered for is giving Branch Rickey permission to sign Jackie Robinson. "I don't believe in barring Negroes from baseball just because they are Negroes," Happy said in taking his stand. When Happy Chandler sided with Branch Rickey, it was the two of them against the entire league. Happy knew that he was taking an unpopular stand and, eventually, it cost him his job.

The next commissioner was Ford Frick, who took over in 1951. He was the National League president for several years and, before that, he had been a sportswriter and radio commentator. The thing that he is remembered for is putting the asterisk on Roger Maris' home run record, when he broke Babe Ruth's season record in 1961.

After Frick came Spike Eckert and Bowie Kuhn. When Bowie left, Peter Ueberroth was brought in because he was so successful with the Olympics. He was not a big baseball man per se, but he was a fine person and a young, talented businessman. He had made money for the Olympics and for the city of Los Angeles. So he knew how to make money and he made a lot of money for the baseball owners. But by the time his five years were over, they said that was enough. He had alienated so many owners that he didn't run for a second term. He knew there was no sentiment and he didn't have the votes.

The next baseball commissioner was the perfect person for the job, Bart Giamatti. He had been the president of the National League, so he understood baseball. And he was highly educated and had been the president of Yale University. He had the personality, was a wonderful man, and was a great baseball fan. It's just too bad that he didn't live very long after becoming commissioner. I think the Pete Rose situation and the stress that resulted from it helped to hasten his death. Because it was just crushing and was too much for his heart.

After Giamatti was Faye Vincent. He was a friend of Giamatti's and when he came in, he wanted to do the right thing. He wanted to represent the players *and* the owners. But the owners didn't think he was enough of their friend so they wanted him out. He said he didn't need that pressure and stepped aside. Now, he lives in Connecticut with his family, his health is good, and he is really enjoying himself.

Bowie Kuhn is living in Florida and doing fine. Bowie, his secretary Mary Sotos, and I all retired at the same time in 1984. I was sixty-five. I had taken a lot of long bus rides, had a tough career in the major leagues, and had been away from my family much of that time. I decided that I would enjoy the rest of my life. I had already bought a house in Florida and I couldn't wait to move down. Now I can just relax and enjoy myself until it's time to leave this earth. I'm not sorry I made that decison.

Some youngsters have taken over baseball now, and that's the way it should be. Milwaukee Brewers' owner Bud Selig has been voted the temporary commissioner for the next five years. Bud has a history of dedicated service and, if given a chance, he will do an outstanding job. I had sixteen good years and I enjoyed every minute of it.

29 Baseball Pinnacle

Regarded as one of Negro leagues' best hitters, star slugger of Newark Eagles won 1946 Negro League batting title. Led N. L. in runs batted in and paced "miracle" Giants in hitting in 1951 drive to pennant. Batted .458 and stole home in 1951 World Series.

—Hall of Fame Plaque, Cooperstown, New York

THE ONE DAY that I will never forget is August 6, 1973. That is the day I was inducted into Baseball's Hall of Fame at Cooperstown, New York. Being elected for this honor is the highest tribute that can be paid to a player. During my professional baseball career that spanned more than twenty years, I had countless thrills on and off the baseball diamond. I had played in three World Series, two in the major leagues with the New York Giants and one with the Newark Eagles in the Negro leagues.

But this was a different kind of a thrill from the World Series. It was a sense of accomplishment. It meant that the long bus rides, the hard training, and all the unfavorable conditions that I had faced had finally paid off. Because I was being rewarded with the highest honor that could be bestowed on me as a baseball player. This certainly was the crowning point of my life, and I was deeply appreciative. It was a wonderful feeling but, at the same time, I felt very humble about it.

That day, as I looked out over the crowd, I thought about all that had happened in my life and the chain of events that led to me being there. Because, when I was a youngster growing up, the major leagues were not even open to black Americans and, as I sat there waiting for my name to be called, I thought about all the battles that

I had experienced in high school, playing football, basketball, baseball, and track. And I thought about many of my white teammates that I had played with then and, yet, how I couldn't play with white players in the major leagues after I graduated from high school.

I had to start my baseball career in the old Negro leagues and we used to play against many of the white clubs. On those occasions, I wondered what it would be like to play in the major leagues and get my name in the record books. The white players that I played against would tell us, "The way you guys can play, you should be in the majors." And I would say, "Well, why don't you guys speak out, and maybe they'll give us a chance." But that was not the way things were back then. That was just not the mindset of the times, and I don't harbor any ill feelings against anybody because of that. All I ever wanted was a chance and to get a fair shake. But that never did happen until Branch Rickey came along and gave Jackie Robinson a chance.

I thought about all the great black players who never got that chance. Players like Josh Gibson, Buck Leonard, Oscar Charleston, Ray Dandridge, Willie Wells, Leon Day, Biz Mackey, Cool Papa Bell, Martin Dihigo and all the others that I had seen. There are easily twenty-five or thirty players who were truly superstars, and I wondered what kind of records *they* would have made had they been given the opportunity to play in the major leagues.

I thought about this and I considered myself lucky that the Hall of Fame committee for the Negro leagues thought enough of me to select me as a member of this prestigious group. I also felt very fortunate that I was young enough to still play in the major leagues after the color line was eliminated, and was able to play in two World Series. I was lucky enough to be on the '51 New York Giants when Bobby Thomson hit the "shot heard 'round the world" that won the pennant for us, and I was lucky enough to play on the '54 New York Giants Championship team that swept the Cleveland Indians four straight in the World Series. During those years, I was able to see the emergence of Willie Mays, one of the best rookies I had ever seen, and it was great to watch him develop his skills and become a superstar.

And while I was waiting to deliver my speech, I thought about all those great players who had gone in before me. Babe Ruth, Ty Cobb, Honus Wagner, Rogers Hornsby, Walter Johnson, Christy

Mathewson, Joe DiMaggio, Ted Williams, Stan Musial, and all the other greats who played the game so well. Finally, my name would have to be mentioned along with theirs.

I was honored to be in the same company with these great players who had made such tremendous contributions during their careers. But at the same time, I felt a little twinge of regret because each of these men played in the major leagues for their entire careers. I wondered what kind of numbers I *could* have put in the record book if I had been able to spend my entire career in the majors.

But more than anything else, it made me feel good inside because I knew, when I was eighteen years old, that I was ready to play in the major leagues. Yet, I didn't reach the majors until I was nearly past my prime. I just wish that people could have seen me before I went into the service, when I was considered second to none in the Negro leagues. And I didn't feel at all embarrassed by the fact that a special committee had to vote me in. I was just so happy that it finally happened, I didn't care how it happened, just that it *did* happen.

And, most of all, I thought about growing up and how my father struggled to do the very best he could for a family of ten. And how he kept us together and taught us the value of a close family relationship. I thought about how hard he and my mother worked down South, and how little we had when we come up North. And how they taught us to play hard, but to play clean and to play fair. I wished that they could have been there that day because they would have been so proud.

Not only was my father a great baseball fan but he was responsible for me being what I became. I used to take him to the ball games with me and I remember how he really enjoyed going to the baseball parks. Even though he was in his early eighties, he still enjoyed the games. I just wished that he could have been there to see me be inducted because he probably would have been the happiest guy in the world.

With these thoughts in my mind, I was very happy to be able to go to the microphone and tell everybody what was in my heart. I tried to be relaxed because I didn't want to make any mistakes when I addressed all the wonderful people there. When I got up to speak, I gave most of the credit to my father. I said that there were only a few people in life that I could really depend on, and my father was the one person that I depended on most of all. He was my hero. He stood up in face of all the adversity and was the one that I really admired.

As I mentioned that from the podium, it was a very emotional time for me, and my voice did crack a couple of times. And I said, "He's up there now. He's looking down and I'm sure he and my mother are both smiling very widely because they know that the good things that they taught me have finally been rewarded." That's how I felt then and that's how I feel now.

Aside from my own personal sentiments, the entire ceremony was very impressive. The other two modern-day players who were inducted with me were Warren Spahn and Roberto Clemente. Spahn was a superb pitcher, and is a good friend and a nice person. He was selected by the Baseball Writers Association and everybody knew what Warren had done in his career. He was the winningest left-hander of all time with 363 victories and was truly a superstar. I hit a few homers off him and I didn't mind batting against him, but no hitter was really effective against Spahnie. He didn't have that overpowering speed but, most of the time, he would get you out with that great screwball, those off-speed pitches, and uncanny control. I was pleased to have one of the greatest left-handers of all time on the platform with me that day.

Also there was Mrs. Vera Clemente, representing her late husband Roberto, who had been killed in a plane crash in Puerto Rico on New Year's Eve in 1972, while taking a load of food to the impoverished people of Nicaragua. They waived the five-year waiting period so he could go in right away, like they did for Lou Gehrig when his fatal illness was diagnosed in 1939.

When Clemente was a youngster, I was playing in Puerto Rico with the San Juan Senadores and he was a protégé of mine. He would come to the ball park and I would let him take my bag in so he could get into the ball game free. He watched me and saw how I played the game. He told me he admired, not only the way I hit the ball, but also the way I threw the ball. He wanted to throw the way that I did and later, when he had one of the best throwing arms in baseball, I considered it a compliment. We used to communicate with each other often and he and I became real close until the day he died.

There were three others, selected by the Veterans Committee, who were inducted with us. George "Highpockets" Kelly was the only one still living. I never saw him play but I had heard about his career with the Giants, back in the days when Frankie Frisch was there. The other two men were Mickey Welch, a nineteenth-century player, and Billy Evans, the distinguished umpire. Both of them were represented by a family member.

It was a wonderful day and I felt just great to finally make it. I was very proud and that was just about the happiest moment of my life. I was pleased that I was able to have my family there and to be able to introduce them. My wife Dee, my older daughter Pam, my younger daughter Patti, and her fiancé Craig S. Gordon, who is now her husband, were all there. My good friend and college roommate, Ernie Young, and his wife were also there and I felt very happy that they were able to attend.

It sure was a wonderful feeling. I compare it with the feeling of getting married, experiencing the birth of your first child, or graduating from medical school and hanging out your shingle for the first time. After all the playing, practicing, and traveling that I had done, it had finally paid off. And that feeling stayed with me for a very long time.

That weekend left me with such wonderful memories. When I think about it now, I still get a thrill. I don't think I have missed going back for the ceremonies but one time since I was inducted. As I said, the only thing missing at my induction were my parents. My father passed away in 1963 and my mother in 1970. But I know that they were looking down from up there and heard everything I said.

30 Honor and Recognitions

Monte is a very influential source for the Negro League baseball players. He has done a wonderful job reaching back and helping them gain recognition and secure benefits.

—Buck O'Neil, Kansas City Monarchs

THE FORMATION OF the Negro leagues committee for the Hall of Fame resulted from a conversation that Dick Young and Roy Campanella had one day in Cooperstown. Young asked Campanella, "In the old Negro leagues how many players do you think were of Hall of Fame caliber?" Without giving it any real thought, Campanella said, "Oh, three or four." Just like that. As a result, Dick Young wrote to the commissioner and told him that there should be a committee set up to review and to possibly select the men who in our estimation should be into the Hall of Fame.

Bowie Kuhn asked me to be the chairman of that committee. I selected Eddie Gottleib, Eppie Barnes, Roy Campanella, Judy Johnson, Wendell Smith, Sam Lacy, Dick Young, Joe Reichler, and Alex Pompez. We were asked to formulate a list of players to be considered for induction. When we got down to the business of reviewing all the players, we came up with about thirty men who would qualify. These men were real stars and ones that we had seen play.

Everyone on that committee had seen some of these guys play and they knew that by all circumstances, they would have made the Hall of Fame if they had been given the chance. People might ask, "Then, why did Campanella say three or four?" Campy just said that as a public relations statement. He didn't want to scare anybody off by saying fifteen or twenty.

The committee members conferred and, after reviewing the names carefully, we made up a list and put them in alphabetical order. From that list, Satchel Paige was the first player selected by the committee. He was inducted in 1971, and the next year we put in Josh Gibson and Buck Leonard together. I was the committee's choice in 1973 and then Cool Papa Bell (1974), Judy Johnson (1975), Oscar Charleston (1976), John Henry Lloyd (1977), and Martin Dihigo (1977) were selected. Altogether, we put in nine players before the committee was abolished.

We had a meeting one day and it was decided that we had done our job and the committee should be disbanded, with the duties being taken over by the Veterans Committee. I'm not going to say who made that decision. Just the committee was present that day, including Dick Young, who was a nonvoting member. He was there to make sure everything was done properly and he would give the committee publicity. Joe Reichler was also a very respected member, and he was looking out for the best interests of baseball and the commissioner's office. It was a blue chip committee and performed admirably in my estimation.

In the years since our committee was disbanded, the Veterans' Committee added Rube Foster (1981), Ray Dandridge (1987), and Leon Day (1995), making an even dozen former Negro League players in the Hall of Fame. I'm glad Leon was finally elected while he was still living, but he should have been in years ago. As it was, he had only six days to enjoy the news before he passed away March 13, 1995. He was in the hospital and unconscious most of that time, but at least he knew that he had finally been recognized.

Leon has to be near the top of the list of my all-time favorites. When I was asked to speak at his funeral, I opened my remarks by saying, "Every time I'm asked to say something, I feel not eloquent enough because this great player - this great man - deserves special words." I always get a little teary when I start to think about him and talk about him. I don't know anybody who disliked Leon Day. He had a way about him that made you like him. And he was just a special kind of player and a special kind of person.

I attended the Hall of Fame induction ceremonies and his wife Geraldine, accepting the honor on his behalf, said that she knew

Leon was with her. As I sat there I was very proud of the fact that he made it.

However, there must be at least twenty or more deserving players out there who are still being overlooked. I'm talking about men like Smokey Joe Williams, Willie Wells, Biz Mackey, Bullet Rogan, Willie Foster, Turkey Stearnes, Mule Suttles, John Beckwith, Louis Santop, Hilton Smith, Raymond Brown, Dick Redding, Dick Lundy, and Christobal Torriente.

I was elected by the Negro League Committee because I came in the category of not being allowed to play before 1947. We were at one of the hotels in New York and when my name came up, the others said, "Well, Monte Irvin is a member of the committee and we're discussing *all* the ball players. If this man had been able to come up to the majors at the beginning of his career, he would certainly have made the Hall of Fame." And I was asked to leave the room as we were discussing it. One of the other fellows took over as chairman when they voted whether I belonged. And it was decided that I definitely belonged under the rules of the Negro leagues Committee for the Hall of Fame.

I knew after that meeting that my selection was going to be announced. The official announcement was made later at a press conference in one of the hotels in New York. I had the press conference and, when the commissioner came over, I was asked some questions by the reporters present. They asked how I felt. I told them I was very happy and I felt like I was on cloud nine. My wife was there and they took several pictures. I couldn't believe it because it was something that I never figured would ever happen. I never even figured that I would ever make the big leagues because the feeling against blacks was so intense at that time. So who would have thought that I could ever get a chance?

One of the guys in the office came over to me and said, "Now that you've been elected to the Hall of Fame, your life will change remarkably." And it has been just wonderful, because I've had opportunities to do things and to go places that I never thought was possible.

Being in the Hall of Fame has changed my life in many ways but, even before then, I had the same kind of opportunities when I worked in the commissioner's office. I had a chance to act as host at the winter meetings, and to attend all the All Star games and the World Series. I also had an opportunity to go to the White House in 1969, when it was the centennial of baseball, to meet with President Nixon. Later, during his term in office, President Reagan invited all the Hall of Famers to the White House for a special luncheon.

Then, on February 19, 1992, President Bush invited Leon Day, Jimmy Crutchfield, Josh Gibson, Jr., and myself to be honored at a presidential program in the East Room of the White House, recognizing February as black history month. Among the distinguished dignitaries present for the ceremonies were General Colin Powell, chairman of the Joint Chiefs of Staff, and Judge Clarence Thomas, newest Supreme Court justice. We were sitting in the front row, and President Bush welcomed the four of us in his opening remarks. To have him call our names and get up and take a bow was simply outstanding. Afterward, he personally greeted each of us at a reception in the Abraham Lincoln Room.

I had previously met President Bush at an old-timers' game in Denver, where he played some at first base and took a turn at bat. As I recall, he got a base hit in that game. I understand that he had been a pretty good college baseball player at Yale in his undergraduate years.

In February 1995 George Bush and I met again when he hosted a luncheon for Ted Williams, when they recognized the twenty greatest hitters ever. He spoke at the ceremony and suggested that his wife, Barbara, might make a good commissioner. She is a very nice person, and I admire President Bush for the recognition that he gave to the former Negro league players during his presidency.

To honor those fellows, who never got a chance to play in the major leagues and let them finally experience the feeling of being wanted was most gratifying. It made me feel very good to hear the President tell the players that it was not their fault that they didn't make it, but that it was just a sign of the times.

That is one way that all of this has been possible. I'm just so happy that in my small way, I can give something back for the good things that have happened to me. I would like to continue to be active in helping these ex-Negro leaguers get recognition and to see that they will be helped financially. There's not too many of us around, and I'd like to raise some more money so that these fellows can enjoy their old age comfortably. And, possibly to get some more of these men who so richly deserve it inducted into the Hall of Fame. That is my immediate goal and if I can accomplish that, I will be very happy.

31 Sundown Stars

Some of the best athletes in the world were playing Negro League baseball. The supply was greater than the demand, and we just didn't have enough places for all of them. There was some outstanding baseball being played in our leagues.

—Buck O'Neil, Kansas City Monarchs

There were many Satchels, there were many Joshs.

—Satchel Paige, Kansas City Monarchs

IN TALKING ABOUT all the other great black players, Cool Papa Bell once said, "There's a whole lot of unwritten baseball." If the major leagues had started to take black players a generation sooner, they would have gotten the cream of the crop. Some of those players at that time were unbelievably good. I'm talking about players as good as Willie Mays, Hank Aaron, Ernie Banks, Frank Robinson, Bob Gibson, and the rest of those players who began their major-league careers in the fifties. They were also as good as the young stars of today, like Barry Bonds, Frank Thomas, Ken Griffey, Jr., and all these other young fellows. We had the same kind of players back then and, in fact, some of them might have been a little better. That's the kind of talent that existed during that time.

It's amazing how much they accomplished under such dire circumstances. The hardships were terrible but the guys knew that in order to succeed, they had to endure. During that time, that was the mindset of the country. But, in spite of all that, they played and they played well. The most amazing thing is a lack of bitterness on their part. But you can't miss what you never had. However, they would like some recognition now.

There was so much great talent in those days. It's just too bad that some of those great fellows didn't get a chance to play in the major leagues. And it's a crime that no one important on the white side saw them in action or recorded their feats. The test of a man's merit should be his ability. Most of them never got a chance, and the sad thing is that no one will ever know just what records they would generally have achieved and how great they would have been. They can be measured only in terms of what they accomplished on the baseball diamonds to which they were restricted.

The local white newspapers usually wouldn't carry box scores of those games, and they would just mention them a little bit. But the Negro press would generally have a detailed account of the game plus the box score. The *Pittsburgh Courier, Chicago Defender, Baltimore Afro-American, Philadelphia Tribune*, and some other newspapers provided pretty good coverage of weekend games. But these papers were weeklies, so by the time they came out, other games had already been played and not reported. So the league did not get as much publicity as it deserved. I think later on in New York, the *Daily News* and the *Daily Mirror* began to carry a little better stories, but most white papers still would not even carry the story.

It's tough to compare players since the complete statistics don't exist. Researchers are compiling data from microfilm but it is not complete, so you have to rely on those of us who played against these players and just take our word for it. Buck O'Neil and Buck Leonard are still around, and they remember farther back than I do. George Giles and Jimmy Crutchfield were the same way before they passed away. And if they told you about a guy and said he was good, that meant he was potentially a Hall of Famer, or very close to it. Roy Campanella had a great saying. If Campy told you a guy could *play*, that meant he was very good or a Hall of Famer. And if Campy said he could *really play*, that meant he definitely belonged in the Hall of Fame.

Maybe the only way that these deserving players can be granted their rightful place at Cooperstown is to renew the special Negro leagues committee. In the eighteen years since the first one was abolished, only three players from that era have been inducted. I have been very disappointed in the Veterans' Committee for their lack of responsiveness to this injustice. We are overlooking players who, by today's standards, would go in on the first ballot.

Major leaguers who barnstormed against us knew that there was great talent on the black All-Star teams. Even if these were exhibition games, the white teams didn't want to lose. The black teams did all right against the white players, and won about two out of every three games played. Our players proved themselves in every way they could. Still most fans know little, if anything, about these great ball players. There were just so many whose contributions to baseball have not been acknowledged.

Rube Foster made many contributions to our national pastime and is recognized as the father of Negro baseball. He was the one who got the league started and kept it going. Rube had passed away before I got a chance to meet him. But all the people that I talked to about him told me how great he was as a player, as a manager, and as an organizer.

They used to call Smokey Joe Williams the black Walter Johnson. They said he was even better than Satchel Paige, if that is possible. Smokey Joe was one of the best, but he was an old-timer and got very little publicity. So the media and major-league fans know virtually nothing about him. But if you ever saw him play, then you would know about him. When I saw him he was near the end of his career, and was only pitching once in a while.

After Smokey Joe stopped playing ball, he became a bartender in Harlem and it was a very popular spot. Roy Campanella and I would go over there where he worked and listen to some of the stories he used to tell. We knew that he was bonafide because of the way he could explain things. We would listen to him for hours.

Satchel Paige needs no introduction to anyone. He ranks with the top pitchers of all time, black or white. Even when he got older, his fastball was by you and gone, and I've never seen better control. There were some other great right-handed pitchers like Bullet Joe Rogan and Cannonball Dick Redding. They both were before my time, but those who saw them say they ranked with the best. When I was playing, we had Leon Day, who ranked right up there with anyone, along with Raymond Brown and Bill Byrd from our league, and Hilton Smith from the other league. And Johnny Taylor should be mentioned, too.

Rube Foster had a half-brother, Willie Foster, who was a great pitcher. Some consider him the greatest black left-hander of all time, but few people know about him. There were other great players that nobody ever heard about. Slim Jones is a good example. Nobody has ever heard of him, but if you ever hit against Slim Jones, then you would always remember him. He was a left-hander and could throw as hard as Lefty Grove.

There are a couple of left-handers that I faced who also need to be mentioned. Roy Partlow, in his prime, was as good a pitcher as you ever want to see, and there was another great southpaw by the name of Barney Brown. Neither of them ever got the publicity they deserved, but they were there and they could *play*. Nip Winters and Andy Cooper are two other left-handers who were supposed to be tops, but they were before my time.

Everyone knows about Josh Gibson. I played both with him and against him. I played with him in the All-Star game, and against him in the league. He had superhuman power. He could hit the ball as far to right field as he could to left. You could just see the muscles rippling as you talked to him. Josh was not only a great hitter, but he had a rifle for an arm and could run like a deer. He was just great to be around. He would tell a lot of stories, and had a special way of saying anything. You couldn't make him mad, but he also knew he was the best. He'd say, "Well, you got me today, but tomorrow old Josh will get you."

Campy was always the first to tell you that, in the All-Star game, Josh would be the starting catcher, and Campy would have to play third base or in the outfield. Later on, when Josh was gone, then Campy moved behind the plate. Campy would also tell you that his mentor, Biz Mackey, was the best receiver he ever saw, even much better than Campy himself. The old-timers always talked about Louis Santop and Bruce Petway from the deadball era, who were top catchers.

Buck Leonard was the top black first baseman of all time. Even when Buck was well past his prime, Luke Easter had to play the outfield when he joined the Homestead Grays because he couldn't move Buck off first base. Before Buck came along, Ben Taylor was considered the top black first baseman. Mule Suttles was our first baseman, when I first joined the Eagles. He was in the twilight of his career, but he still was a home run hitter who could hit the ball as far as anybody, including Josh Gibson. He might not hit it as often as Josh, but he was a great slugger.

The top players at second base were Bingo DeMoss, Newt Allen, and Sammy T. Hughes. Sammy T. could do it all. He used to drink second base. He was tall, rangy, could run, and hit with some power. That's what made him so effective. And he was a nice, quiet team player like Piper Davis. He and Piper played practically the same way. Both covered a lot of ground but Sammy T. had more power. He was quick and smooth like Charlie Gehringer.

At a reunion in Arlington, Texas, a few years back, Willie Wells said that the best second baseman was Newt Allen. Willie said that he got the ball and threw it and didn't even have to look. He was quick and had a good arm. But I only saw him once or twice and he was on the way out then. I never saw Bingo DeMoss but those who did see him said that he was a terrific player and could do it all.

John Henry Lloyd was regarded as one of the best players in baseball history. That's the quality of players I'm talking about. Lloyd was a shortstop and is called the black Honus Wagner, but he was before my time. The best shortstop that I ever saw was Willie Wells and he was comparable to Lloyd. Dick Lundy was right there with them, too, but he was mostly just coaching when I came into the league. John Beckwith played several positions, including shortstop, but he was best known as a slugger. He is another player who was before my time.

At the hot corner, Judy Johnson and Oliver Marcelle were considered the best until Ray Dandridge came along. I never did see Marcelle, but I saw Judy a couple of times when he was in his twilight years. He was a popular and stylish third baseman and could hit and field. But I couldn't really judge them like I can Dandridge. He was one of the greatest infielders I have ever seen, both as a third basemen and a second baseman. But how many people had ever heard of Ray Dandridge before he was elected to the Hall of Fame? When they started to look at his stats and get opinons of guys who played with him or played against him, they said, "Gee whiz, he must have been good. If everybody says that, it must have been true." And it *was*. He was an original.

Oscar Charleston is in center field on my all-time Negro league team, for hitting, running, fielding, throwing, and hitting for power. Oscar is considered by many to be the greatest of all the black baseball players. They said he was just like Willie Mays, and may have been even a little better. Nobody can beat Willie fielding in my estimation, but Oscar was a great hitter.

Before a game, Charleston used to put on a hitting and fielding exhibition. They'd get a guy at homeplate with a fungo to hit line drives, and Oscar would run under those line drives and then throw a strike to home plate. This was the way they attracted fans. They used to say, "Come out and see the Oscar Charleston show." He was very strong and a great hitter. He was a left-handed hitter but, like Ted Williams, he didn't care anything about left-handed pitchers, he could hit them too. Charleston was a great all-around player.

Cool Papa Bell is a little better known because he had that magical name. And he seemed to work a little magic on the field, too. He could run, he could hit, and he could *play*. Satchel helped to publicize him with some of the stories that he told. Cool Papa was very quick. Satchel said that Cool could turn off the lights and get in the bed before the room got dark.

When I saw him he was nearing the end of his career. Quincy Trouppe, who lived in St Louis when Cool Papa played there with the St. Louis Stars, said that he was faster than Sam Jethroe. And Jethroe was the fastest player that I had seen circling the bases when he really had to score. Jethroe was called The Jet and he ranked right up there along with Richie Ashburn, Bill Bruton, Maury Wills, George Case, and some of the others who were exceptionally quick. But Quincy said Cool Papa was faster than any of those guys.

I was just a youngster the first time I saw Turkey Stearnes at Sprague Field on Bloomfield Avenue in Newark. He was batting first that day, and usually the leadoff batter will take the first pitch, but on the first pitch he hit the ball over the centerfield fence. This made a distinct impression on me. From then on, I became a Turkey Stearnes fan. He's not in the Hall of Fame but he should be. He could run, was a good hitter, had a good arm, and was a great outfielder.

One of the best outfielders that I played against was Wild Bill Wright. He was a big, strong player who could hit, throw, and *run*. He never had a slump because when he needed a hit, he could drag or push a bunt and beat it out. He could do everything.

Rap Dixon was a stylist and could also do it all. But I only heard about him. Other players from the early years that I've heard about but never saw, are Pete Hill, Spot Poles, and Christobal Torriente, who were all outstanding outfielders.

Martin Dihigo was the most versatile player I ever saw. He could play any position, and play it well. If I had to put him at a position, I would have to put him on the mound. When I saw him in 1942 with Torreon in Mexico, he was almost unbeatable. He had a good curve, was smart and had good control. If I played him in the outfield, I would put him in right field because of his powerful arm. It's just too bad that major-league fans didn't get a chance to see him and all those other great ball players.

32 The Future

Monte and I have been married for fifty-three years and, of course, I know him better than anybody else. He is a wonderful husband, a loving father, and he simply adores our grandchildren. He's just the greatest!

—Dee Irvin

THERE IS AN increased awareness all across America about the Negro leagues. In the last several years, several ball parks have been named after some of us players. In Atlantic City, Pop Lloyd Field is being restored, and there are four of us Hall of Famers who have parks named after them. There's a park in Rocky Mount, North Carolina, named after Buck Leonard, one in Kansas City named after Satchel Paige, and in Newark the West Side Park was renamed after Ray Dandridge.

On June 6, 1986, the Grove Street Oval was recognized as an historic site, and John C. Hatcher, the mayor of East Orange, New Jersey, who had played there as a youngter, read a proclamation redesignating the park as Monte Irvin Field in my honor. After the ceremonies, they had a reception for me at Upsala College and later The Society for American Baseball Research (SABR) placed a commemorative plaque at the entrance to the field, denoting the historic significance of the ball park.

The fact that I was honored in that way made me very grateful. I hope that by naming this park after me, it will be an inspiration to some of the youngsters coming along today. We didn't have an easy time. We knew it was tough but it made us better men. Some little league teams have started to use the names of the old Negro League teams, and this has created a growing interest among black youth about the history of black baseball.

I would advise youngsters who are playing baseball today to stick to it. Stay with it. We had to overcome many obstacles during our lifetimes, but young people don't have these barriers now. All they have to do now is learn their trade well. There is equal opportunity and if you work hard and do the things that you're supposed to do, you can certainly succeed.

That is the same advice and hope that I have for my grandchildren. I want them to be happy and to be successful in whatever they choose to do in life. Nothing gives me more joy than to see my family content and doing well in their endeavors.

My wife, Dee, and I were married on March 31, 1942, so we have been married fifty-three years. We still enjoy pretty good health and hope to have many more happy years together. My older daughter, Pamela, doesn't have any children. But our younger daughter, Patti, has given us two wonderful grandchildren, Stacie and Erika. They live in Houston, where their dad is a doctor, and they really enjoy living there.

Dee and I look forward to going to Houston to visit with them as often as we can, and their coming to stay with us in Florida every summer. It's important to try to keep strong family ties and to raise your children as best as you can. So far we've been very lucky with our daughters and granddaughters. They have never given us any trouble.

I think what has really kept me going for a long time is the fact that I have two of the finest grandchildren anywhere. To see them come on the scene and grow up kind of keeps you young and spry, and just being with them keeps you hopeful. I just hope that I can live a few more years to see them grow up into young ladies, go on to college, and carve out a wonderful life for themselves.

I got a good start in life because of my parents and I want to pass what they taught me on down to my children and grandchildren. My philosophy is good because my father's philosophy was good. My father's philosophy was simply to follow the Golden Rule. He believed that if you treat a person right, sooner or later, you'll win that person over.

Because of my parents' influence and the upbringing that I had, I never really encountered problems of any consequence when I was growing up. I excelled in sports, was a good student, watched my conduct and wasn't a carouser. I went to church and to Sunday school, and was respectful of my elders.

My philosophy of life, has always been to do the right thing. It's just as easy to do the right thing as to do the wrong thing. If you lie, you have to tell two or three other lies to cover up the first one. And unless you're a real good liar, you're going to forget and sooner or later you'll get caught. So, why lie? Tell the truth, don't cheat, and don't steal. Treat people right. Always try to make a bad situation better.

I just think that if you work hard, have hope, and have a purpose, you can get the job done. I have always believed that to be happy yourself, you have to make someone else happy. I still stand by that today. When you give some happiness, happiness will automatically come back to you. When you do something good and feel good inside, you can stay on a high in life. The rest is easy. If you do good, then good will be returned to you.

Index

D

E

F

G

M

N

O

P

R

S

T

U

V

W

Y

About James A. Riley

James A. Riley is a foremost authority on the history of baseball's Negro leagues. His landmark reference volume, *The Biographical Encyclopedia of the Negro Baseball Leagues* (1994), is recognized as the most comprehensive work chronicling this era of baseball history. He has also written *The All-Time All-Stars of Black Baseball* (1983), *Dandy, Day, and the Devil* (1987), and *Buck Leonard: The Black Lou Gehrig* (1995). His forthcoming books include *The History of the Negro Baseball Leagues, The Chronological Encyclopedia of the Negro Baseball Leagues* and *The Statistical Encyclopedia of the Negro Baseball Leagues.*

He has contributed to many compilations including, *Insiders Baseball* (1983), *Biographical Dictionary of American Sports: Baseball* (1987), *The Ballplayers* (1990), *Baseball Chronology* (1991) and *Biographical Dictionary of American Sports: 1989-1992 Supplement* (1992), *Biographical Dictionary of American Sports: 1992-1995 Supplement for Baseball, Football, Basketball and other sports* (1995), *African-American Sports Greats: A Biographical Dictionary* (1995). He has also contributed to *The Baseball Research Journal* (1981, 1982, 1985, 1991), *Oldtyme Baseball News* (1989–95), *Negro Leagues Baseball Museum Yearbook* (1993–94), *The Diamond* (1993–94), *Athlon Baseball* (1994–95), and *All-Star Game: Official Major League Baseball Program* (1993–94); has served as an editor on the Negro League Section of *The Baseball Encyclopedia* (1990); is listed in *International Authors and Writers Who's Who (Fourteenth Edition, 1995–96).* A two-time recipient (1990 and 1993) of the *SABR-MacMillan Research Award* for his scholarship on the Negro leagues, he has appeared in television documentaries *A League Second to None* (ESPN) and *Safe at Home Plate* (PBS) and guested on radio sports talk shows across the country.

Counted among his forebears are frontiersman Daniel Boone, President Andrew Johnson, and an obscure Cherokee named Crow. The transplanted Tennessean has made the Sunshine State his home since graduating from college in 1961. He and his wife, Dottie, reside in Rockledge, Florida.